KT-495-942

Step-by-Step
VEGETARIAN
COOKBOOK

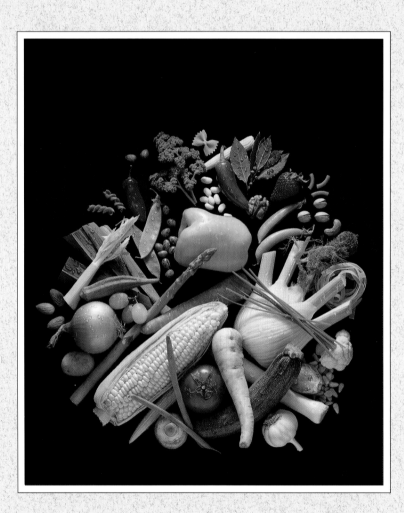

Photography by Peter Barry
Recipes styled by Bridgeen Deery and Wendy Devenish
Edited by Kate Cranshaw and Jillian Stewart
Designed by Amanda Sedge

3511
This 1994 edition published by Tiger Books International PLC, London
Copyright © 1994 CLB Publishing, Godalming, Surrey
Printed and bound in Singapore
All rights reserved
ISBN 1-85501-402-5

Step-by-Step
VEGETARIAN
COOKBOOK

Contents

Introduction

There is nothing strange about vegetarian eating. Vegetarians are not cranks, they simply prefer, either for moral, health, or taste reasons, to eat food that does not include meat, poultry, game or fish. In fact, vegetarianism is on the increase, spurred by the publicity given to the cruelties of intensive livestock farming and the advantages of reducing animal fat intake and cholesterol levels. Lower incidence of heart disease and fewer intestinal disorders are just two of the many perceived health benefits of a balanced vegetarian diet.

The market has responded to the trend towards vegetarianism. Supermarkets are full of high quality fruit and vegetables in ever increasing varieties. The choice of dairy products has also increased, with great emphasis being given to different varieties of yogurt and the increasing range of vegetarian cheeses. Supermarkets and healthfood stores now stock an array of wonderful "meat substitutes" such as grains, pulses, nuts, and soya bean derivatives. The choice of vegetarian foods has never been greater nor the variety more stimulating. For many people vegetarian cooking has become an exciting, creative pastime, and even the basis for a new way of life.

Before embarking on a vegetarian diet, it is important to have an understanding of your nutritional requirements. As with any diet, the less refined or processed the ingredients the better. Pulses and nuts are a good standby in the kitchen cupboard, but they do deteriorate with time, and notice should be taken of the "use by" date. As a basic guide to a sensible vegetarian diet, it is advisable to eat beans and nuts, grains, dairy produce, vegetables and fruit daily. Typical complementary pairs include: beans and grains – serve a lentil dish with rice; nuts and vegetables – nuts go well with green vegetables such as spinach; cheese and vegetables – top a vegetable casserole with cheese; fruit and yogurt – either whipped together or the yogurt used as a sauce.

Suddenly changing one's eating habits from a traditional meat diet to one in which meat is totally excluded is not always easy. Indeed, many people adopt a gradual approach, initially avoiding red meats in favour of chicken and fish, and progressing to vegetarianism at their own pace. Even if becoming completely vegetarian is not the goal, many people are increasingly including a few vegetarian meals in their weekly menus. Whatever your eating habits, you are sure to find something to tempt you among this mouthwatering selection of imaginative vegetarian recipes. They may just be the inspiration you have been looking for to change the eating habits of a lifetime.

Chapter 1
VEGETARIAN SOUPS

CREAM OF CUCUMBER WITH MINT

SERVES 4

This delicious summer soup can be eaten hot, or chilled and served on ice for a refreshing change.

INGREDIENTS

3 large cucumbers
1 litre/1¾ pints vegetable stock
Salt and freshly ground black pepper
2-3 sprigs fresh mint
280ml/½ pint single cream
60ml/4 tbsps natural yogurt, to garnish

Step 7 *Chop the mint leaves finely before adding to the soup.*

1 Cut one of the cucumbers in half and chop one half into small dice. Set the small dice to one side.
2 Peel the remaining half and the other 2 cucumbers and roughly chop them into small pieces.
3 Put the peeled cucumber, stock and seasoning into a large saucepan.
4 Remove the mint leaves from the sprig and add the stalks only to the pan. Bring gently to the boil, reduce the heat and simmer gently for 25 minutes

or until cucumber is tender.
5 Remove the mint stalks from the soup, and using a liquidiser or food processor, purée the soup until smooth.
6 Return to the rinsed out pan and stir in the single cream and reserved diced cucumber. Reheat gently for about 5 minutes.
7 To serve, finely chop the mint leaves and add to the soup. Stir a spoonful of yogurt into each bowl before serving.

Cook's Notes

TIME
Preparation takes about 15 minutes, cooking time is about 30 minutes.

VEGETARIAN SUITABILITY
This recipe is suitable for lacto-vegetarians only.

VARIATION
Use a mixture of half stock and half pale ale for an interesting variation.

PARSNIP AND CARROT SOUP

SERVES 4

A delicious and wholesome country soup which makes use of that favourite vegetable, the humble parsnip.

INGREDIENTS

225g/8oz parsnips, peeled and sliced
225g/8oz carrots, peeled and sliced
280ml/½ pint vegetable stock
570ml/1 pint milk
Salt and freshly ground black pepper
Pinch of ground nutmeg
1 small bunch chives, snipped
60ml/4 tbsps single cream

Step 2 *Blend the soup to a smooth purée using a liquidiser or food processor.*

1 Cook the parsnips and carrots in the stock for about 15 minutes until tender.
2 Place in liquidiser or food processor and purée until smooth. Return to the rinsed out pan.

3 Add the milk, season with salt, pepper and nutmeg, and stir in the chives. Reheat gently until just simmering.
4 Stir in the cream and serve.

Cook's Notes

 TIME
Preparation takes about 10 minutes, cooking time is about 20 minutes.

 VEGETARIAN SUITABILITY
This recipe is suitable for lacto-vegetarians only.

PREPARATION
If a very smooth soup is required, the puréed soup can be strained through a metal sieve before the chives are added.

SERVING IDEA
Serve with crisp French sticks and a vegetarian cheese.

FREEZING
This soup will freeze for up to 3 months if frozen before the final addition of the cream. This can be added just before serving.

CHEDDAR CHEESE SOUP

SERVES 4

An unusual soup that is ideal for using up any left over cheese.

INGREDIENTS

*225g/8oz vegetarian Cheddar cheese or a mixture of
    different types of hard vegetarian cheeses*
45g/1½oz butter or vegetable margarine
1 carrot, peeled and diced
2 sticks celery, trimmed and chopped
30g/1oz plain flour
420ml/¾ pint vegetable stock
570ml/1 pint milk
1 bay leaf
¼ tsp dried thyme
Chopped parsley, to garnish

1 Grate the cheese finely and, if using more than one type, mix together.
2 Melt the butter or margarine in a pan and sauté the carrot and celery until just soft.
3 Stir in the flour and cook for about 30 seconds. Remove from the heat and gradually add the stock and milk. Add the bay leaf and thyme.
4 Return to the heat and cook gently until thickened slightly, stirring constantly.
5 Add the cheese a little at a time, stirring until the cheese has melted.
6 Remove the bay leaf and serve the soup sprinkled with chopped parsley.

Cook's Notes

TIME
Preparation takes about 10 minutes, cooking time is about 20 minutes.

VEGETARIAN SUITABILITY
This recipe is suitable for lacto-vegetarians only.

SERVING IDEA
Serve with caraway or rye bread.

TOMATO AND LEEK SOUP

SERVES 4-6

This delicious combination of leeks and sweet tomatoes is sure to become a firm favourite.

INGREDIENTS

2 large leeks, washed, trimmed and finely sliced
570ml/1 pint fresh tomato juice
Dash of Tabasco or soy sauce
¼ tsp celery seasoning
Shake of garlic powder
4 fresh tomatoes, skinned and sliced
Salt and freshly ground black pepper

1 Cook the leeks in about 280ml/½ pint of boiling water for 15 minutes or until tender.
2 Remove about half the leeks from the cooking liquid and set aside.
3 Purée the remaining leeks with the cooking liquid, in a liquidiser or food processor.

Step 3 *Purée half the leeks in the cooking liquid, using a liquidiser or food processor.*

4 Return the puréed leeks to the rinsed out pan and add another 280ml/½ pint water.
5 Stir in the tomato juice, Tabasco or soy sauce, celery seasoning and garlic powder.
6 Heat gently to simmering point then add the reserved leeks and tomato slices, season with salt and pepper. Cook gently for 3-4 minutes and serve hot.

Cook's Notes

 TIME
Preparation takes about 10 minutes, cooking time is about 20 minutes.

 SERVING IDEA
Serve with crusty French bread and vegetarian Cheddar cheese.

VEGETARIAN SUITABILITY
This recipe is suitable for vegans.

 VARIATION
If leeks are not available use large Spanish onions in their place.

FREEZING
This soup will freeze for up to 6 weeks. Freeze in a rigid 2-litre/3-pint container.

SPRING VEGETABLE SOUP

SERVES 4-6

Spring vegetables combine to produce a delightfully light soup with a glorious fresh flavour.

INGREDIENTS

1 litre/1¾ pints vegetable stock
120g/4oz fresh shelled peas
3 carrots, peeled and cut into thin 5 cm/2-inch strips
120g/4oz fresh French beans, cut into 2.5cm/1-inch pieces
120g/4oz fresh asparagus, cut into 2.5cm/1-inch pieces
1 head green cabbage, finely shredded
3 spring onions, sliced
1 red pepper, seeded and sliced
60ml/4 tbsps white wine (optional)
Salt and freshly ground black pepper

1 Bring the stock to the boil in a large pan, add the peas, simmer gently for 10 minutes, and then add the carrots and simmer for another 10 minutes.
2 Stir in the beans, asparagus and cabbage and cook for 5 minutes.
3 Finally add the spring onions, red pepper and white wine if using.
4 Cook for 5 minutes then season to taste before serving.

Cook's Notes

 TIME
Preparation takes about 25 minutes, cooking time is about 30 minutes.

VEGETARIAN SUITABILITY
Suitable for vegans.

SERVING IDEA
Serve with crunchy French toast.

 PREPARATION
Trim away the hard core of the cabbage and only use the finely shredded leaves in this recipe.

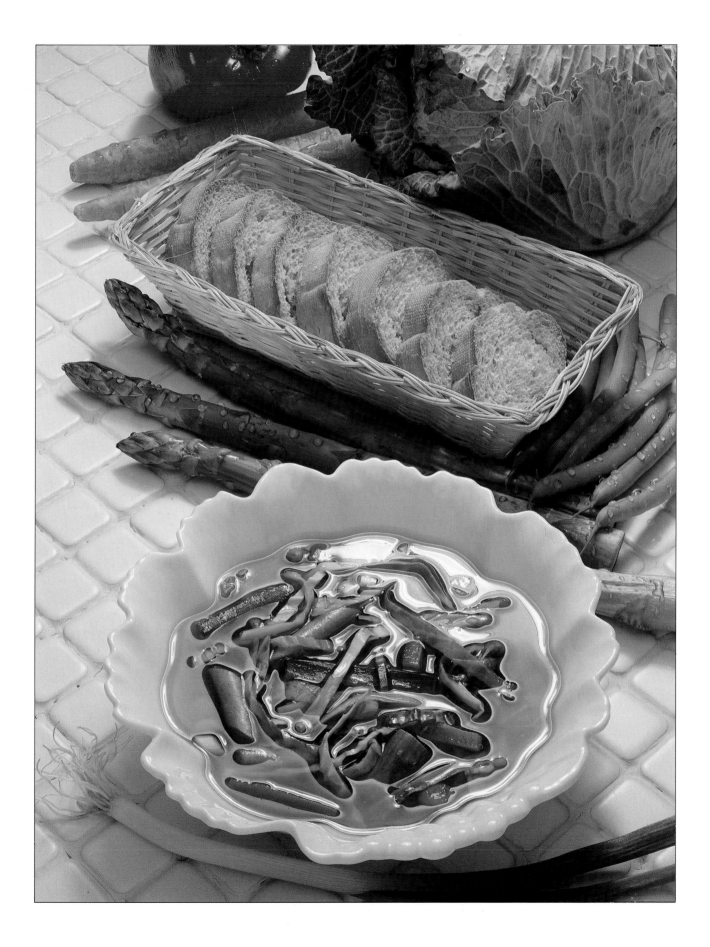

PURÉE OF ASPARAGUS SOUP

<u>SERVES 4</u>

This thick and creamy soup makes full use of the delicate flavour of fresh summer asparagus.

INGREDIENTS

1.4kg/3lbs asparagus, fresh or frozen and thawed
1 litre/1¾ pints vegetable stock
¼ tsp ground mace
Salt and freshly ground black pepper
280ml/½ pint single cream
140ml/¼ pint whipped cream
Sprinkling of ground mace

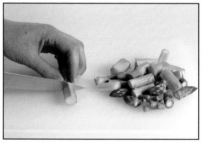

Step 1 *Chop the spears into 2.5cm/1-inch pieces.*

1 Trim the thick ends from the asparagus and cut away any tough outer skin. Chop the spears into 2.5cm/1-inch pieces.

Step 1 *Trim the thick ends from the asparagus, and cut away any tough outer skin. Use a potato peeler or very sharp knife to avoid cutting away too much of the tender, fleshy asparagus.*

2 Bring the stock to the boil in a large pan, add the asparagus, mace and seasoning, and cook for about 10 minutes or until asparagus is just tender.

3 Using a liquidiser or food processor, blend the asparagus in the cooking liquid until it becomes a smooth purée.

4 Return the asparagus to the rinsed out pan and stir in the single cream. Reheat gently but do not allow to boil or the cream will curdle.

5 Garnish each serving with a spoonful of the whipped cream and a dusting of the ground mace.

Cook's Notes

TIME
Preparation takes about 15 minutes, cooking time is about 15 minutes.

VEGETARIAN SUITABILITY
This recipe is suitable for lacto-vegetarians only.

SERVING IDEA
Serve with slices of wholemeal bread for a luxurious first course.

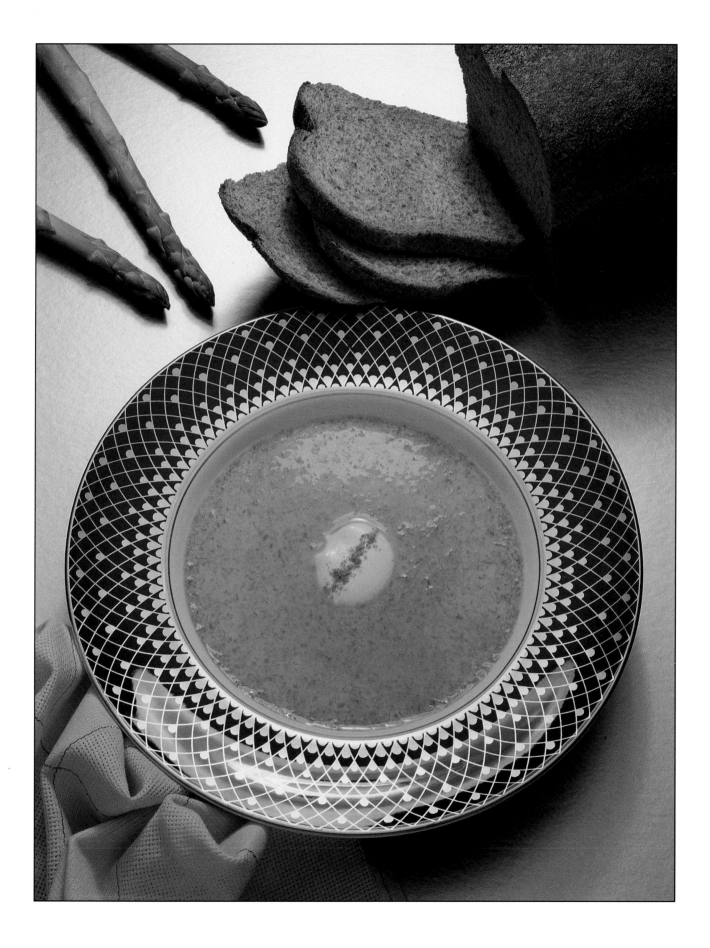

CREAMY SPINACH SOUP

SERVES 4-6

The wonderful combination of spinach and cream in this soup could not fail to please even the most fussy guest.

INGREDIENTS

900g/2lbs fresh spinach, trimmed and well washed

30g/1oz butter or vegetable margarine

1 shallot, peeled and finely chopped

30g/1oz plain flour

700ml/1¼ pints vegetable stock

¼ tsp dried marjoram

1 bay leaf

Pinch of grated nutmeg

Salt and freshly ground black pepper

Squeeze of lemon juice

420ml/¾ pint milk

140ml/¼ pint single cream

Slices of lemon or chopped hard boiled egg, to garnish

Step 6 Blend the soup in a liquidiser or a food processor until it is a smooth purée. This may have to be done in several batches.

1 Cook the spinach until just wilted in a covered saucepan with just the water that is left clinging to the leaves.

2 Melt the butter or margarine in a large pan and sauté the shallot until soft.

3 Stir the flour into the pan and cook for about 30 seconds. Remove from the heat and gradually add the stock.

4 Add the marjoram, bay leaf and nutmeg. Return to the heat and cook gently until thickened slightly, stirring constantly.

5 Remove the bay leaf and discard. Add the spinach to the pan. Season with salt and pepper and add the lemon juice.

6 Purée the soup in a liquidiser or food processor until smooth.

7 Return to the rinsed out pan and stir in the milk. Bring gently to simmering point.

8 Just before serving stir in the cream. Serve garnished with lemon slices or chopped hard boiled eggs.

Cook's Notes

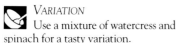 TIME
Preparation takes about 15 minutes, cooking time is about 20 minutes.

VEGETARIAN SUITABILITY
This recipe is suitable for lacto-vegetarians only.

FREEZING
This soup will freeze successfully for up to 3 months without the cream and garnish.

VARIATION
Use a mixture of watercress and spinach for a tasty variation.

 SERVING IDEA
Serve with crunchy wholemeal croutons.

Mushroom and Sherry Cream Soup

Serves 4

This unusual soup is hearty and filling; ideal for a cold day.

INGREDIENTS

900g/2lbs mushrooms, trimmed and chopped
5-6 slices stale bread, crusts removed
700 ml/1¼ pints vegetable stock
1 sprig of fresh thyme
1 bay leaf
½ clove garlic, crushed
Salt and freshly ground black pepper
420ml/¾ pint single cream
60ml/4 tbsps sherry
140ml/¼ pint whipped cream
Grated nutmeg, to garnish

---

1 Place the mushrooms in a large pan and crumble the bread over them.
2 Add the stock, thyme, bay leaf, garlic, salt and pepper. Bring to the boil, reduce the heat and simmer gently for 20 minutes or until mushrooms are soft, stirring occasionally.
3 Remove the bay leaf and thyme. Using a liquidiser or food processor, blend the soup until a smooth purée is formed.
4 Return to the rinsed out pan. Whisk in the single cream and sherry.
5 Reheat gently but do not allow to boil. Garnish each serving of soup with a spoonful of the whipped cream and a sprinkling of nutmeg.

Cook's Notes

TIME
Preparation takes about 20 minutes, cooking time is about 25 minutes.

VEGETARIAN SUITABILITY
This recipe is suitable for lacto-vegetarians only.

PREPARATION
If preferred, the bread can be made into breadcrumbs before adding to the soup.

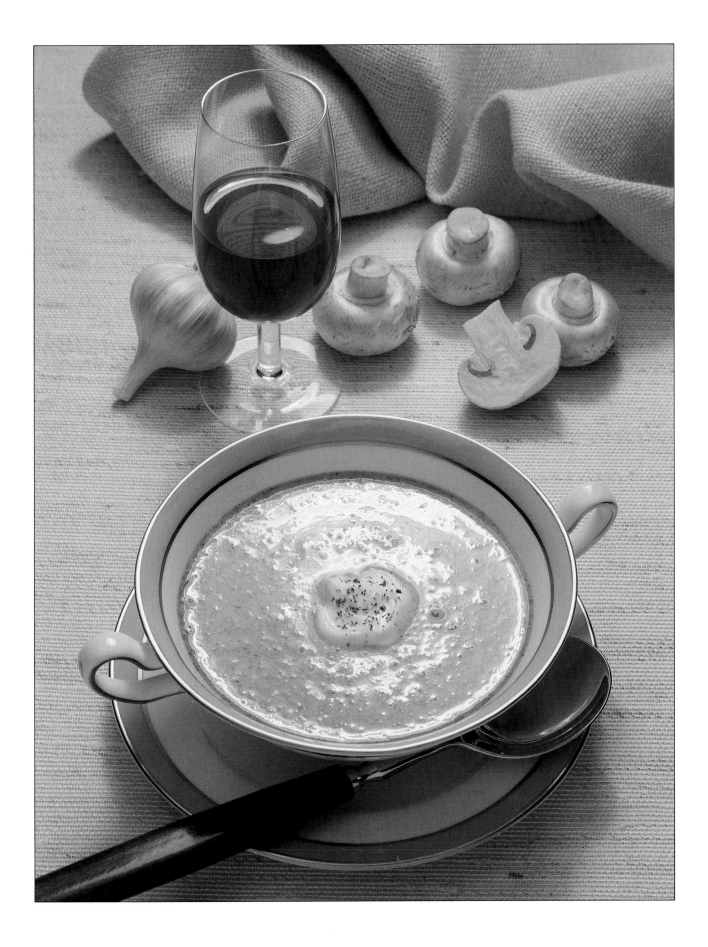

SWEETCORN AND RED PEPPER SOUP

SERVES 4

This creamy soup has a definite bite to its flavour and can be made with either fresh or canned sweetcorn kernels.

INGREDIENTS

4 medium potatoes, scrubbed and cut into even-sized pieces
1 bay leaf
570ml/1 pint vegetable stock
15g/½oz butter or vegetable margarine
1 onion, peeled and chopped
1 large red pepper, deseeded and chopped
1 red chilli, deseeded and chopped
225g/8oz sweetcorn kernels
570ml/1 pint milk
Salt and freshly ground black pepper
Fresh chopped parsley, to garnish

1 Place the potatoes in a saucepan with the bay leaf and cover with the stock. Bring to the boil and simmer gently for 15 minutes until tender.

Step 2 Blend the potatoes and stock in a liquidiser or food processor until smooth.

2 Remove the bay leaf, then pour the potatoes and stock into a liquidiser or food processor and blend until smooth.
3 Melt the butter or margarine in another pan and add the onion, red pepper and chilli. Sauté gently for 5-10 minutes or until soft.
4 Add the puréed potatoes to the pan along with the sweetcorn and milk, stir to blend thoroughly.
5 Reheat gently and season to taste. Serve garnished with chopped parsley.

Cook's Notes

 VARIATION
Substitute soya milk for fresh milk, but do not boil the soup after this addition, and use non-dairy margarine for vegans.

 TIME
Preparation takes about 20 minutes, cooking time is about 30 minutes.

 SERVING IDEA
Serve with fresh, crusty rolls.

COOK'S TIP
Great care must be taken when preparing fresh chillies. Use clean rubber gloves and do not get the juice near eyes or mouth. Rinse eyes with lots of clear cold water should you accidentally get juice in them.

BEETROOT AND SOUR CREAM SOUP

SERVES 4

This delicious and unusual soup is worthy of any occasion.

INGREDIENTS

450g/1lb fresh beetroot
225g/8oz turnips, peeled and cut into even-sized pieces
1 litre/1¾ pints vegetable stock
1 bay leaf
Salt and freshly ground black pepper
280ml/½ pint soured cream
1 tbsp grated fresh or bottled horseradish
Snipped chives, to garnish

1 Boil the beetroot in salted water for about 30-40 minutes or until beetroots are soft. (Large older beetroot may take longer.)
2 Remove from the pan and leave until cold enough to handle. Carefully remove the skins and any roots from the cooked beetroots, using a small knife.
3 Cut the cooked beetroot into small pieces and put these along with the turnips, stock, bay leaf, salt and pepper into a large saucepan.

Step 2 Carefully remove the skins and any roots from the cooked beetroots.

4 Bring to the boil, then reduce the heat and simmer gently for 20 minutes or until the turnip is tender. Remove the bay leaf and discard.
5 Using a liquidiser or food processor, blend the soup until it becomes a smooth purée. Return to the rinsed out pan.
6 Reserve 60ml/4 tbsps of the soured cream and stir the remainder into the soup along with the horseradish.
7 Reheat gently for a few minutes but do not allow the soup to boil.
8 Serve the soup topped with the reserved cream and a sprinkling of snipped chives.

Cook's Notes

TIME
Preparation takes about 20 minutes, cooking time is about 1 hour.

VEGETARIAN SUITABILITY
This recipe is suitable for lacto-vegetarians only.

 FREEZING
This soup will freeze for up to 2 months.

SERVING IDEA
Serve this soup with warm granary bread.

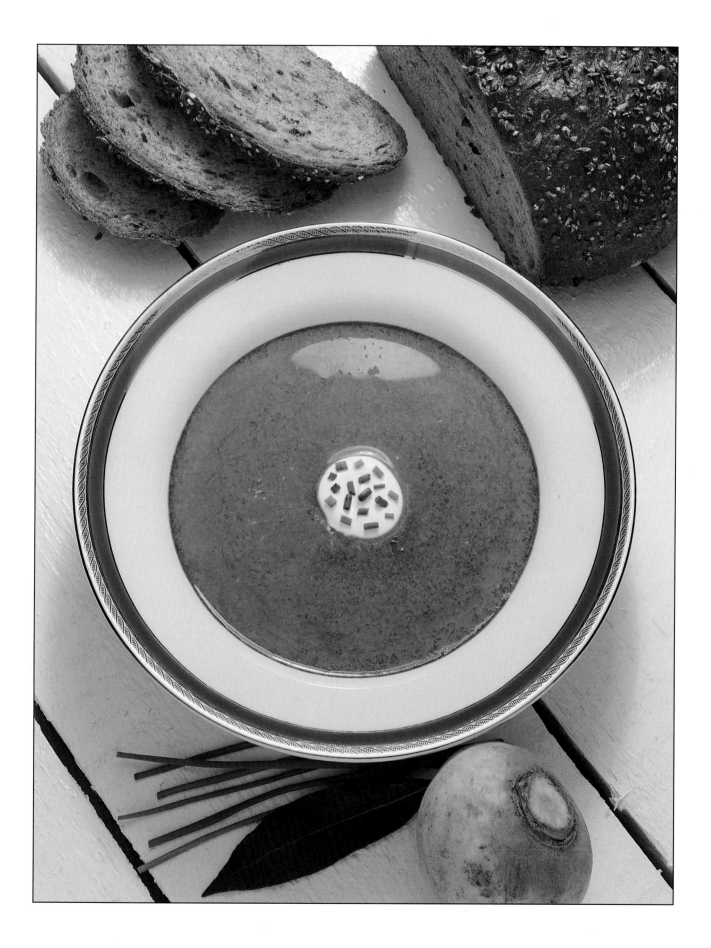

VEGETABLE SOUP

SERVES 4

This hearty vegetable soup makes the most of traditional and unusual vegetables.

INGREDIENTS

2 tbsps vegetable oil

1 large carrot, peeled and diced

1 large turnip, peeled and diced

2 leeks, washed and thinly sliced

2 potatoes, scrubbed and diced

570ml/1 pint vegetable stock

450g/1lb can plum tomatoes, chopped

1 bay leaf

¼ tsp dried savoury or marjoram

60g/2oz soup pasta

Salt and freshly ground black pepper

90g/3oz fresh or frozen sliced green beans

120g/4oz okra, trimmed and sliced

60g/2oz frozen sweetcorn niblets

60g/2oz frozen peas

1 tbsp chopped parsley

1 Heat the oil in a large saucepan and add the carrot, turnip, leeks and potatoes. Sauté gently for about 10 minutes or until softened.

2 Stir in the stock, tomatoes, bay leaf, savoury or marjoram, soup pasta, salt and pepper. Bring gently to the boil, reduce the heat and simmer gently for 20 minutes.

3 Add the beans and okra and cook for a further 10 minutes. Finally add the sweetcorn, peas and parsley. Cook for 5 minutes before serving.

Cook's Notes

VEGETARIAN SUITABILITY
This recipe is suitable for lacto-vegetarians. The recipe can be adapted for vegans by omitting the soup pasta and replacing it with brown rice.

TIME
Preparation takes about 20 minutes, cooking time is about 45 minutes.

VARIATION
Use any combination of vegetables in season to vary this soup.

PREPARATION
If tinned tomatoes are not available, add 340g/12oz fresh tomatoes and 140ml/¼ pint vegetable stock or water instead.

TOMATO AND DILL BISQUE

SERVES 4

This sophisticated soup, with its delicate flavour, is an elegant starter to serve at a summer lunch or dinner.

INGREDIENTS

900g/2lbs fresh tomatoes
1 tbsp vegetable oil
1 onion, peeled and chopped
2 large sprigs fresh dill
2 tbsps tomato purée
Salt and freshly ground black pepper
850ml/1½ pints vegetable stock
140ml/¼ pint double cream
2 tsps chopped fresh dill
60ml/4 tbsps natural yogurt
4 slices fresh tomato
4 small sprigs fresh dill

Step 1 *Scoop out the tomato seeds over a sieve and bowl in order to collect the juice.*

1 Cut the tomatoes in half over a bowl and remove and discard the seeds, reserving any juice that is produced.

2 Heat the oil in a saucepan and sauté the onion until softened.

3 Add the tomato flesh, tomato juice, dill sprigs, tomato purée, salt, pepper and stock. Bring gently to the boil and simmer for 10 minutes.

4 Remove the sprigs of dill and using a liquidiser or food processor, purée the soup until smooth.

5 Strain the puréed soup back into the pan through a sieve to remove the skins.

6 Stir in the double cream and chopped dill, and reheat gently, stirring constantly. Do not allow to boil at this point.

7 Garnish each serving with a spoonful of the yogurt, a tomato slice and a sprig of dill.

Cook's Notes

TIME
Preparation takes about 20 minutes, cooking time is about 20 minutes.

VEGETARIAN SUITABILITY
This recipe is suitable for lacto-vegetarians only.

VARIATION
Use sprigs of fresh basil instead of dill for a delicious variation.

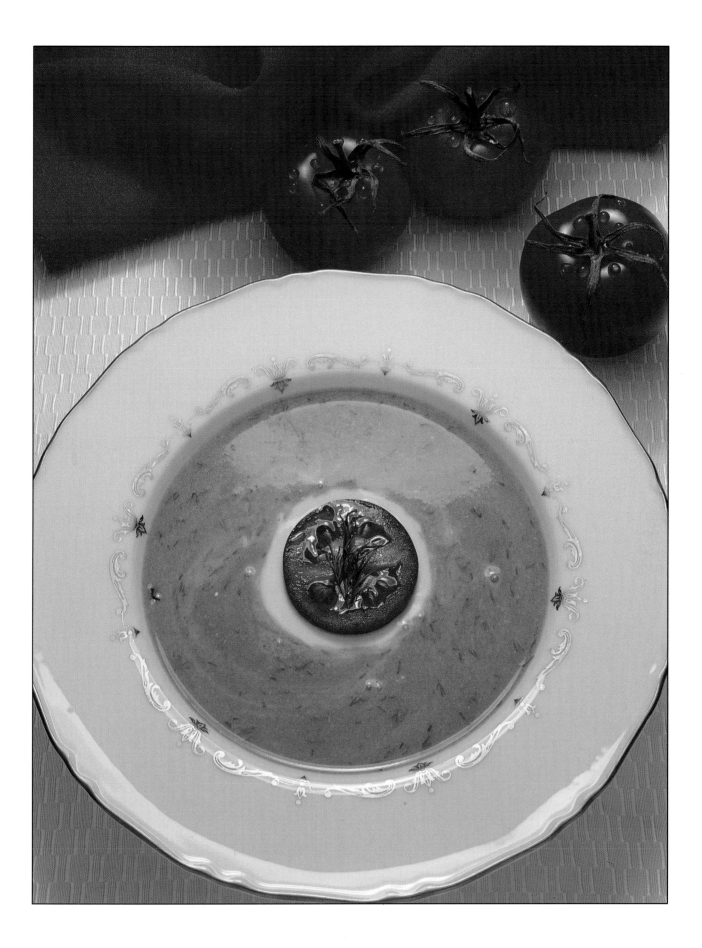

CHESTNUT SOUP

SERVES 4

This unusual soup is high in protein and dietary fibre, and is so delicious that it will become a firm family favourite.

INGREDIENTS

30g/1oz butter or vegetable margarine

2 sticks of celery, trimmed and finely chopped

2 large onions, peeled and chopped

225g/8oz unsweetened chestnut purée

850ml/1½ pints homemade vegetable stock

Salt and freshly ground black pepper

Wholemeal croutons, to garnish

1 Melt the butter or margarine in a large saucepan and sauté the celery and onion until just soft.

2 Blend the chestnut purée with a little of the stock and add to the pan along with the remaining stock. Season with salt and pepper.

3 Bring gently to the boil, reduce the heat and simmer gently for 35 minutes.

4 Serve garnished with the croutons.

Cook's Notes

 PREPARATION
If unsweetened chestnut purée is unavailable, cook 225g/8oz shelled chestnuts in 140ml/¼pt boiling water until they are soft, and purée these in a liquidiser or food processor.

 VEGETARIAN SUITABILITY
Suitable for vegans.

❄ FREEZING
This soup will freeze for 1 month.

🕐 TIME
Preparation takes about 15 minutes and cooking time is about 40 minutes.

GREEN PEA SOUP

SERVES 4

*Pale green and creamy, this delicious soup is made with frozen peas,
making it possible to enjoy the taste of summer all year round.*

INGREDIENTS

30g/1oz butter or vegetable margarine

1 shallot, peeled and finely chopped

30g/1oz plain flour

280ml/½ pint vegetable stock

420ml/¾ pint milk

450g/1lb frozen peas

¼ tsp dried marjoram

1 tbsp chopped fresh parsley

Salt and freshly ground black pepper

1 small bunch fresh mint

140ml/¼ pint single cream

Step 4 *Blend the soup in a liquidiser or food processor until smooth.*

1 Melt the butter or margarine in a saucepan and sauté the shallot until soft.

2 Stir in the flour and cook gently for about 1 minute, remove the pan from the heat and gradually add the stock and milk.

3 Reserve about 90g/3oz of the peas and add the rest to the pan, along with the marjoram, parsley and seasoning. Return to the heat and cook gently until thickened slightly.

4 Pour the soup into a liquidiser or food processor and purée until smooth.

5 Using a sharp knife, chop the mint very finely. Stir the mint along with the cream into the puréed soup. Stir in the reserved peas and reheat gently before serving.

Cook's Notes

SERVING IDEA
Serve this soup with crusty rolls and a crumbly vegetarian Cheshire cheese.

COOK'S TIP
Liquidise the soup a little at a time to ensure a smooth texture.

TIME
Preparation takes about 10 minutes, cooking time is about 15 minutes.

SALAD SOUP

A delicious, unusual soup which is as refreshing as its name implies.

INGREDIENTS

2-3 medium potatoes, peeled and diced

420ml/¾ pint vegetable stock

6 spring onions, finely chopped

½ head lettuce, washed and shredded

120g/4oz fresh spinach leaves, washed, trimmed and
  shredded

1 bunch watercress, washed, trimmed and chopped

½ cucumber, peeled and grated or diced

570ml/1 pint milk

2 tbsps chopped fresh parsley

Pinch of nutmeg

Pinch of cayenne pepper

Salt and freshly ground black pepper

140ml/¼ pint single cream

Natural yogurt and slices of cucumber, to garnish

1 Cook the potatoes in the stock for 15 minutes or
until tender.

Step 3 *Purée the soup
using a liquidiser or food
processor. Purée a little of
the soup at a time to
ensure an even texture.*

2 Add all the remaining vegetables and cook for a
further 5 minutes.

3 Pour into a liquidiser or food processor and
purée until smooth. Return to the rinsed out pan.

4 Stir in the milk and parsley and season with
nutmeg, cayenne pepper, salt and pepper.

5 Add the cream and reheat gently, but do not
allow to boil.

6 Just before serving garnish with swirls of natural
yogurt and slices of cucumber.

Cook's Notes

TIME
Preparation takes about 10
minutes, cooking time is about 25
minutes.

SERVING IDEA
Serve with hot garlic bread.

FREEZING
This soup will freeze well for up
to 3 months.

VICHYSSOISE

SERVES 4

This classic French soup is both simple and economical to make.

INGREDIENTS

3 large leeks
45g/1½oz butter or vegetable margarine
2-3 medium potatoes, peeled and sliced
850ml/1½ pints vegetable stock
140ml/¼ pint milk
Salt and freshly ground black pepper
3 tbsps soured cream
Snipped chives, to garnish

1 Wash and trim the leeks discarding the green parts. Slice the white part of the leeks thinly.
2 Melt the butter or margarine in a large pan and sauté the leeks and potatoes for 10 minutes, stirring frequently until just softened.

Step 1 *Discard the green part of the leeks and slice the white parts thinly.*

3 Add the stock and bring gently to the boil. Reduce heat and simmer for 30 minutes.
4 Allow to cool slightly, pour the soup into a liquidiser or food processor and blend until smooth.
5 Return to the rinsed out pan. Stir in the milk, season and bring gently to simmering point. Chill before serving, garnished with soured cream and snipped chives.

Cook's Notes

TIME
Preparation takes about 15 minutes, cooking time is about 45 minutes.

SERVING IDEA
Vichyssoise is traditionally served chilled, but serve this soup hot for a delicious change when it becomes known simply as leek and potato soup.

VEGETARIAN SUITABILITY
This recipe is suitable for lacto-vegetarians only.

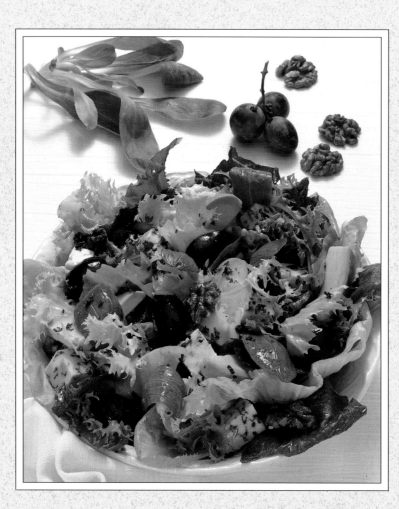

Chapter 2
VEGETARIAN STARTERS

STUFFED ARTICHOKES

<u>SERVES 4</u>

*Many people shy away from artichokes, but they are simple to prepare
and absolutely delicious.*

Step 2 *Trim away any tough, inedible leaves that remain and cut out as much of the fluffy 'choke' as possible, to form a good artichoke shell.*

INGREDIENTS

4 globe artichokes

15g/½oz butter or vegetable margarine

1 shallot, peeled and finely chopped

450g/1lb fresh spinach, stalks removed and washed

60g/2oz breadcrumbs

1 free-range egg, beaten

140ml/¼ pint double cream

Pinch each of ground nutmeg and cayenne pepper

Salt

60g/2oz vegetarian Cheddar cheese, finely grated

60ml/4 tbsps double cream

1 Cut the tops off each artichoke to about halfway down and trim the stalk end to allow the artichoke to sit upright.

2 Trim away any outer tough, inedible leaves and cut out as much of the fluffy 'choke' as possible to form a firm shell.

3 Cook in lightly salted, boiling water for about 10 minutes or until the hearts are tender.

4 Drain and cool. Trim any remaining 'choke' away.

5 Melt the butter or margarine in a large pan and sauté the shallot until soft.

6 Add the spinach with just the water that remains clinging to the leaves after washing. Cover, and cook until the spinach wilts.

7 Remove from the heat, add the breadcrumbs, egg, cream, nutmeg, cayenne and salt.

8 Pile equal amounts into the centre of the artichokes and place in the top of a steamer. Cover and steam for 10 minutes or until the filling just sets.

9 In a small bowl mix together the cheese and the remaining cream, then spoon this on top of each of the filled artichokes and steam for 1 minute.

10 Sprinkle with a little ground nutmeg and serve.

Cook's Notes

TIME
Preparation takes about 20 minutes, cooking time is about 25 minutes.

VEGETARIAN SUITABILITY
This recipe is suitable for lacto-vegetarians only.

VARIATION
Use any other variety of vegetarian hard cheese for the topping.

GARLIC MUSHROOMS

SERVES 4

An established favourite, this can also be served as a light snack.

INGREDIENTS

60g/2oz butter or olive oil

2 cloves garlic, crushed

¼ tsp chopped fresh thyme

¼ tsp chopped fresh parsley

¼ tsp chopped fresh sage

3 tbsps white wine

Salt and freshly ground black pepper

675g/1½lbs mushrooms, cleaned and quartered

8 slices French bread

2 tbsps snipped chives

Fresh herb sprigs, to garnish

1 Heat the butter or oil in a frying pan and sauté the garlic until soft and beginning to turn golden.
2 Stir in the herbs, wine, seasoning and mushrooms and cook over a low heat for 10 minutes or until the mushrooms are cooked but not too soft.
3 Warm the bread in a low oven if wished and serve the mushrooms piled onto the bread.
4 Sprinkle with chopped chives and garnish with sprigs of fresh herbs.

Cook's Notes

TIME
Preparation takes about 15 minutes, cooking time is about 15 minutes.

SERVING IDEA
Serve with sliced tomatoes.

VEGETARIAN SUITABILITY
This recipe is suitable for vegans if oil is used instead of the butter.

VARIATION
Wild mushrooms are often available at good greengrocers or in supermarkets; they make a delicious full flavoured variation to this recipe.

PREPARATION
This recipe can be prepared well in advance and reheated just before serving.

CELERIAC À LA MOUTARDE

SERVES 4

This delicious starter could also be used as a light lunch or supper for two.

INGREDIENTS

1 large root celeriac, peeled
60g/2oz butter or vegetable margarine
30g/1oz plain flour
570ml/1 pint milk
60ml/4 tbsps Dijon mustard
1 tsp celery seasoning
Freshly ground black pepper
30g/4 tbsps dry breadcrumbs

Step 1 *Cut the celeriac into 5mm/¼-inch slices, and then cut each slice into 2.5cm/1-inch strips.*

1 Cut the celeriac into 5mm/¼-inch thick slices and then into sticks about 2.5cm/1-inch long.
2 Cook in lightly salted, boiling water for about 20 minutes or until just tender, then drain.
3 Meanwhile, melt 45g/1½oz of the butter or margarine in a saucepan. Stir in the flour and cook for about 30 seconds.
4 Remove from the heat and gradually add the milk, stirring well after each addition.
5 Return to the heat and stir in the mustard, celery seasoning and pepper. Cook gently until thickened, stirring constantly.
6 Add the celeriac to the sauce and stir to coat well. Transfer to a serving dish and keep it warm.
7 Melt the remaining butter or margarine in a small frying pan and fry the breadcrumbs until golden. Sprinkle the crumbs over the celeriac and serve immediately.

Cook's Notes

TIME
Preparation takes about 10 minutes, cooking time is about 30 minutes.

PREPARATION
If the sauce goes lumpy, rub it through a nylon sieve.

SERVING IDEA
Serve with a small mixed salad.

TOMATO CHARTREUSE

SERVES 4

This delicately flavoured starter is ideal for a warm summer's day.

INGREDIENTS

2-3 tbsps agar agar
Juice of ½ lemon
340ml/12 fl oz tomato juice
2 tsps tomato purée
1 bay leaf
Salt and freshly ground black pepper
3 tbsps olive or vegetable oil
3 spring onions, finely chopped
90g/3oz mushrooms, sliced
1 tbsp white wine vinegar
Pinch of mixed dried herbs
Cucumber slices, to garnish

1 Dissolve the agar agar in the lemon juice.
2 Combine the tomato juice, tomato purée, bay leaf and seasoning in a small saucepan and bring gently to the boil.
3 Allow to stand for 2 minutes, then remove the bay leaf.
4 Stir in the dissolved agar agar and whisk well to make sure the agar agar is evenly blended.
5 Dampen a 700ml/1¼ pint mould or individual moulds and pour in the tomato mixture. Chill in the refrigerator until set.

6 Heat the oil in a small frying pan and fry the spring onions and mushrooms until soft.
7 Allow the mushrooms to cool completely, then combine them with the vinegar and herbs. Season with salt and pepper.
8 Carefully loosen the tomato chartreuse with a round-bladed knife.
9 Hold a plate over the top of the mould and carefully turn both the plate and the mould over, shaking gently to drop the tomato chartreuse onto the plate.
10 Arrange the mushroom mixture on top and serve garnished with cucumber slices.

Step 8 Carefully loosen the tomato chartreuse with a round-bladed knife.

Step 9 Gently shake the mould to allow the chartreuse to drop out.

Cook's Notes

TIME
Preparation takes about 10 minutes, plus setting. Cooking time is about 5 minutes.

VEGETARIAN SUITABILITY
This recipe is suitable for vegans.

ASPARAGUS WITH ORANGE HOLLANDAISE

SERVES 4

Simplicity is often the making of a classic dish, and serving fresh asparagus in this way is certainly a classic combination.

INGREDIENTS

900g/2lbs asparagus spears
Grated rind and juice of ½ orange
Juice of ½ lemon
1 bay leaf
Blade of mace
60g/2oz butter
3 free-range egg yolks, beaten
Salt and freshly ground black pepper
Strips of blanched orange rind, to garnish (optional)

1 Trim away any thick, tough ends from the asparagus and rinse them well.
2 Bring a sauté pan of lightly salted water to the boil. Move the pan so that is half on and half off the direct heat (take care not to spill the water). Place the asparagus in the pan so that the tips are in the part of the pan off the direct heat.
3 Cover the pan and bring back to the boil. Cook asparagus for about 10 minutes or until just tender, drain and keep warm.

4 Meanwhile, prepare the sauce. Heat the orange juice, lemon juice, bay leaf and mace in a small pan to almost boiling and allow to stand for a few moments.
5 Melt the butter in the top of a double boiler or in a bowl placed over a pan of gently simmering water.
6 Whisk the beaten egg yolks into the butter and add the orange rind.
7 Strain the juice into the butter and egg mixture and whisk well.
8 Cook gently until the sauce thickens, whisking constantly.
9 Once the sauce has reached the desired consistency, immediately remove it from the heat and stand the pan or bowl in cold water to prevent further cooking.
10 Arrange the asparagus on serving plates and pour equal amounts of sauce over each serving. Garnish with strips of orange rind if wished.

Cook's Notes

TIME
Preparation takes about 10 minutes, cooking time is about 15 minutes.

VEGETARIAN SUITABILITY
This recipe is suitable for lacto-vegetarians only.

SERVING IDEA
Serve with thin slices of wholemeal bread.

GOURMET'S WARM SALAD

SERVES 4

This colourful salad is ideal as a sophisticated starter for a special meal.

INGREDIENTS

Mixed salad leaves, e.g. frisée, chicory, radicchio, lamb's
*   lettuce, watercress or iceberg lettuce*
2 avocados
175g/6oz black grapes
15g/4 tbsps chopped fresh mixed herbs
120g/4oz walnut pieces
120g/4oz vegetarian blue cheese, diced or crumbled
3 tbsps walnut oil and grapeseed oil, mixed
2 tbsps lemon vinegar
Pinch of unrefined sugar

1 Tear the larger salad leaves into small pieces and place in a large bowl.
2 If using lamb's lettuce separate the leaves and leave whole. Remove any tough stalks from the watercress. Add all the leaves to the bowl.
3 Peel the avocados, cut into neat slices and add

Step 4 *Remove the pips from the halved grapes using the point of a sharp knife.*

to the salad leaves.
4 Cut the grapes in half and remove pips, add the grapes to the salad along with the herbs, walnuts and cheese.
5 Put the oils, vinegar and sugar into a screw top jar. Screw down the top well and shake vigorously until the dressing is well blended.
6 Pour the dressing into a large frying pan and heat until bubbling. Quickly add to the salad and toss well, taking care not to break up the avocado.
7 Arrange on serving plates and serve at once.

Cook's Notes

TIME
Preparation takes about 15 minutes, cooking time is about 2 minutes.

VEGETARIAN SUITABILITY
This recipe is suitable for lacto-vegetarians only. See 'variation' for vegan alternative.

PREPARATION
It is important to tear the salad leaves by hand as the edges will discolour if they are cut with a knife.

VARIATION
For a delicious vegan alternative, substitute the cheese with 175g/6oz wild mushrooms that have been cooked in 2 tbsps white wine, drained then chilled.

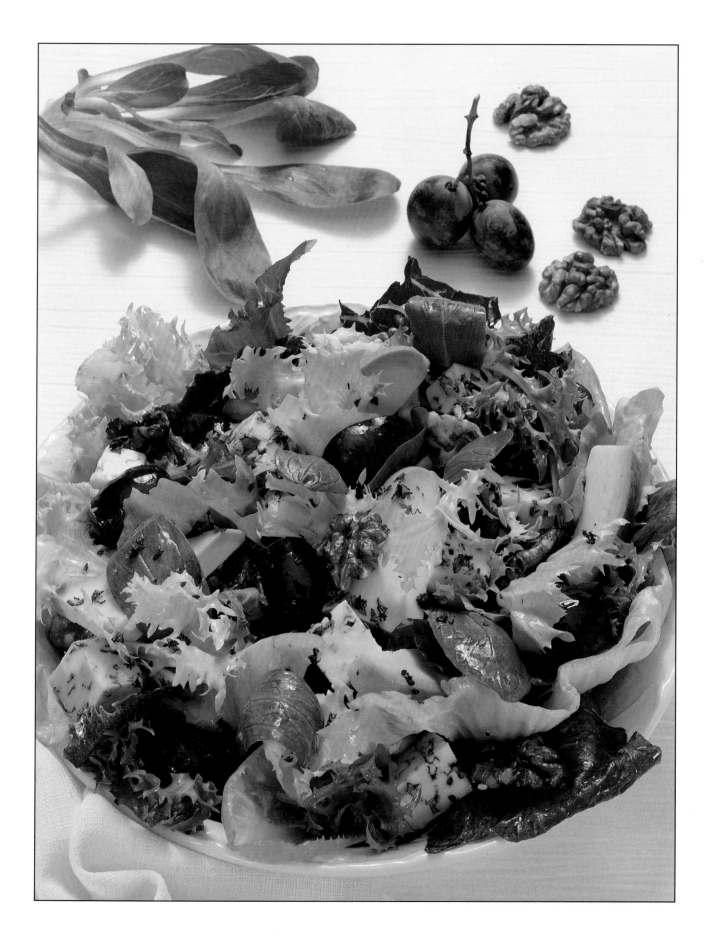

SPICY HOT GRAPEFRUIT

SERVES 4

This simple starter makes an ideal first course, or even a refresher between main courses.

INGREDIENTS

2 ruby grapefruits
1 tsp ground allspice
2 tsps unrefined caster sugar (optional)
Lemon balm or mint leaves, to decorate

1 Cut the grapefruits in half.
2 Using a small, sharp, serrated knife or a grapefruit knife, cut around the edges of each half between the flesh and the pith.
3 Carefully cut down between each segment and inner thin skins.
4 Take hold of the inner pithy core and gently twist to remove, and at the same time pull away the thin inner skins which have been cut away from the grapefruit segments.
5 Remove any pips.
6 Sprinkle each grapefruit half with equal amounts of the allspice and sugar, if using.

Step 3 *Cut between the fleshy segments and the thin inner skin.*

Step 4 *Gently twist out the pithy inner core, pulling the segment skins out with it.*

7 Place under a medium, preheated grill for 3-4 minutes to heat through.
8 Garnish with lemon balm or mint leaves.

Cook's Notes

⏰ TIME
Preparation takes about 15 minutes, cooking time is about 5 minutes.

🍃 VEGETARIAN SUITABILITY
This recipe is suitable for vegans.

📐 PREPARATION
The grapefruit halves can be prepared well in advance. Cover closely with cling film to prevent drying out.

🔪 VARIATION
Sprinkle each grapefruit with ground ginger instead of the allspice and pour a teaspoon of ginger wine or sherry over each half.

STUFFED TOMATOES PROVENÇAL

SERVES 4

A refreshing starter, ideal as a first course to a rich meal.

INGREDIENTS

4 large ripe tomatoes
30g/1oz butter or vegetable margarine
1 clove garlic, crushed
1 shallot, peeled and finely chopped
225g/8oz mushrooms, finely chopped
1 tbsp white wine or vegetable stock
45g/1½oz fresh white breadcrumbs
1 tsp chopped fresh parsley
1 tsp chopped fresh basil
¼ tsp dried thyme
1 tsp Dijon mustard
Salt and freshly ground black pepper

1 Preheat the oven to 180°C/350°F/Gas Mark 4.
2 Cut the tops off the tomatoes and carefully scoop out the flesh and seeds.
3 Place in a sieve and strain off excess juice. Chop the flesh.
4 Melt the butter or margarine in a saucepan and sauté the garlic and shallot until soft.
5 Stir in the mushrooms and wine or stock and cook gently for 4 minutes.
6 Remove from the heat and stir in the breadcrumbs, herbs, mustard, seasoning and tomato flesh, mixing well.
7 Fill each tomato with the mixture and place in a shallow ovenproof dish. Place caps on top.
8 Bake for 10 to 12 minutes and serve hot.

Cook's Notes

TIME
Preparation takes about 15 minutes, cooking time is about 15 minutes.

PREPARATION
If preferred the skins can be removed from the tomatoes before the centres are scooped out.

SERVING IDEA
Serve garnished with a mixed green salad.

VINAIGRETTE DE JARDIN

SERVES 4

Healthy, fresh vegetables with a tangy dressing make this an interesting starter or a delicious side dish.

INGREDIENTS

120g/4oz mange tout peas
2 courgettes, washed and sliced
120g/4oz broccoli florets
120g/4oz cauliflower florets
2 carrots, peeled and sliced
4 tomatoes
1 yellow pepper, seeded and sliced
4 spring onions, trimmed and cut into diagonal strips
90ml/6 tbsps olive oil
2 tbsps white wine vinegar
1 tbsp Dijon mustard
1 tbsp chopped fresh herbs (e.g. chives, parsley, basil)
Salt and freshly ground black pepper

1 Bring a pan of lightly salted water to the boil and cook the mange tout peas for 3 minutes or until just tender.
2 Remove with a draining spoon and place in a bowl of iced water.
3 Cook the courgettes in the water for 2 minutes, remove and add to the mange tout. Cook the broccoli, cauliflower and carrots for 5 minutes.

4 The vegetables should be tender but still crisp. Allow to cool completely, drain and set aside.
5 Cut a small cross in the stalk end of each tomato and plunge them into boiling water for a few seconds. Remove the tomatoes from the water with a draining spoon and peel away the skins using a small, sharp knife.
6 Quarter the tomatoes and remove and discard the seeds. Cut the tomato flesh into thin slices.
7 Put the tomatoes, pepper and spring onions into a large bowl, add the drained blanched vegetables and toss to mix well.
8 Put the oil, vinegar, mustard, herbs and seasoning into a small bowl and mix together thoroughly until thick and pale.
9 Pour the dressing over the vegetables and toss to mix well. Leave to marinate for 3-4 hours before serving.

Step 6 *Quarter the skinned tomatoes, and remove and discard the seeds.*

Cook's Notes

TIME
Preparation takes about 15 minutes, plus marinating. Cooking time is about 10 minutes.

VEGETARIAN SUITABILITY
This recipe is suitable for vegans.

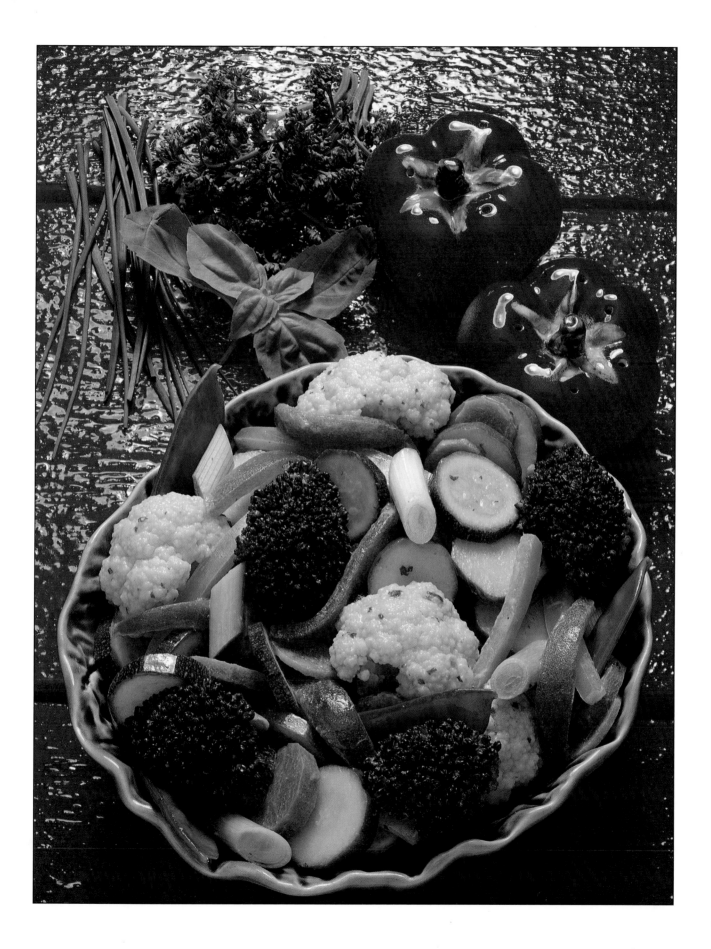

COURGETTE AND CARROT TERRINE

SERVES 6-8

This colourful terrine makes a sophisticated starter which is sure to impress family or guests.

INGREDIENTS

6-8 large, green cabbage leaves
1-2 carrots, peeled and cut into thin sticks
1-2 courgettes, washed and cut into thin sticks
340g/12oz low-fat curd cheese
4 slices white bread, crusts removed, made into crumbs
2 free-range eggs, beaten
140ml/¼ pint double cream, lightly whipped
2 tbsps snipped fresh chives
Salt and freshly ground black pepper
280ml/½ pint natural yogurt
140ml/¼ pint mayonnaise
2 tomatoes, skinned, seeded and cut into dice
2 tbsps lemon juice or dry white wine
Pinch unrefined sugar (optional)

1 Preheat the oven to 160°C/325°F/Gas Mark 3.
2 Trim the thick spine away from the cabbage leaves by cutting a triangular section out of each.
3 Blanch cabbage leaves in boiling water for 2 minutes, then refresh in cold water.
4 Blanch the carrot sticks for 4 minutes in boiling water, then refresh in cold water.
5 Repeat with the courgette, blanching for only 1 minute.
6 Combine the cheese, breadcrumbs, eggs, cream, chives and seasoning. Mix well.
7 Drain the blanched vegetables well and pat dry with kitchen paper.
8 Leaving at least 5cm/2 inches of leaf hanging over the edges, carefully line a 900g/2lb loaf tin with the cabbage leaves. Overlap each leaf slightly to ensure that no gap appears when the terrine is turned out.
9 Put one quarter of the cheese mixture into the tin and spread out evenly.
10 Place a layer of carrots over the cheese mixture. Top with a quarter of the cheese mixture.
11 Arrange a layer of courgettes over the cheese and top with some more of the cheese mixture.
12 Repeat until all the vegetable and cheese mixtures are used.
13 Fold the cabbage over the terrine to enclose the filling completely. Cover with a sheet of non-stick baking parchment, then cover with foil.
14 Place in a roasting tin filled with enough hot water to come halfway up the sides of the terrine. Bake for 1½ hours or until the terrine feels firm to the touch.
15 Cool the terrine completely and chill before turning out.
16 Combine the yogurt, mayonnaise, tomatoes, lemon juice or wine, sugar if using, and a little more seasoning to make a sauce.
17 Cut the terrine into slices and serve with the sauce.

AUBERGINE CAVIAR

SERVES 4

This novel starter is an interesting and different way of serving this delicious vegetable.

INGREDIENTS

1 large or 2 small aubergines
Salt
60ml/4 tbsps walnut oil
1 clove garlic, crushed
Juice of ½ lemon
Pinch of cayenne pepper
2 hard-boiled, free-range eggs (optional)
1 small onion, finely chopped
4-8 slices French bread, toasted
2 tbsps chopped fresh parsley

1 Remove the stalk from the aubergine and cut in half lengthways.
2 Using a small sharp knife, score and cut the flesh on each half of the aubergine, at about 5mm/¼-inch intervals, diagonally, first in one direction, then the other.
3 Sprinkle each cut surface with a little salt and leave to stand for 30 minutes, to draw out any bitterness and excess water.
4 Rinse the aubergines thoroughly and pat dry with kitchen paper.

5 Cut the aubergine into chunks. Heat the oil in a frying pan and fry the aubergine and garlic until the aubergine is tender. This will take about 10 minutes.
6 Place the aubergine in a food processor along with the lemon juice, cayenne and some salt, and process to chop finely.
7 Adjust the seasoning and chill thoroughly.
8 Cut the eggs in half and separate the yolks from the whites.
9 Push the yolks through a nylon sieve.
10 Finely chop the egg white.
11 Pile the aubergine caviar onto the French bread and top with chopped onion, then egg white, then egg yolk.
12 Sprinkle with chopped parsley and serve.

Step 2 *Score the cut half of each aubergine half using a sharp knife. Cut criss-cross lines deeply into the flesh in a diamond pattern, taking care not to cut through the skins.*

Cook's Notes

 TIME
Preparation takes about 15 minutes, plus standing. Cooking time is about 10 minutes.

 SERVING IDEA
Serve with a side salad.

VEGETARIAN SUITABILITY
This recipe is suitable for lacto-vegetarians, or vegans if the egg is omitted.

VARIATION
Use a 5cm/2-inch piece of cucumber instead of the egg in this recipe, chopping it into very small dice and sprinkling with a little black pepper before using it as a garnish.

PASTA AND ASPARAGUS SALAD

<u>SERVES 4</u>

This elegant green salad is a wonderful way of making the most of asparagus, that most luxurious of vegetables.

Step 6 *Pour the dressing over the vegetables and pasta and stir gently to coat well.*

INGREDIENTS

120g/4oz tagliatelle
450g/1lb asparagus, trimmed and cut into 2.5cm/1-inch
    pieces
2 courgettes, cut into 5cm/2-inch sticks
2 tbsps chopped fresh parsley
2 tbsps chopped fresh marjoram
1 lemon, peeled and segmented
Grated rind and juice of 1 lemon
90ml/6 tbsps olive oil
Pinch of unrefined sugar
Salt and freshly ground black pepper
Crisp lettuce leaves
Frisée leaves

1 Cook the pasta in plenty of lightly salted, boiling water for 10 minutes or as directed on the packet.
2 Drain and refresh in cold water. Drain again and leave to cool completely.
3 Cook the asparagus in lightly salted, boiling water for 4 minutes, then add the courgettes and cook for a further 3-4 minutes or until the vegetables are just tender. Drain and refresh in cold water. Drain again and leave to cool.
4 Place the cooked pasta, vegetables, herbs and lemon segments into a large bowl and mix together, taking care not to break up the vegetables.
5 Mix together the lemon rind and juice, oil, sugar and salt and pepper, to make the dressing.
6 Arrange the lettuce and frisée on serving plates. Just before serving, pour the dressing over the vegetables and pasta and toss to coat well.
7 Pile equal quantities of the pasta salad into the centre of the salad leaves and serve immediately.

Cook's Notes

 TIME
Preparation takes about 15 minutes, plus cooling, cooking time is about 20 minutes.

VEGETARIAN SUITABILITY
This recipe is suitable for vegans as long as there is no egg in the pasta.

COOK'S TIP
Put the ingredients for the dressing into a screw-top jar and shake vigorously to blend thoroughly.

BROCCOLI AND HAZELNUT TERRINE

SERVE 6-8

This colourful, crunchy terrine is full of protein and flavour.

INGREDIENTS

6-8 large whole spinach leaves

450g/1lb broccoli

2 free-range eggs, beaten

175g/6oz low-fat curd cheese

280ml/½ pint double cream, lightly whipped

4 slices white bread, crusts removed, made into crumbs

1 shallot, peeled and finely chopped

Pinch dried thyme

Pinch of ground nutmeg

Salt and freshly ground black pepper

120g/4oz hazelnuts, lightly toasted, then finely chopped

280ml/½ pint mayonnaise

140ml/¼ pint natural yogurt

Grated rind and juice of 1 lemon

Pinch of cayenne pepper

1 Preheat the oven to 170°C/325°F/Gas Mark 3.

2 Trim away any coarse stalks from the spinach, taking care to leave the leaves whole. Wash the leaves, blanch in boiling water for 1 minute, drain and refresh in cold water. Drain again and pat dry.

3 Leaving at least 5cm/2 inches of leaf hanging over the edges, carefully line a 900g/2lb loaf tin with the spinach leaves. Overlap each leaf slightly to ensure that no gaps appear when the terrine is turned out.

4 Chop the broccoli finely.

5 Put the eggs, cheese, cream, breadcrumbs, shallot, thyme, nutmeg, salt and pepper into a bowl and combine well.

6 Stir in the broccoli and hazelnuts, mixing well to combine thoroughly.

7 Spoon the mixture into the lined loaf tin, packing it down well, but taking care not to dislodge the spinach leaves.

8 Carefully fold the spinach over the top of the terrine mixture. Cover with a sheet of non-stick baking parchment and then cover with foil.

9 Place in a roasting tin and add enough hot water to come halfway up the sides of the loaf tin. Bake for 1 hour, or until the terrine feels firm to the touch.

10 Cool the terrine completely, and chill before turning out.

11 In a bowl mix together the mayonnaise, yogurt, lemon rind and juice, cayenne pepper and a little salt. Serve the sauce with slices of the terrine.

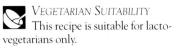

Cook's Notes

TIME
Preparation takes about 20 minutes, cooking time is about 1 hour.

VEGETARIAN SUITABILITY
This recipe is suitable for lacto-vegetarians only.

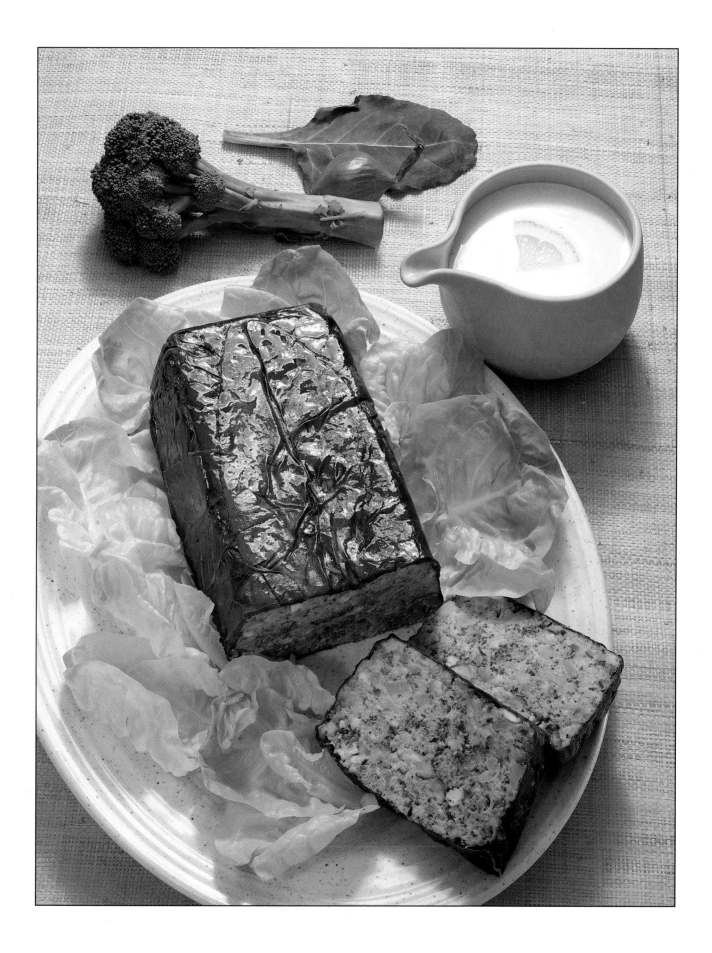

DANISH EGG SALAD

SERVES 4

This delicious starter is also ideal for a light lunch or supper for two.

Step 9 *Shred the omelette into 5mm/¼-inch wide and 5cm/2-inch long strips.*

INGREDIENTS

1 free-range egg
1 tbsp single cream
Salt and freshly ground black pepper
Knob butter or vegetable margarine
225g/8oz fresh or frozen peas
280ml/½ pint soured cream
60ml/4 tbsps mayonnaise
2 tbsps chopped fresh dill
Pinch of paprika
Salt
6 sticks celery, trimmed and diced
120g/4oz vegetarian cheese of your choice, diced
120g/4oz diced cucumber
3 spring onions, chopped
½ head Chinese leaves, shredded

1 Beat together the egg, cream and seasoning in a small bowl.
2 Melt the butter or margarine in a frying pan and pour in the egg mixture, tilt the pan so that the egg coats the base in a thin layer.
3 Cook gently for 1-2 minutes or until the egg is set. Carefully flip over and cook the other side.

4 Remove from the pan and allow to cool.
5 Cook the peas and refresh in cold water, drain and set aside.
6 Whisk together the soured cream, mayonnaise, dill, paprika and a little salt. Reserve a few tablespoons.
7 Mix the remaining dressing with the peas, celery, cheese, cucumber and spring onions.
8 Arrange the Chinese leaves on a serving dish and pile the vegetable mixture into the centre.
9 Using a sharp knife, shred the omelette and use to garnish the salad. Drizzle over the reserved soured cream dressing before serving.

Cook's Notes

TIME
Preparation takes about 20 minutes, cooking time is about 10 minutes.

VEGETARIAN SUITABILITY
This recipe is suitable for lacto-vegetarians only.

VARIATION
Use finely chopped tarragon in place of dill in this recipe and a mild vegetarian brie for a delicious French version.

MUSHROOM AND ARTICHOKE SALAD

SERVES 4

Wild mushrooms are becoming more readily available, and this recipe provides a delightful way of serving them.

INGREDIENTS

2-3 artichokes, depending on size
1 slice of lemon
1 bay leaf
6 black peppercorns
225g/8oz mixed wild mushrooms, e.g. shiitake or oyster
2 tbsps vegetable oil
Radicchio, iceberg lettuce and watercress leaves, mixed
2 tbsps snipped fresh chives
90ml/6 tbsps olive oil
2 tbsps white wine vinegar
1 tbsp Dijon mustard
Salt and freshly ground black pepper
Sprigs fresh dill or chervil, to garnish

1 Trim the pointed leaves off the artichokes with a sharp knife. Remove the stem.
2 Place the lemon slice, bay leaf and peppercorns in a saucepan of water and bring to the boil. Add the artichokes and cook for 30-40 minutes or until tender and the bottom leaves pull away easily.
3 Stand each artichoke upside-down to drain completely.
4 Slice the mushrooms. Heat the vegetable oil in a frying pan and fry the mushrooms for 5 minutes, or until just tender. Set aside.
5 Tear the salad leaves into small pieces and place in a bowl with the snipped chives.
6 Whisk together the olive oil, vinegar, mustard and seasoning until thick and pale coloured.
7 Remove the leaves from the drained artichokes and arrange them attractively on plates.
8 Arrange the leaf salad over the artichoke.
9 Cut away and discard the fluffy 'chokes' from the artichoke hearts. Trim the hearts and cut these into pieces.
10 Mix together the artichoke hearts, mushrooms and half the dressing. Spoon some onto each plate. Garnish with dill or chervil, and serve the remaining dressing separately.

Cook's Notes

TIME
Preparation takes about 20 minutes, cooking time is about 40 minutes.

VEGETARIAN SUITABILITY
This recipe is suitable for vegans.

PREPARATION
The mushrooms and artichokes can be prepared well in advance and kept in the refrigerator until needed.

Chapter 3

SNACKS AND SALADS

STUFFED POTATOES

<u>SERVES 4</u>

An unusual way of serving this popular vegetable meal.

INGREDIENTS

4 large baking potatoes, scrubbed
4 free-range eggs
60g/2oz butter or vegetable margarine
120g/4oz button mushrooms, sliced
1 shallot, peeled and finely chopped
1 tbsp plain flour
420ml/3/4 pint milk
60g/2oz vegetarian Cheddar cheese, grated
Pinch each of dry mustard and cayenne pepper
Salt and freshly ground black pepper
1 bunch watercress, chopped
Grated cheese, cayenne and watercress, to garnish

1 Preheat the oven to 200°C/400°F/Gas Mark 6.
2 Prick the potatoes a few times with a fork and place them directly on the oven shelves. Bake for 3/4-1 hour, or until soft when squeezed.
3 Reduce the oven temperature to 170°C/325°F/Gas Mark 3 and keep potatoes warm.
4 Poach the eggs in gently simmering water for 3½-5 minutes until the white and yolk is just set. Remove from the pan and keep in cold water.

5 Melt 15g/½oz of the butter or margarine in a small pan and fry the mushrooms and shallot for 5 minutes until just beginning to soften.
6 Melt the remaining fat in another pan, stir in the flour and cook for about 1 minute. Remove from the heat and gradually add 280ml/½ pint of the milk, stirring well after each addition.
7 Return to the heat and cook gently until sauce thickens. Stir in the cheese, and continue cooking until cheese melts. Add the mustard, cayenne, salt and pepper.
8 When the potatoes are cooked, cut a slice off the top and scoop out the flesh with a spoon, leaving a border to form a firm shell.
9 Put equal amounts of the mushroom mixture into each potato and top with a well drained egg. Spoon the cheese sauce mixture over the top.
10 Heat the remaining milk until almost boiling. Mash the potato flesh, then gradually beat in the hot milk and watercress. Pipe or spoon the potato over the sauce in the potato shell.
11 Sprinkle the top with a little extra cheese and return to the oven for 15 minutes to warm through.
12 Serve garnished with cayenne and watercress.

Cook's Notes

TIME
Preparation takes about 20 minutes, cooking time is about 1½ hours.

VEGETARIAN SUITABILITY
This recipe is suitable for lacto-vegetarians only.

SERVING IDEA
Serve with coleslaw or any other salad.

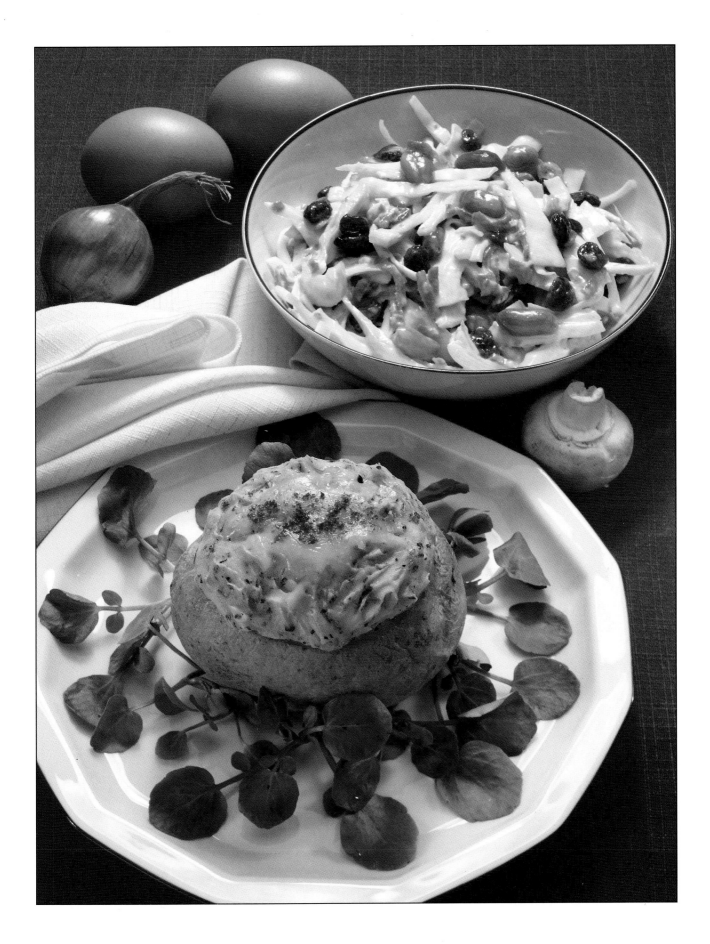

SPANISH BARLEY

<u>SERVES 4</u>

Paprika gives this dish its distinctive taste. It is a colourful and delicious main dish that is equally good served hot or cold.

INGREDIENTS

340g/12oz barley
700ml/1¼ pints vegetable stock or water
2 tbsps olive or vegetable oil
1 large Spanish onion, peeled and chopped
1 clove garlic, crushed
1 green pepper, seeded and chopped
1 tsp paprika
Salt and freshly ground black pepper
400g/14oz can chopped tomatoes
Tomato slices and chopped parsley, to garnish

1 Place the barley and stock in a saucepan and bring gently to the boil, simmer for 25 minutes or until the barley is tender, drain and discard any excess liquid.

2 Heat the oil in a saucepan and fry the onion, garlic and pepper until soft.
3 Stir in the paprika and cook gently for 1 minute.
4 Stir in the cooked barley, seasoning and tomatoes, stirring well.
5 Cook gently for 10 minutes until the juice from the tomatoes has been absorbed.
6 Serve garnished with tomato slices and a sprinkling of chopped fresh parsley.

Step 1 *Drain the cooked barley and discard the excess water.*

Cook's Notes

 TIME
Preparation takes about 5 minutes, cooking time is about 40 minutes.

VEGETARIAN SUITABILITY
This recipe is suitable for vegans.

FREEZING
This recipe will freeze well for up to 3 months. The flavour of the paprika will be enhanced during this time.

SERVING IDEA
Serve with a tomato and basil salad.

 VARIATION
Add 90g/3oz pitted sliced black olives and 120g/4oz cubed vegetarian Wensleydale cheese for a delicious, lacto-vegetarian alternative.

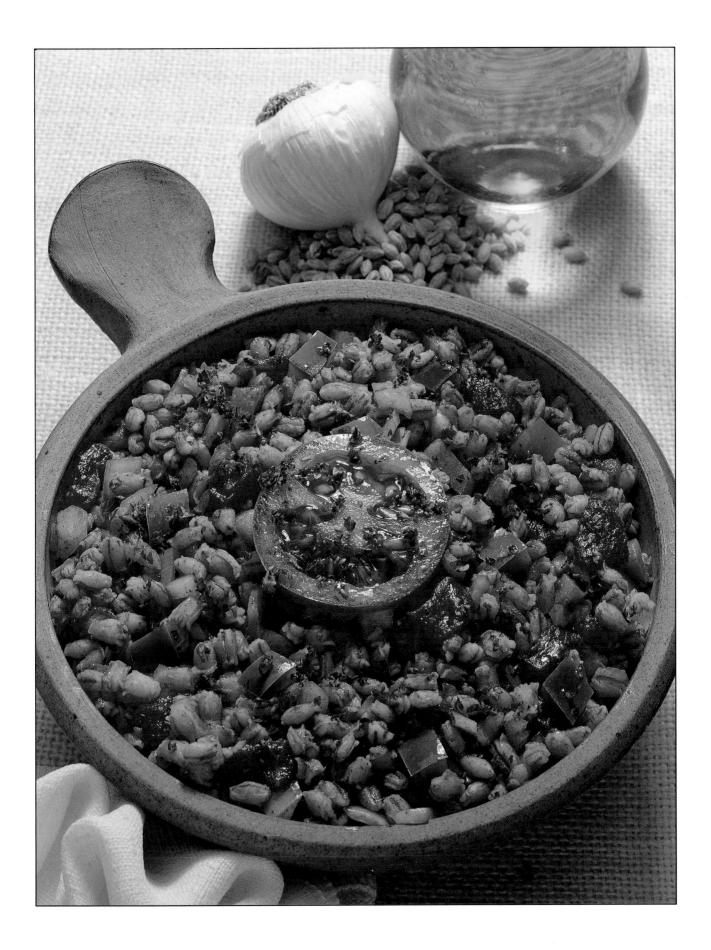

PASTA PRIMAVERA

SERVES 4

Primavera is Italian for springtime, and this recipe certainly tastes its best when tender young spring vegetables and herbs are used.

INGREDIENTS

450g/1lb pasta shapes

225g/8oz asparagus

120g/4oz green beans, trimmed and cut into diagonal slices

2 carrots, peeled and sliced

60g/2oz butter or vegetable margarine

60g/2oz mushrooms, sliced

3 tomatoes, skinned, seeded and chopped

6 spring onions, trimmed and sliced

140ml/¼ pint double cream

Salt and freshly ground black pepper

2 tbsps chopped fresh parsley

2 tsps chopped fresh tarragon

1 Cook the pasta in plenty of lightly salted, boiling water for 10 minutes or as directed on the packet.

2 Meanwhile, trim any wood ends from the asparagus and cut each spear diagonally into 2.5cm/1-inch pieces, leaving the actual tips whole.

3 Blanch the asparagus, beans and carrots for 3 minutes in boiling water, then drain well.

4 Melt the butter or margarine in a large pan and add the blanched vegetables and mushrooms. Sauté for 3 minutes, then stir in the tomatoes and spring onions.

5 Add the cream, seasoning and herbs and bring to the boil. Boil rapidly for a few minutes until the cream thickens slightly.

6 When the pasta is cooked, drain well and add to the pan, toss to combine all the ingredients thoroughly and serve immediately.

Cook's Notes

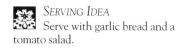

TIME
Preparation takes about 15 minutes, cooking time is about 20 minutes.

VEGETARIAN SUITABILITY
This recipe is suitable for lacto-vegetarians only

SERVING IDEA
Serve with garlic bread and a tomato salad.

VARIATION
Use wild mushrooms in place of the button mushrooms.

CAULIFLOWER AND CABBAGE IN CHEESE SAUCE

SERVES 4

*A delicious combination of flavours and textures lifts this recipe above
its more usual counterpart, cauliflower cheese.*

INGREDIENTS

1 cauliflower
1 small green cabbage
60g/2oz butter or vegetable margarine
60g/2oz wholemeal flour
570ml/1 pint milk
120g/4oz vegetarian Cheddar cheese, grated
90g/3oz walnuts, finely chopped
Salt and freshly ground black pepper
Pinch of ground nutmeg

1 Break the cauliflower into small florets. Wash and thickly shred the cabbage.
2 Bring a saucepan of water to the boil, add the cauliflower, cook for 5 minutes and then add the cabbage. Cook for a further 5 minutes or until both the vegetables are just tender.

3 Meanwhile, melt the fat in a small saucepan and stir in the flour. Cook for 1 minute.
4 Remove from the heat and gradually add the milk, stirring well. Return to the heat and cook, gently stirring, continuously until thickened.
5 Add the cheese and nuts and cook until the cheese melts. Add salt, pepper and nutmeg.
6 When the vegetables are cooked, drain well and transfer to a serving dish. Pour the sauce over and sprinkle with a little more nutmeg.

Step 1 *Break the cauliflower into small florets, and cut away any thick stalks or leaves.*

Cook's Notes

TIME
Preparation takes about 15 minutes, cooking time is about 15 minutes.

VEGETARIAN SUITABILITY
This recipe is suitable for lacto-vegetarians only.

SERVING IDEA
Serve as a vegetable accompaniment for up to 8 people.

FRESH AND DRIED BEANS PROVENÇALE

<u>SERVES 4</u>

This attractive dish is full of flavour and is high in protein too.

INGREDIENTS

225g/8oz dried flageolet beans, soaked
450g/1lb tomatoes, skinned and chopped
1 clove garlic, crushed
2 tsps dried basil
1 tsp dried oregano
½ tsp dried rosemary
450g/1lb fresh or frozen green beans, trimmed

1 Drain the beans and place in a saucepan with enough fresh water to cover them by 2.5cm/1 inch.

Bring to the boil, boil rapidly for 10 minutes, then reduce the heat and simmer gently for 1-1½ hours or until the beans are soft.

2 Drain and set aside until required.

3 Place the tomatoes, garlic and herbs in a saucepan and cook over a low heat for 10 minutes or until the tomatoes soften and the juice begins to flow.

4 Cut the green beans into 2.5cm/1-inch lengths and add to the pan along with the cooked flageolet beans. Cook gently for 15 minutes or until the flavours are well combined.

Cook's Notes

TIME
Preparation takes about 15 minutes, plus about 3 hours soaking. Cooking time is about 2 hours.

VEGETARIAN SUITABILITY
This recipe is suitable for vegans.

COOK'S TIP
Canned flageolet beans are now easily available and require no pre-cooking, so reduce the overall cooking time dramatically. Use 450g/1lb canned, drained beans in this recipe.

SERVING IDEA
Serve this casserole over cornmeal or cooked rice. Lacto-vegetarians can sprinkle grated vegetarian cheese over the top just before serving.

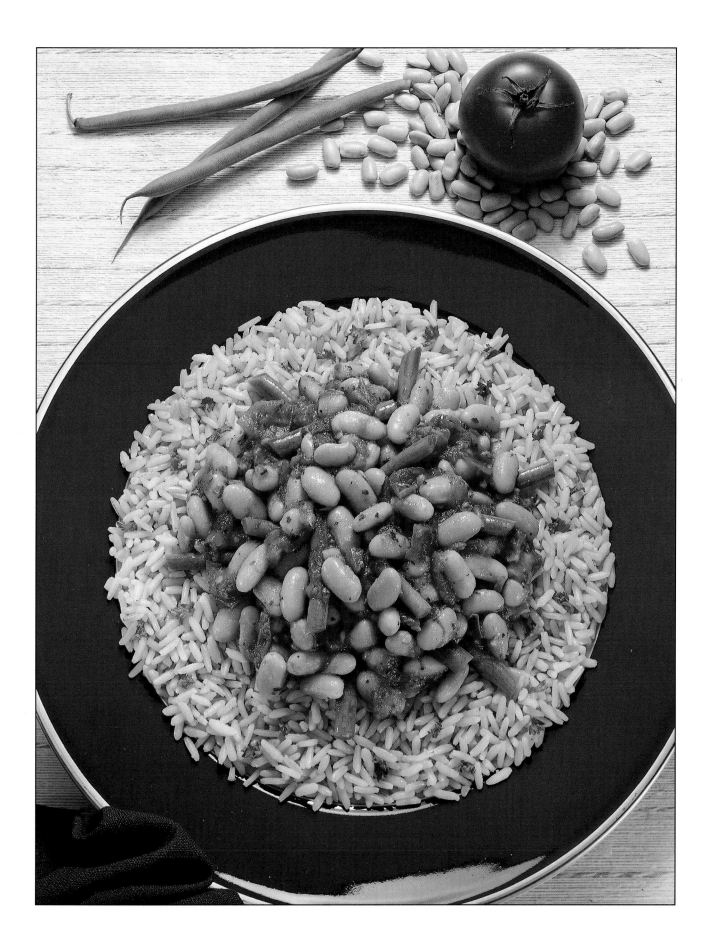

RED LENTIL AND MUSHROOM LOAF

<u>SERVES 4-6</u>

*This delicious and highly nutritious vegetable loaf is equally good served
hot or cold.*

INGREDIENTS

175g/6oz red lentils
340ml/12 fl oz vegetable stock or water
1 free-range egg
2 tbsps double cream
90g/3oz mushrooms, chopped
120g/4oz curd or cream cheese
1 clove garlic, crushed
1 tbsp chopped fresh parsley
Salt and freshly ground black pepper
400g/14oz can chopped tomatoes
1 tbsp tomato purée
Pinch of unrefined sugar
1 tbsp chopped fresh tarragon

1 Preheat the oven to 180°C/350°F/Gas Mark 4.
2 Rinse the lentils and place in a saucepan with the stock or water.
3 Bring gently to the boil, and boil rapidly for 10 minutes. Reduce the heat and continue to cook until the lentils are soft and the liquid has been absorbed.
4 Using a potato masher mash the lentils to a thick purée.
5 Beat the egg and cream together and add to the lentil purée, along with the mushrooms, cheese, garlic, parsley and seasoning.
6 Mix all the ingredients together thoroughly.
7 Press the lentil mixture into a greased and lined 450g/1lb loaf tin. Bake for 1 hour or until firm to the touch.
8 Put the tomatoes, tomato purée, sugar and half the tarragon into a small saucepan and cook for 5 minutes. Purée in a food processor or push through a sieve to form a smooth sauce.
9 Stir in the remaining tarragon and season to taste.
10 Slice the loaf and serve with the tomato sauce and a mixed salad.

Cook's Notes

TIME
Preparation takes about 15 minutes, cooking time is about 1 hour, 20 minutes.

VEGETARIAN SUITABILITY
This recipe is suitable for lacto-vegetarians only.

SPAGHETTI WITH PINE NUTS

This crunchy, flavoursome combination makes good use of store-cupboard ingredients.

INGREDIENTS

340g/12oz spaghetti
90ml/6 tbsps olive oil
1 large onion, peeled and sliced
1 clove garlic, crushed
120g/4oz pine nuts
400g/14oz can artichoke hearts, drained
12 tbsps chopped fresh parsley
60g/2oz vegetarian Cheddar cheese, grated (optional)

1 Cook the spaghetti in plenty of lightly salted, boiling water for 10 minutes or as directed on the packet.
2 Just before the spaghetti is cooked, heat the oil in a frying pan and fry the onion and garlic until beginning to brown.
3 Add the pine nuts and cook for 1 minute. Chop the artichoke hearts into bite-sized pieces and add to the pan with the parsley. Heat gently for a few minutes.
4 When the spaghetti is cooked, drain well and add to the pan. Toss until the spaghetti is well coated in the oil.
5 Stir in the grated cheese if using, reserving a little to sprinkle on top.
6 Transfer to a serving dish and sprinkle with the remaining cheese. Serve immediately.

Step 3 *Chop the artichoke hearts into bite-sized pieces.*

Cook's Notes

TIME
Preparation takes about 5 minutes, cooking time is about 15 minutes.

VEGETARIAN SUITABILITY
This recipe is only suitable for lacto-vegetarians if the cheese is used.

COOK'S TIP
If fresh pasta is used, start cooking the onion and garlic immediately as the cooking time is much shorter.

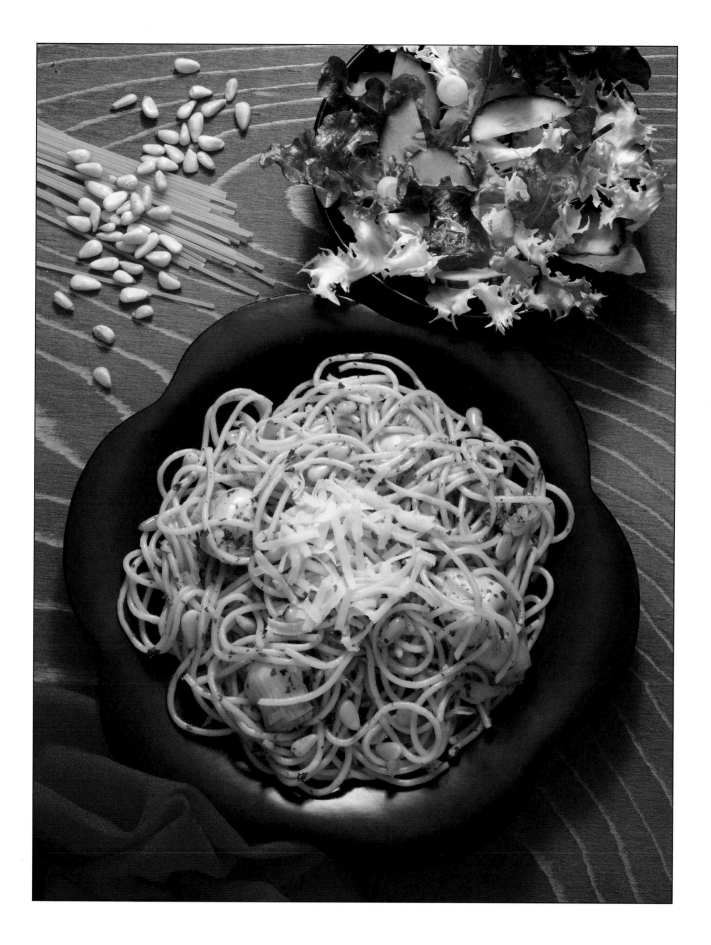

PANCAKES PROVENÇALE

SERVES 4

These moreish pancakes are quick and easy to make.

INGREDIENTS

60g/2oz plain flour
Pinch salt
1 free-range egg
140ml/¼ pint milk
Oil for frying
2 green peppers, seeded and diced
1 red pepper, seeded and diced
1 large onion, peeled and finely chopped
1 clove garlic, crushed
1 small courgette, diced
3 tomatoes, skinned, seeded and chopped
1 tsp chopped fresh basil
2 tbsps tomato purée
30g/1oz vegetarian Cheshire or Wensleydale cheese,
*   crumbled*
Salt and freshly ground black pepper
Fresh herbs and tomato slices, to garnish

1 Put the flour and salt into a bowl. Make a well in the centre and add the egg and a little of the milk.

2 Using a wooden spoon, gradually incorporate the flour into the egg mixture to form a smooth paste. Gradually beat in the remaining milk.
3 Heat a little oil in a heavy-based frying pan and spoon in a little of the batter, swirl to coat the base of the pan. Cook for about 1 minute or until the underside is golden.
4 Flip or toss the pancake over and cook the other side. Slide the pancake out of the pan and keep warm. Repeat with the remaining batter. You should end up with 8 pancakes.
5 Heat 2 tbsps oil in a small pan and fry the peppers, onion and garlic until beginning to soften.
6 Stir in the courgette and tomatoes and cook for 2 minutes. Add the basil, tomato purée, cheese and seasoning, and cook gently until cheese begins to melt.
7 Divide the vegetable mixture between the pancakes and roll or fold the pancakes to enclose the filling.
8 Serve immediately garnished with sprigs of fresh herbs and tomato slices.

Cook's Notes

TIME
Preparation takes about 20 minutes, cooking time is about 30 minutes.

VEGETARIAN SUITABILITY
This recipe is suitable for lacto-vegetarians only. See variation for vegan alternative.

VARIATION
Omit the cheese from the filling and substitute halved pitta bread for the pancakes to make a vegan variation.

VEGETABLE PILAU

SERVES 4-6

*Lightly spiced and fragrant, this traditional Indian rice dish will serve 4
as a lunch or supper on its own or 6 as part of a larger Indian meal.*

INGREDIENTS

60g/2oz butter or 60ml/4 tbsps vegetable oil

1 onion, peeled and finely sliced

225g/8oz long grain rice

1 small piece cinnamon stick

4 cardamoms, husks removed and seeds crushed

4 cloves

½ tsp ground coriander

¼ tsp ground turmeric

¼ tsp garam masala

1 bay leaf

Salt and freshly ground black pepper

570ml/1 pint vegetable stock or water

½ aubergine, cut into dice

60g/2oz frozen cauliflower florets

120g/4oz frozen mixed vegetables

1 Melt the butter or heat the oil in a large saucepan and fry the onion until beginning to soften.

2 Stir in the rice, spices, bay leaf and seasoning and fry for 2 minutes, stirring constantly.

3 Add the stock or water, stir well, bring gently to the boil and cook for 5 minutes.

4 Add the remaining ingredients and cook for a further 5-7 minutes or until rice is tender and most of the liquid has been absorbed.

5 Leave covered for 5 minutes until the remaining liquid has been absorbed, stir to separate the grains and serve.

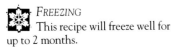 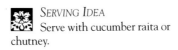

Cook's Notes

TIME
Preparation takes about 10 minutes, cooking time is about 20 minutes.

VEGETARIAN SUITABILITY
This recipe is suitable for vegans if oil is used.

COOK'S TIP
Sprinkle with chopped coriander to enhance the taste and give a superb fragrance to this dish.

FREEZING
This recipe will freeze well for up to 2 months.

SERVING IDEA
Serve with cucumber raita or chutney.

GARBURE

SERVES 4

*This thick, tasty vegetarian version of a classic French country
soup-stew makes a warming lunch or supper dish.*

INGREDIENTS

225g/8oz haricot beans, soaked overnight

2 tbsps vegetable oil

1 large potato, scrubbed and diced

4 carrots, peeled and sliced

2 leeks, washed and chopped

1 tsp dried marjoram

1 tsp dried thyme

½ tsp paprika

850ml/1½ pints vegetable stock

Salt and freshly ground black pepper

1 small cabbage, finely shredded

1 Drain the soaked beans and place in a saucepan with enough fresh water to cover them by 2.5cm/1 inch. Bring to the boil, boil rapidly for 10 minutes, then reduce the heat and simmer gently for 1 hour or until the beans are soft.

2 Drain and set aside until required.

3 Heat the oil in a saucepan and sauté the potato, carrots and leeks for 5 minutes.

4 Stir in the herbs and paprika and cook for 1 minute. Add the beans and vegetable stock and simmer gently for 20 minutes. Stir well and season to taste.

5 Scatter the shredded cabbage over the beans, cover and continue cooking for 15-20 minutes or until the cabbage is cooked.

Cook's Notes

TIME
Preparation takes about 20 minutes, plus overnight soaking. Cooking time is about 1¾ hours.

VEGETARIAN SUITABILITY
This recipe is suitable for vegans.

SERVING IDEA
Serve ladled over thick slices of wholemeal bread.

PREPARATION
Great care must be taken when cooking any dried beans. They should be well soaked, preferably overnight, then thoroughly cooked with at least 10 minutes rapid boiling before being eaten.

CURRIED VEGETABLES

SERVES 6-8

This wholesome vegetable curry includes an interesting combination of unusual vegetables, nuts and spices.

INGREDIENTS

2 tbsps groundnut oil
1 large onion, peeled and chopped
1 green chilli, seeded and very finely chopped
1 small piece root ginger, peeled and grated
2 cloves garlic, crushed
½ tsp ground coriander
½ tsp ground cumin
1 tsp ground turmeric
2 potatoes, peeled and diced
1 small cauliflower, washed and cut into florets
1 aubergine, cut into small cubes
400g/14oz can tomatoes, drained
225g/8oz okra, trimmed, washed and thickly sliced
280ml/½ pint vegetable stock
120g/4oz roasted, salted cashew nuts
25g/4 tbsps desiccated coconut
60ml/4 tbsps natural yogurt (optional)

1 Heat the oil in a saucepan and fry the onion, chilli, ginger and garlic for 5 minutes or until beginning to soften.
2 Add the spices and cook for a further minute.
3 Stir in the potatoes and cauliflower and cook for 5 minutes, then stir in all the remaining ingredients, except the natural yogurt.
4 Cover and simmer gently for 30-40 minutes or until all the vegetables are tender and the flavours well blended.
5 Serve topped with natural yogurt if wished.

Cook's Notes

TIME
Preparation takes about 30 minutes, cooking time is about 50 minutes.

VEGETARIAN SUITABILITY
This recipe is suitable for lacto-vegetarians and vegans if the natural yogurt is not used.

PREPARATION
Great care must be taken when preparing chillies. Try not to get the juice into the eyes or mouth, and rinse with lots of cold water if this does happen.

COOK'S TIP
Wear rubber gloves when preparing chillies, to help prevent the juice getting onto your fingers and from there into your eyes or mouth.

FREEZING
This recipe freezes well for up to 3 months.

SERVING IDEA
Serve on its own with chapattis, or boiled brown rice, or as part of a larger Indian meal.

BEANS WITH TREE EARS AND BAMBOO SHOOTS

SERVES 4

Tree ears are Chinese black fungi. These are usually sold dried and are available from most ethnic shops or delicatessens.

INGREDIENTS

6 Chinese tree ears, broken into small pieces
340g/12oz green beans
2 whole pieces canned bamboo shoots
2 tbsps vegetable oil
2 tsps cornflour
2 tbsps soy sauce
60ml/4 tbsps vegetable stock
Dash of sesame oil
Salt and freshly ground black pepper

Step 2 Trim the tops and tails from the green beans, and then slice into 5cm/2-inch diagonal pieces.

Step 3 Slice the bamboo shoots and cut them into thin triangular pieces.

1 Put the tree ears in a bowl and pour over enough hot water to cover them and allow to stand for 30 minutes.

2 Trim the tops and tails from the green beans and cut into 5cm/2-inch diagonal pieces.

3 Slice the bamboo shoots and cut into thin triangular pieces with a sharp knife.

4 Heat the oil in a large frying pan and sauté the beans and bamboo shoots for 3 minutes.

5 Stir in the drained tree ears and sauté for another couple of minutes.

6 Mix together the cornflour and soy sauce, then stir in the stock, add to the pan and stir-fry until sauce thickens.

7 Add a dash of sesame oil and season with salt and pepper. Serve immediately.

Cook's Notes

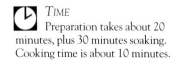 TIME
Preparation takes about 20 minutes, plus 30 minutes soaking. Cooking time is about 10 minutes.

 VEGETARIAN SUITABILITY
This recipe is suitable for vegans.

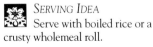 SERVING IDEA
Serve with boiled rice or a crusty wholemeal roll.

GRATIN OF VEGETABLES OLIVER

SERVES 4

*Fresh summer vegetables with a crunchy nut topping combine to make
a substantial lunch or supper dish.*

INGREDIENTS

90g/3oz butter or vegetable margarine
225g/8oz black olives, pitted and chopped
120g/4oz dry breadcrumbs
175g/6oz vegetarian Cheddar cheese, grated
120g/4oz walnuts, chopped
2 tsps chopped fresh basil
Pinch cayenne pepper
2 tbsps oil
4 medium carrots, peeled and sliced
1 head broccoli, trimmed and cut into small florets
225g/8oz French beans, trimmed
4 courgettes, sliced
2 red peppers, seeded and sliced
8 spring onions, trimmed and sliced
Salt and freshly ground black pepper

1 Melt the butter or margarine in a small pan. Add the olives, breadcrumbs, cheese, walnuts, basil and cayenne pepper. Stir to coat in the butter and set aside.

2 Heat the oil in a wok or large frying pan and fry the carrots for 5 minutes.

3 Add the broccoli and French beans and stir-fry for 3 minutes.

4 Add the courgettes, peppers and spring onions and continue to stir-fry for about 5 minutes or until the vegetables are just cooked, but still crisp.

5 Season with salt and pepper and transfer to a gratin dish.

6 Sprinkle the vegetables with the breadcrumb mixture and place under a preheated grill for a few minutes until the cheese melts.

Cook's Notes

TIME
Preparation takes about 15 minutes, cooking time is about 20 minutes.

VEGETARIAN SUITABILITY
This recipe is suitable for lacto-vegetarians, but could be adapted for vegans by omitting the Cheddar cheese and using a suitable margarine.

SERVING IDEA
Serve with a hot tomato salad.

BLACK-EYED BEAN AND ORANGE SALAD

SERVES 4

This colourful salad has a fresh taste which is given a delicious peppery 'bite' by the addition of watercress.

INGREDIENTS

225g/8oz black-eyed beans, soaked
1 bay leaf
1 slice of onion
Juice and grated rind of 1 orange
75ml/5 tbsps olive or grapeseed oil
6 black olives, pitted and quartered
4 spring onions, trimmed and chopped
2 tbsps each chopped fresh parsley and basil
Salt and freshly ground black pepper
4 whole oranges
1 bunch watercress, washed

1 Place the beans, bay leaf, and onion slice into a saucepan, add enough water to cover by 2.5cm/1 inch and bring to the boil. Boil rapidly for 10 minutes, reduce the heat and simmer gently for about 50 minutes-1 hour, until the beans are tender. Drain well.

Step 3 Add the cooked, drained beans to the dressing in the bowl and mix thoroughly to coat the beans evenly with the dressing mixture.

2 Put the orange juice, rind and oil in a large bowl and whisk together with a fork. Stir in the olives, spring onions and chopped herbs.
3 Add the cooked beans to the dressing and season. Mix thoroughly to coat the beans well.
4 Peel and segment the oranges, chop the segments of 3 of the oranges and add to the beans.
5 Arrange the watercress on individual serving plates and pile equal amounts of the bean and orange salad onto this.
6 Arrange the remaining orange segments on the plate and serve immediately.

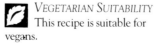

Cook's Notes

TIME
Preparation takes about 20 minutes, plus soaking. Cooking time is about 1 hour.

VEGETARIAN SUITABILITY
This recipe is suitable for vegans.

SERVING IDEA
Serve in split wholemeal pitta bread or in taco shells.

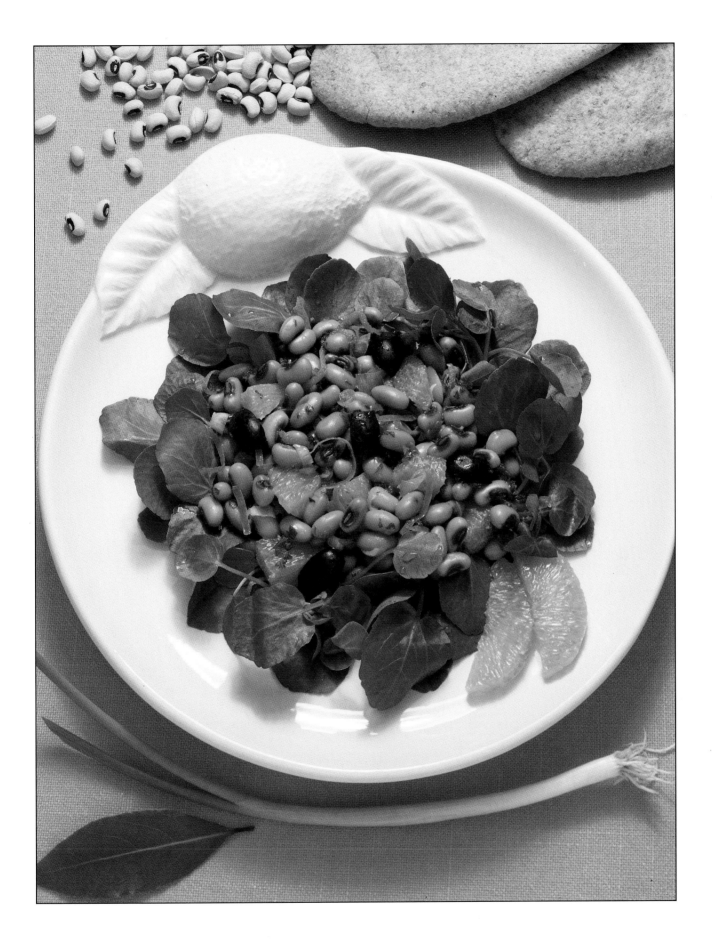

RED BEAN CREOLE

<u>SERVES 4</u>

This bright and colourful dish is ideal served on its own or as part of a larger meal.

INGREDIENTS

175g/6oz long-grain brown or white rice

30g/1oz butter or vegetable margarine

1 green pepper, seeded and sliced

120g/4oz mushrooms, sliced

Pinch of cayenne pepper

Pinch of ground nutmeg

340g/12oz cooked red kidney beans

140ml/¼ pint vegetable stock

4 firm tomatoes, skinned, seeded and cut into strips

4 spring onions, trimmed and chopped

Salt and freshly ground black pepper

Chopped fresh parsley, to garnish

1 Cook the rice in plenty of lightly salted, boiling water as directed on the packet. Drain the rice and rinse under boiling water.

2 Melt the butter or margarine in a large saucepan and sauté the pepper and mushrooms for 5 minutes or until just beginning to soften.

3 Add the rice, cayenne, nutmeg, beans and stock. Cook gently for 10 minutes, stir in the remaining ingredients and cook for a further 5 minutes or until all the ingredients are heated through.

4 Serve garnished with chopped parsley. This dish is delicious served with Ratatouille.

Cook's Notes

TIME
Preparation takes about 20 minutes, cooking time is about 40 minutes.

VEGETARIAN SUITABILITY
This recipe is suitable for vegans if a non-dairy margarine is used instead of the butter.

PREPARATION
Dried kidney beans can be used. You will need about 175g/6oz. Soak overnight before cooking and remember to boil rapidly for at least 10 minutes.

BUTTER BEAN, LEMON AND FENNEL SALAD

SERVES 4

This interesting combination of textures and flavours makes an unusual lunch or supper dish.

INGREDIENTS

225g/8oz butter beans, soaked overnight

1 lemon

1 large bulb fennel, thinly sliced

60ml/4 tbsps vegetable or soya oil

Pinch of unrefined sugar

Salt and freshly ground black pepper

Lettuce and radicchio leaves, to serve

1 Place the butter beans in a saucepan, add enough water to cover them by 2.5cm/1 inch and bring to the boil. Boil rapidly for 10 minutes, reduce the heat and simmer gently for about 2 hours or until the beans are tender. Drain well.

2 Pare the rind from the lemon, taking care not to include too much white pith. Cut the rind into very thin strips.

3 Blanch the lemon rind for 5 minutes in boiling water, then remove with a draining spoon to kitchen paper.

4 Add the fennel to the water (reserve the green tops) and blanch for 2 minutes, the fennel should be just cooked but still crunchy to the bite.

5 Squeeze the juice from the lemon and place in a bowl with the lemon rind strips, oil, sugar and seasoning and whisk together well with a fork.

6 Chop the fennel tops and add to the dressing.

7 Mix the cooked beans and fennel in a large bowl, then add the dressing and toss to coat. Serve on a bed of lettuce and radicchio leaves.

Step 5 Briskly whisk the lemon juice, oil, sugar and seasoning together in a small bowl, until the dressing is thick.

Cook's Notes

TIME
Preparation takes about 10 minutes, plus soaking. Cooking time is about 2 hours.

VEGETARIAN SUITABILITY
This recipe is suitable for vegans.

SERVING IDEA
Serve with boiled new potatoes or jacket potatoes.

PEASE PUDDING

SERVES 4

*This traditional English dish is delicious eaten as a light lunch or supper,
or as an accompaniment to a larger meal.*

INGREDIENTS

225g/8oz dried peas or green split peas, soaked overnight
1 carrot, peeled and finely chopped
1 onion, peeled and finely chopped
1 free-range egg, beaten
½ tsp dried marjoram
½ tsp dried savoury
Salt and freshly ground black pepper
1 tbsp arrowroot
140ml/¼ pint milk
30g/1oz butter or vegetable margarine
Tomato slices and chopped fresh parsley, to garnish

1 Drain the soaked peas and place in a saucepan with enough fresh water to cover them by 2.5cm/1 inch. Bring to the boil, reduce the heat and simmer gently for 1 hour or until the peas are soft.
2 Preheat the oven to 180°C/350°F/Gas Mark 4.
3 Drain the cooked peas, reserving some of the liquid. Blend in a food processor or liquidiser with enough of the reserved water to form a thick, smooth purée.

4 Put the pea purée in a large bowl and add the carrot, onion, egg, herbs and seasoning. Mix well to combine the ingredients thoroughly.
5 Mix the arrowroot with a little of the milk. Put the remaining milk, butter or margarine and arrowroot mixture in a small saucepan and heat gently, stirring continuously, until thickened.
6 Pour the sauce into the pea mixture and stir well.
7 Divide the mixture between four individual dishes and place in a roasting tin.
8 Fill the tin with enough hot water to come half way up the sides of the dishes and bake for 40-45 minutes or until the pease pudding has set and is firm to the touch.
9 Turn out onto serving dishes and garnish with slices of tomato and chopped parsley.

Cook's Notes

TIME
Preparation takes about 20 minutes, plus overnight soaking. Cooking time is about 2 hours.

VEGETARIAN SUITABILITY
This recipe is suitable for lacto-vegetarians only.

COOK'S TIP
If you do not have a liquidiser or food processor, the pea purée can be made by pushing the cooked peas through the mesh of a wire sieve with a wooden spoon.

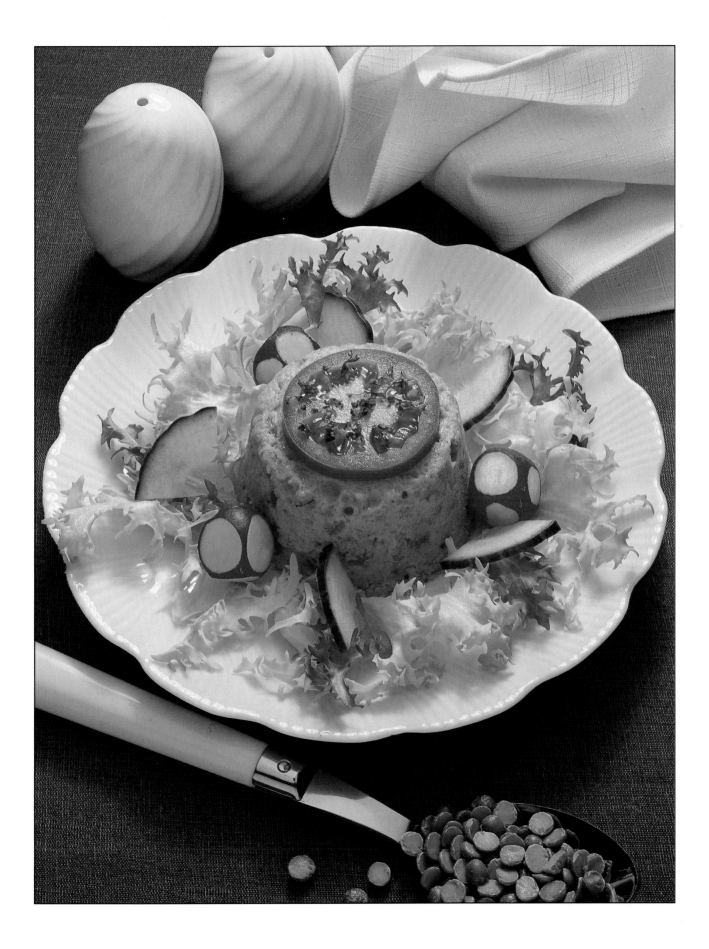

SPINACH AND PEPPER CASSEROLE

SERVES 4

*This hearty, warm casserole makes a substantial lunch or supper, or
could be used as an accompanying vegetable for up to 8 people.*

INGREDIENTS

450g/1lb spinach, washed, trimmed and roughly chopped
2 tbsps oil
1 red pepper, seeded and sliced
1 green pepper, seeded and sliced
4 sticks celery, trimmed and thinly sliced
2 onions, peeled and finely chopped
30g/1oz sultanas
Pinch paprika
Pinch unrefined sugar
Pinch of ground cinnamon
Salt
2 tbsps tomato purée
1 tsp cornflour
30g/1oz vegetarian Cheddar cheese
2 tbsps fresh breadcrumbs

1 Cook the spinach in a covered pan until just wilted, with just the water that clings to the leaves after washing.

2 Drain the spinach well, reserving the cooking liquid to make the sauce.

3 Heat the oil in a frying pan and fry the peppers, celery and onions for about 10 minutes, or until softened.

4 Mix together the sultanas, paprika, sugar, cinnamon, salt, tomato purée and cornflour. Make the reserved cooking liquid up to 140ml/¼ pint and stir into the cornflour mixture.

5 Add to the vegetables and cook, stirring until the sauce thickens.

6 Spoon the vegetable mixture into a flameproof casserole dish. Mix together the cheese and breadcrumbs and sprinkle over the vegetables. Place under a preheated grill until the cheese melts and the crumbs are golden.

Cook's Notes

TIME
Preparation takes about 15 minutes, cooking time is about 20 minutes.

VEGETARIAN SUITABILITY
This recipe is suitable for lacto-vegetarians only.

SERVING IDEA
Serve with a rice salad.

PASTA, PEAS AND PEPPERS

<u>SERVES 4</u>

This very colourful salad is simple, but is substantial enough to be a meal in itself.

INGREDIENTS

225g/8oz mixed, plain and wholemeal pasta shells
225g/8oz frozen peas
1 green pepper, seeded and sliced
1 red pepper, seeded and sliced
1 yellow pepper, seeded and sliced
140ml/¼ pint vegetable or olive oil
60ml/4 tbsps white wine vinegar
1 tbsp Dijon or wholegrain mustard
2 tsps poppy seeds
2 tsps chopped fresh parsley
1 tsp chopped fresh thyme
Salt and freshly ground black pepper
4 spring onions, trimmed and shredded
120g/4oz vegetarian Cheddar cheese, finely grated

Step 4 *Whisk the dressing ingredients together until they become thick and pale coloured.*

1 Cook the pasta in plenty of lightly salted, boiling water for 10 minutes or as directed on the packet.

2 Drain the pasta and cool under running cold water. When cold drain well.

3 Cook the peas and peppers in boiling water for 5 minutes. Drain and add to the pasta.

4 Place the oil, vinegar, mustard, poppy seeds, herbs and a little seasoning in a bowl and whisk vigorously, until the dressing is thick and pale coloured.

5 Pour the dressing over the pasta and vegetables. Toss well and chill in the refrigerator.

6 Stir the spring onions and cheese into the salad and serve immediately.

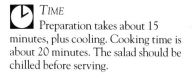
Cook's Notes

TIME
Preparation takes about 15 minutes, plus cooling. Cooking time is about 20 minutes. The salad should be chilled before serving.

VEGETARIAN SUITABILITY
This recipe is suitable for lacto-vegetarians, but could be served to vegans if the cheese is omitted. Make sure that the pasta does not contain any egg.

VARIATION
Use 60g/2oz salted peanuts instead of cheese in this recipe.

CHICK PEAS AND BULGUR WHEAT

SERVES 4

High in protein and flavour, this simple lunch dish is sure to become a family favourite.

INGREDIENTS

1 tbsp vegetable oil

2 small onions, peeled and chopped

1 red pepper, seeded and chopped

450g/1lb cooked chick peas

120g/4oz bulgur wheat

120ml/4 fl oz tomato purée

420ml/¾ pint vegetable stock or water

Onion rings, to garnish

1 Heat the oil in a saucepan and fry the onions and pepper until soft but not coloured.

2 Stir in the chick peas and bulgur wheat. Stir in the tomato purée, then gradually add the stock or water.

3 Bring gently to the boil, cover, and simmer gently for 10-15 minutes or until the bulgur wheat is tender and the liquid has been absorbed.

4 Transfer to a serving dish and garnish with onion rings.

Cook's Notes

TIME
Preparation takes about 10 minutes, cooking time is about 20 minutes.

SERVING IDEA
Serve with a crunchy carrot and peanut coleslaw.

VEGETARIAN SUITABILITY
This recipe is suitable for vegans.

COOK'S TIP
The chickpeas should be boiled for at least 30 minutes. As an alternative, use 450g/1lb canned chickpeas, which will require no pre-cooking.

VARIATION
Use green peppers in place of the red peppers in this recipe, and add ½ tsp chilli powder for a spicy variation.

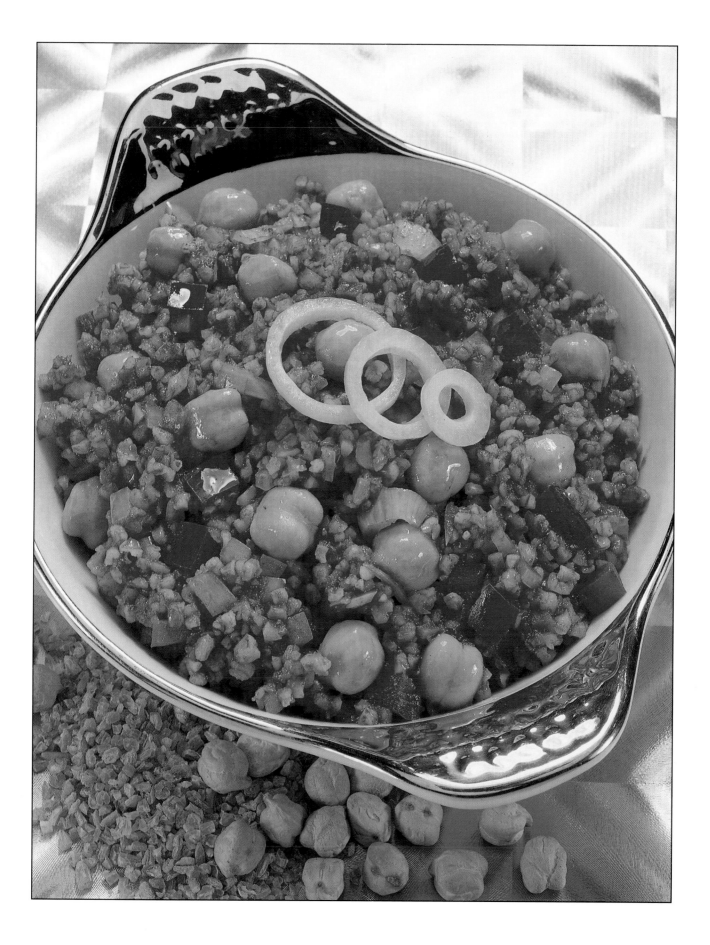

MACARONI AND BLUE CHEESE

SERVES 4

The classic combination of apples and blue cheese sets this delicious variation of macaroni cheese apart from its humble origins.

INGREDIENTS

340g/12oz wholemeal macaroni
90g/3oz butter or vegetable margarine
90g/3oz plain flour
570ml/1 pint milk
1 tsp dried or fresh chopped tarragon
225g/8oz vegetarian blue cheese, crumbled or grated
Salt and freshly ground black pepper
2 tbsps vegetable oil
2 apples, cored and chopped
2 onions, peeled and chopped
1 clove garlic, crushed
Sprig of fresh tarragon, to garnish

1 Cook the macaroni in plenty of lightly salted, boiling water for 12 minutes or as directed on the packet. Drain well.
2 Meanwhile, melt the butter or margarine in a saucepan, stir in the flour and cook for 1 minute.
3 Remove from the heat and gradually stir in the milk. Return to the heat and cook gently until the sauce thickens, stirring constantly.
4 Stir in the tarragon and blue cheese and cook until the cheese melts, taste and season with salt if needed and freshly ground pepper.
5 In a smaller pan heat the oil and fry the apples, onions and garlic for 5 minutes until just soft.
6 Mix the apple and onion into the sauce then stir in the drained pasta, return to the heat to warm through the pasta if necessary. Serve garnished with a sprig of fresh tarragon.

Cook's Notes

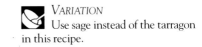

TIME
Preparation takes about 5 minutes, cooking time is about 20 minutes.

VEGETARIAN SUITABILITY
This recipe is suitable for lacto-vegetarians only.

VARIATION
Use sage instead of the tarragon in this recipe.

WHOLEMEAL VEGETABLE QUICHE

<u>SERVES 4</u>

This wholesome lunch or supper dish is equally good served hot or cold.

INGREDIENTS

175g/6oz wholemeal plain flour
90g/3oz butter or vegetable margarine
About 2 tbsps cold water
2 tbsps olive or vegetable oil
1 small red pepper, seeded and diced
120g/4oz courgettes, diced
2 spring onions, trimmed and sliced
1 tomato, skinned, seeded and chopped
2 free-range eggs
140ml/¼ pint milk
Salt and freshly ground black pepper
Tomato slices and chopped parsley, to garnish

1 Preheat the oven to 200°C/400°F/Gas Mark 6.
2 Place the flour in a bowl and rub in the butter or margarine until the mixture resembles fine breadcrumbs.
3 Add enough cold water to mix to a firm dough.
4 Roll out the dough and use to line a 20cm/8-inch flan dish.

5 Line the dish with a sheet of greaseproof paper and fill with baking beans or dried pasta, and bake for 16 minutes, removing the paper and beans half way through the cooking time.
6 Reduce the oven temperature to 180°C/350°F/Gas Mark 4.
7 Heat the oil in a small pan and fry the pepper for 2 minutes, add the courgettes and fry for 2 minutes. Add the spring onions and tomato.
8 Spoon the vegetable mixture into the flan case.
9 Beat the eggs and milk together and season well. Pour over the vegetables, return to the oven and bake for 30 minutes or until the filling is just set. Garnish with sliced tomatoes and chopped parsley.

Step 4 *Press the dough evenly into the base and sides of the prepared flan dish, to make a shallow pie case.*

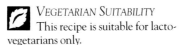

Cook's Notes

 TIME
Preparation takes about 15 minutes, cooking time is about 50 minutes.

VEGETARIAN SUITABILITY
This recipe is suitable for lacto-vegetarians only.

SERVING IDEA
Serve with a fresh mixed salad.

VARIATION
Use any combination of your favourite vegetables in this recipe.

MIXED GRAINS AND SEEDS

SERVES 4

This recipe makes a simple supper dish on its own, or an excellent accompaniment for curries and tomato dishes.

INGREDIENTS

120g/4oz brown rice
60g/2oz wheat grains
90g/3oz rye grains or buckwheat
90g/3oz barley or oat groats
90g/3oz sunflower seeds or pine nuts
90g/3oz sesame seeds
700ml/1¼ pints vegetable stock or water
120g/4oz vegetarian Cheddar cheese, grated
30g/1oz butter or vegetable margarine
Sprig of parsley, to garnish

1 Place the rice, wheat, rye and barley or oat grains in a colander and rinse well under running water.
2 Drain, and place in a large saucepan with the seeds. Pour in the stock or water.
3 Bring gently to the boil. Stir, cover and simmer gently for about 30 minutes, or until the grains are tender and the liquid has been absorbed.
4 Allow to stand for 5 minutes, then add the cheese and butter or margarine, stir to combine well and serve garnished with a sprig of fresh parsley.

Cook's Notes

TIME
Preparation takes about 5 minutes, cooking time is about 30 minutes.

VEGETARIAN SUITABILITY
This recipe is suitable for lacto-vegetarians only. For vegans see variation.

VARIATION
Omit the cheese and butter and stir in 120g/4oz finely chopped spring onions, which have been gently cooked in 2 tbsps olive or walnut oil.

FREEZING
The cooked grains and seeds can be frozen for up to 2 months, but the cheese or onions should not be added until just before they are served.

RATATOUILLE

SERVES 4-6

This delicious classic dish is equally good served hot or cold.

INGREDIENTS

1 large aubergine

Salt

2 tbsps olive oil

1 large onion, peeled and thinly sliced

1 clove garlic, crushed

1 green pepper, seeded and thinly sliced

450g/1lb tomatoes, skinned and chopped

1 tsp chopped fresh thyme

2 tsps chopped fresh basil

Salt and freshly ground black pepper

Sprigs of fresh thyme, to garnish

1 Cut the aubergine in half lengthways and score the cut surface in a diamond fashion with a sharp knife.

2 Sprinkle liberally with salt and allow to stand for 30 minutes, to remove excess moisture.

3 Rinse well and pat dry with kitchen paper.

4 Cut the aubergine halves into thin slices.

5 Heat the oil in a large frying pan and fry the onion and garlic until it begins to soften, but not brown.

6 Add the pepper and aubergine and sauté for 5 minutes.

7 Stir in the remaining ingredients and cook gently for 30 minutes.

8 Adjust seasoning if required and serve hot or cold. Garnish with a sprig of fresh thyme.

Step 1 *Cut the aubergine in half lengthways and score the surface in a diamond pattern, using a sharp knife.*

Cook's Notes

TIME
Preparation takes about 20 minutes, plus standing. Cooking time is about 50 minutes.

VEGETARIAN SUITABILITY
This recipe is suitable for vegans.

SERVING IDEA
Serve in pitta bread or with crusty wholemeal rolls.

VARIATION
Serve as an accompaniment to another vegetarian dish for 8 people.

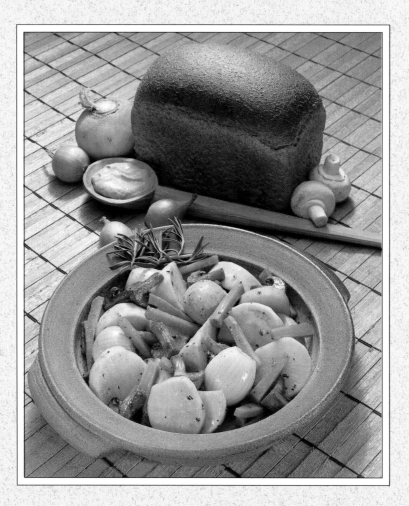

Chapter 4
MAIN MEALS

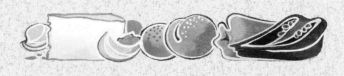

KIDNEY BEAN CURRY

<u>SERVES 4</u>

*The kidney beans are wonderfully enhanced by the flavour of the spices
in this delicious curry.*

INGREDIENTS

2 tbsps vegetable oil

1 large onion, peeled and sliced

2 cloves garlic, crushed

2 green chillies, seeded and chopped

2 tsps grated root ginger

1 tsp chilli powder

1 tsp ground coriander

1 tsp ground cumin

1 tsp garam masala

1 cinnamon stick

400g/14oz can chopped tomatoes

1 bay leaf

450g/1lb canned red kidney beans, drained weight

Salt and freshly ground black pepper

Chopped fresh coriander, to garnish

1 Heat the oil in a large saucepan and fry the onion, garlic and fresh chillies for 5 minutes.

2 Stir in the spices and cook for 1 minute.

3 Add the tomatoes, bay leaf and kidney beans. Season to taste.

4 Cover and simmer gently for 30 minutes or until the flavours are well blended. Remove the cinnamon stick and bay leaf.

5 Garnish with chopped coriander.

Cook's Notes

TIME
Preparation takes about 20 minutes, cooking time is about 35 minutes.

VEGETARIAN SUITABILITY
This recipe is suitable for vegans.

PREPARATION
Great care must be taken when preparing fresh chillies. Wear rubber gloves to prevent the juice being left on the fingers and help prevent the juice getting into your eyes or mouth. If this should happen, rinse with plenty of cold water.

SERVING IDEA
Serve with a cucumber raita if you are a lacto-vegetarian, or hot lime pickle if you are a vegan. Naan bread or chapattis are also excellent accompaniments.

CABBAGE PARCELS

<u>SERVES 4</u>

The nutty texture and flavour of these filled cabbage leaves is ideally complemented by the mushroom and tomato sauce.

INGREDIENTS

120g/4oz soup pasta

8-12 large cabbage leaves, washed

1 hard-boiled, free-range egg, finely chopped

60g/2oz walnuts, chopped

1 tbsp chopped fresh chives

2 tbsps fresh chopped parsley

1 tsp fresh chopped marjoram

Salt and freshly ground black pepper

280ml/½ pint vegetable stock

1 tbsp walnut oil

1 onion, peeled and finely chopped

1 green pepper, seeded and chopped

400g/14oz can chopped tomatoes

120g/4oz button mushrooms, chopped

2 tbsps tomato purée

1 bay leaf

Pinch of unrefined sugar

1 Preheat the oven to 180°C/350°F/Gas Mark 4.

2 Cook the pasta in plenty of lightly salted, boiling water for 8 minutes or as directed on the packet.

3 Remove the thick stems from the base of the

Step 5 *Roll the top of each leaf over the filling and folded sides of the cabbage leaf, tucking it underneath to seal completely.*

cabbage leaves and then blanch the leaves in boiling water for 3 minutes, drain and refresh in cold water.

4 When the pasta is cooked, drain well and mix with the egg, walnuts and herbs, and season.

5 Divide the pasta mixture between the cabbage leaves, fold up to enclose the filling completely and secure with cocktail sticks.

6 Place in a shallow, ovenproof casserole dish and add the stock. Cover and bake for 40 minutes.

7 Heat the oil in a frying pan and fry the onion and pepper for 5 minutes or until soft. Stir in the remaining ingredients, season, and cook gently for 10 minutes.

8 Remove the cabbage parcels from the casserole dish with a draining spoon and serve with the sauce poured over them.

Cook's Notes

TIME
Preparation takes about 30 minutes, cooking time is about 1 hour.

VEGETARIAN SUITABILITY
This recipe is suitable for vegans.

CHEESE AND TOMATO PASTA

SERVES 4

*This favourite Italian classic is perfect served as a lunch or supper dish
and will be popular with all the family.*

INGREDIENTS

225g/8oz tagliatelle verdi
1 tbsp vegetable oil
1 onion, peeled and chopped
120g/4oz mushrooms, finely sliced
1 tbsp tomato purée
400g/14oz can chopped tomatoes
2 tbsps dried mixed herbs
120g/4oz vegetarian Cheddar cheese, grated
Salt and freshly ground black pepper

1 Cook the pasta in plenty of lightly salted, boiling water for 10 minutes or as directed on the packet.
2 Meanwhile, heat the oil in a frying pan and sauté the onion until beginning to soften.
3 Add the mushrooms and fry for 3 minutes. Stir in the tomato purée, tomatoes and herbs and simmer gently while the pasta cooks.
4 When the pasta is cooked, stir most of the cheese into the tomato sauce. Season.
5 Drain the pasta and pile onto a serving dish. Spoon the sauce into the centre and top with the remaining cheese.

Cook's Notes

TIME
Preparation takes about 10 minutes, cooking time is about 20 minutes.

SERVING IDEA
Serve with a mixed Italian salad and hot garlic bread.

VEGETARIAN SUITABILITY
This recipe is suitable for lacto-vegetarians only.

VARIATION
Use any variety of pasta shapes in this recipe.

COOK'S TIP
Fresh pasta is now readily available and very quick to cook. You will need about twice the weight of dried pasta.

NUT AND HERB BULGUR

SERVES 4

Bulgur wheat cooks in a similar way to rice and can be used as an alternative to many rice dishes.

INGREDIENTS

1 tbsp walnut oil

1 tbsp vegetable oil

1 red pepper, seeded and cut into short sticks

1 onion, peeled and chopped

30g/1oz pine nuts

120g/4oz cucumber, diced

1 tbsp chopped fresh coriander

1 tbsp chopped fresh mint

2 tbsps chopped fresh parsley

225g/8oz bulgur wheat

420ml/¾ pint vegetable stock

Mint sprigs, to garnish

1 Heat the oils in a large saucepan and fry the pepper, onion and pine nuts for 5 minutes.
2 Add the cucumber, herbs and bulgur wheat, then pour in the stock.
3 Bring gently to the boil, stir, cover and simmer gently for 10-15 minutes or until the stock has been absorbed, stirring occasionally.
4 Serve hot or cold garnished with sprigs of mint.

Cook's Notes

TIME
Preparation takes about 10 minutes, cooking time is about 20 minutes.

VEGETARIAN SUITABILITY
This recipe is suitable for vegans.

SERVING IDEA
Serve with a mixed salad.

VARIATION
Use brown rice instead of bulgur wheat in this recipe and increase cooking time accordingly.

STUFFED AUBERGINES

<u>SERVES 2</u>

When filled with this delicious stuffing, these interesting vegetables make a substantial hot meal.

INGREDIENTS

2 large aubergines
2 tbsps vegetable oil
1 onion, peeled and finely chopped
1 clove garlic, crushed
1 green pepper, seeded and chopped
60g/2oz mushrooms, chopped
400g/14oz can chopped tomatoes
1 tbsp tomato purée
2 tsps chopped fresh basil
Pinch of unrefined sugar
Salt and freshly ground black pepper
30g/1oz wholemeal breadcrumbs
½ tsp dried oregano
30g/1oz walnuts, chopped and lightly toasted
60g/2oz vegetarian Cheddar cheese, grated (optional)
Salad garnish, to serve

1 Cut the aubergines in half and score the flesh in a criss-cross pattern with a sharp knife.
2 Sprinkle liberally with salt and set aside for 30 minutes.
3 Preheat the oven to 190°C/375°F/Gas Mark 5.
4 Rinse aubergines, scoop out the flesh leaving a border to form a firm shell.
5 Blanch the aubergine shells in boiling water for 3 minutes, drain and set aside. Chop the flesh.
6 Heat the oil in a frying pan and fry the onion and garlic until softened.
7 Stir in the pepper, mushrooms and aubergine flesh and fry for 5 minutes. Add the tomatoes, tomato purée, basil and sugar. Season well.
8 Place the hollowed out aubergine shells in a lightly greased ovenproof shallow dish and pile the tomato mixture into the shells.
9 Mix together the breadcrumbs, oregano, walnuts and cheese, if using. Sprinkle over the aubergines.
10 Bake for 20 minutes. Serve with a salad garnish.

Cook's Notes

TIME
Preparation takes about 20 minutes, plus standing. Cooking time is about 40 minutes.

VEGETARIAN SUITABILITY
This recipe is suitable for vegans if the cheese is omitted.

GLAZED VEGETABLES

SERVES 4

*Using everyday vegetables, this delicious vegetable casserole is
inexpensive and will be a big hit with all the family.*

INGREDIENTS

30g/1oz butter or vegetable margarine

1 tbsp light muscovado sugar

60ml/4 tbsps vegetable stock

2 carrots, peeled and cut into sticks

2 salsify, peeled and cut into rounds

2 turnips, peeled and cut into wedges

*175g/6oz pickling onions or shallots, peeled and cut in half if
large*

120g/4oz large mushrooms, quartered

1 tsp chopped fresh rosemary or thyme

Salt and freshly ground black pepper

2 tsps Dijon mustard

Fresh rosemary, to garnish

1 Melt the butter or margarine and stir in the
sugar and stock. Stir until the sugar dissolves.

2 Add the carrots, salsify, turnips and onions or
shallots and cook over a low heat for about 10
minutes, tossing frequently, until the vegetables
are beginning to soften.

3 Add the mushrooms, herbs, seasoning and
mustard. Cover and cook over a low heat for 10
minutes or until all the vegetables are tender,
tossing occasionally.

4 Serve garnished with fresh rosemary.

Cook's Notes

TIME
Preparation takes about 20
minutes, cooking time is about 20
minutes.

VEGETARIAN SUITABILITY
This recipe is suitable for
vegans, using non-dairy margarine.

SERVING IDEA
Serve with wholemeal bread or
jacket potatoes.

VARIATION
Change the combination of
fresh vegetables to suit the season or
personal taste.

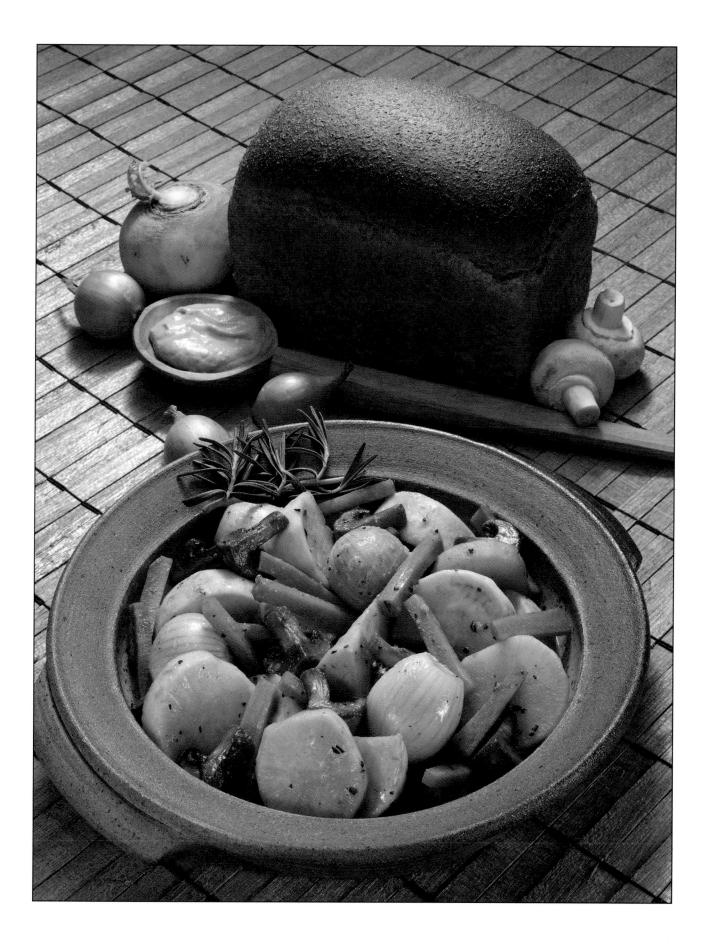

CHEESE SANDWICH SOUFFLÉ

SERVES 4

Unlike a true soufflé, there is no need to rush this dish to the table as it will not sink. It is equally delicious served hot or cold.

INGREDIENTS

1 tbsp wholegrain mustard

8 slices wholemeal bread

2 tomatoes, sliced

175g/6oz vegetarian Cheddar cheese, grated

2 free-range eggs, beaten

570ml/1 pint milk

1 tsp dried basil

Salt and freshly ground black pepper

Parsley sprigs, to garnish

1 Preheat the oven to 180°C/350°F/Gas Mark 4.
2 Spread equal amounts of mustard over four slices of the bread.
3 Arrange the tomato slices over the mustard-spread bread and sprinkle with the grated cheese.
4 Use the remaining four slices to cover the cheese.

5 Place the cheese and tomato sandwiches in a large shallow dish or 4 smaller individual dishes into which they will just fit.
6 Beat together the eggs, milk and basil, season well. Pour over the bread, allow to stand for 30 minutes to allow the bread to soak up the milk mixture.
7 Bake for 40-45 minutes or until the milk mixture is set. Serve garnished with sprigs of parsley.

Step 6 *Pour the egg and milk mixture over the cheese and tomato sandwiches, and allow to stand for 30 minutes.*

Cook's Notes

TIME
Preparation takes about 10 minutes, plus 30 minutes standing. Cooking time is about 45 minutes.

VEGETARIAN SUITABILITY
This recipe is suitable for lacto-vegetarians only.

VARIATION
Use slices of Spanish onion in place of the tomato and vegetarian Stilton in place of the Cheddar cheese.

SERVING IDEA
Serve with braised mushrooms or fennel.

CHICK PEA AND PEPPER CASSEROLE

SERVES 4

This colourful casserole can be made in advance and re-heated before serving.

INGREDIENTS

225g/8oz dried chick peas, soaked overnight

2 tbsps vegetable oil

1 onion, peeled and sliced

1 clove garlic, crushed

1 green pepper, seeded and sliced

1 red pepper, seeded and sliced

½ tsp ground cumin

2 tsps chopped fresh parsley

1 tsp chopped fresh mint

4 tomatoes, seeded and cut into strips

Salt and freshly ground black pepper

1 Drain the soaked peas and place in a saucepan with enough water to cover them by 2.5cm/1 inch. Bring to the boil and boil rapidly for 10 minutes. Reduce the heat and simmer gently for about 2 hours or until the beans are soft.

2 Drain the chick peas and reserve the liquid.

3 Heat the oil in a saucepan and fry the onion, garlic and peppers for 5 minutes, stir in the cumin and fry for 1 minute.

4 Make the reserved liquid up to 280ml/½ pint and add to the pan along with the cooked peas.

5 Add the remaining ingredients and bring gently to the boil. Cover and simmer for 30 minutes.

6 Adjust seasoning if necessary and serve.

Cook's Notes

TIME
Preparation takes about 20 minutes, plus overnight soaking. Cooking time is about 3 hours.

VEGETARIAN SUITABILITY
This recipe is suitable for vegans.

PREPARATION
Ensure that the all dried beans and pulses are fully cooked.

SERVING IDEA
Serve in warm wholemeal pitta breads, and for lacto-vegetarians, top with a mixture of chopped cucumber and natural yogurt.

STIR-FRIED BEANS AND SPROUTS

SERVES 4

High in both protein and fibre, this easy stir-fry makes a flavoursome change.

INGREDIENTS

225g/8oz dried adzuki beans, soaked overnight
2 tbsps vegetable oil
1 large onion, peeled and sliced
1 green pepper, seeded and sliced
225g/8oz bean sprouts
60ml/4 tbsps soy sauce

1 Drain the soaked beans and place in a saucepan with enough water to cover them by 2.5cm/1 inch. Bring to the boil, and boil rapidly for 10 minutes.

Reduce the heat and simmer gently for about 30 minutes or until the beans are soft.
2 Drain the beans and rinse in cold water. Leave them in a colander to drain completely.
3 Heat the oil in a wok or large frying pan and stir-fry the onion and pepper for 4 minutes or until beginning to soften slightly.
4 Add the bean sprouts and stir-fry for 1 minute.
5 Add the cooked beans and soy sauce and fry for a few minutes to warm through.
6 Serve immediately.

Cook's Notes

TIME
Preparation takes about 10 minutes, plus overnight soaking. Cooking time is about 50 minutes.

VEGETARIAN SUITABILITY
This recipe is suitable for vegans.

COOK'S TIP
Save time by cooking beans in bulk and freezing in usable quantities.

SWEET AND SOUR PEANUTS

SERVES 4

This highly nutritious meal is very quick and simple to prepare.

INGREDIENTS

90g/3oz light muscovado sugar

75ml/5 tbsps white wine vinegar

3 tbsps soy sauce

120ml/4 fl oz vegetable stock

1 tbsp arrowroot

1 red pepper, seeded and sliced

120g/4oz bean sprouts

120g/4oz unsalted roasted peanuts

225g/8oz can bamboo shoots, drained and sliced

1 Combine the sugar, vinegar, soy sauce, vegetable stock and arrowroot in a saucepan.

2 Heat gently, stirring constantly, until the mixture thickens slightly.

3 Stir in the remaining ingredients and cook gently for 5 minutes, or until the pepper strips are tender.

Cook's Notes

TIME
Preparation takes about 10 minutes, cooking time is about 10 minutes.

VEGETARIAN SUITABILITY
This recipe is suitable for vegans.

SERVING IDEA
Serve with boiled rice or mixed grains and seeds.

VARIATION
Use cashew nuts instead of the peanuts and add 60g/2oz fresh chopped pineapple.

SAVOURY BREAD PUDDING

SERVES 4

This easy to prepare family meal is both filling and nutritious.

INGREDIENTS

225g/8oz wholemeal bread

60g/2oz sunflower seeds

60g/2oz walnuts or hazelnuts, chopped

1 tbsp dried mixed herbs

420ml/¾ pint vegetable stock

2 tbsps vegetable oil

1 large onion, peeled and chopped

1 clove garlic, crushed

Salt and freshly ground black pepper

1 Preheat the oven to 180°C/350°F/Gas Mark 4.

2 Cut the bread into thick slices and then into cubes.

3 Put the bread, sunflower seeds, nuts, herbs and stock into a bowl and stir until very well combined.

4 Heat the oil in a frying pan and fry the onion and garlic until soft. Stir into the bread mixture. Season well.

Step 2 *Cut the thick slices of bread into 2.5cm/1-inch cubes with a sharp knife.*

Step 3 *Combine the bread, seeds, nuts, herbs and stock in a bowl and stir well.*

5 Pour the bread mixture into a greased shallow ovenproof dish. Cover and bake for 30 minutes.

Cook's Notes

TIME
Preparation takes about 15 minutes, cooking time is about 40 minutes.

VEGETARIAN SUITABILITY
This recipe is suitable for vegans.

VARIATION
For lacto-vegetarians add 120g/4oz grated vegetarian sage Derby cheese and omit the dried herbs.

VEGETABLE CASSOULET

<u>SERVES 4</u>

This warming vegetable stew is an ideal recipe for using delicious autumn vegetables.

INGREDIENTS

225g/8oz haricot beans, soaked overnight

60ml/4 tbsps vegetable oil

2 cloves garlic, crushed

2 leeks, washed and cut into 2.5cm/1-inch pieces

3 carrots, peeled and sliced

4 sticks celery, trimmed and cut into 2.5cm/1-inch pieces

2 turnips, peeled and cut into 2.5cm/1-inch pieces

1 bay leaf

1 tbsp soy sauce

1 tbsp chopped fresh marjoram

Salt and freshly ground black pepper

420ml/¾ pint vegetable stock

30g/1oz butter or vegetable margarine

90g/3oz wholemeal breadcrumbs

1 Drain the soaked beans and place in a saucepan with enough water to cover them by 2.5cm/1 inch. Bring to the boil and boil rapidly for 10 minutes. Reduce the heat and simmer gently for about 1 hour or until the beans are soft. Drain.

2 Preheat the oven to 180°C/350°F/Gas Mark 4.

3 Heat the oil in a large frying pan and fry the garlic and all the prepared vegetables for 5-10 minutes until beginning to brown.

4 Place the cooked beans, bay leaf, soy sauce, marjoram and seasoning into an ovenproof casserole and stir in the browned vegetables and stock.

5 Cover and cook in the oven for 45 minutes.

6 Melt the butter or margarine and stir in the breadcrumbs.

7 Remove the lid from the casserole and sprinkle the breadcrumb mixture over the beans. Bake uncovered for a further 30 minutes or until the breadcrumb topping is crisp.

Cook's Notes

TIME
Preparation takes about 20 minutes, plus overnight soaking. Cooking time is about 2½ hours.

VEGETARIAN SUITABILITY
This recipe is suitable for vegans, if a suitable margarine is used.

VARIATION
Use any combination of vegetables depending on the season.

SERVING IDEA
Serve with jacket potatoes.

VEGETABLE STIR-FRY WITH TOFU

SERVES 4

The inclusion of tofu in the recipe makes it an excellent protein meal.

INGREDIENTS

4 heads of broccoli
120g/4oz baby corn
60ml/4 tbsps vegetable oil
30g/1oz blanched almonds
1 clove garlic, crushed
1 red pepper, seeded and sliced
120g/4oz mange tout peas, trimmed
60g/2oz water chestnuts, sliced
60ml/4 tbsps soy sauce
1 tsp sesame oil
1 tsp sherry
140ml/¼ pint vegetable stock
2 tsps cornflour
120g/4oz bean sprouts
4 spring onions, cut into thin diagonal slices
225g/8oz tofu, cut into cubes
Salt and freshly ground black pepper

1 Remove the florets from the broccoli and set aside. Trim the broccoli stems and slice thinly.
2 Cut the baby corn in half lengthways.
3 Heat the oil in a wok or large frying pan and fry the almonds until browned. Remove with a draining spoon and set aside.
4 Add the garlic, broccoli stems and baby corn to the pan and stir-fry for 1 minute.
5 Stir in the pepper, mange tout peas, water chestnuts and broccoli florets and stir-fry for 4 minutes.
6 Mix the soy sauce, sesame oil, sherry, stock and cornflour together in a small dish and stir until blended.
7 Add to the pan and stir until sauce thickens.
8 Add the bean sprouts, browned almonds, spring onions and tofu and cook for 3 minutes.
9 Season to taste and serve at once.

Cook's Notes

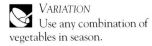 TIME
Preparation takes about 20 minutes, cooking time is about 10-12 minutes.

 VEGETARIAN SUITABILITY
This recipe is suitable for vegans.

VARIATION
Use any combination of vegetables in season.

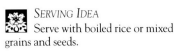 SERVING IDEA
Serve with boiled rice or mixed grains and seeds.

Chapter 5
ENTERTAINING

VEGETABLE NIRAMISH

SERVES 4

This highly fragrant curry is ideal to serve as part of a larger Indian meal. Vary the vegetables according to what you have to hand.

INGREDIENTS

1 small aubergine
Salt
3 tbsps vegetable oil
1 onion, peeled and sliced
1 green chilli, seeded and finely chopped
1 tsp cumin seeds
1 large potato, peeled and cut into chunks
120g/4oz cauliflower florets
1 small green pepper, seeded and sliced
2 small carrots, peeled and thickly sliced
1 tsp each ground coriander, turmeric and chilli powder
140ml/¼ pint vegetable stock
1 tsp chopped fresh coriander
Juice of 1 lime
Chilli 'flower' to garnish

1 Cut the aubergine into chunks, sprinkle liberally with salt and allow to stand for 30 minutes. Rinse well and drain on kitchen paper.

Step 1 *Sprinkle the aubergine chunks liberally with salt, stirring well to ensure that each piece is coated.*

2 Heat the oil in a saucepan and fry the onion, green chilli and cumin seeds for 2 minutes.
3 Stir in the potato and fry for 3 minutes. Add the aubergine, cauliflower, pepper and carrots and fry for another 3 minutes.
4 Stir in the spices and fry for 1 minute, then add the stock. Cover and simmer gently for 30 minutes until all the vegetable are tender, adding a little more stock if needed.
5 Add the coriander and lime juice and simmer for 2 minutes.
6 Serve garnished with a chilli 'flower'.

Cook's Notes

 TIME
Preparation takes about 20 minutes, plus standing. Cooking time is about 40 minutes.

VEGETARIAN SUITABILITY
This recipe is suitable for vegans.

SERVING IDEA
Serve with boiled rice and a simple salad.

WALNUT CUTLETS WITH THREE PEPPER SALPICON

SERVES 4

This colourful dish combines style with high nutritional value.

INGREDIENTS

60g/2oz butter or vegetable margarine
1 shallot, peeled and finely chopped
45g/1½oz plain flour
140ml/¼ pint milk
120g/4oz walnuts, finely chopped or ground
60g/2oz fresh breadcrumbs
1 tsp each chopped fresh parsley and thyme
1 free-range egg, beaten
Dry breadcrumbs for coating
Oil for shallow frying
1 onion, peeled and finely sliced
2 each of green, red and yellow peppers, seeded and sliced
Juice of 1 lemon
90ml/6 tbsps vegetable stock
2 tsps capers
Pinch of cayenne pepper
Salt and freshly ground black pepper
Sprigs of watercress, to garnish

1 Melt half the butter or margarine in a frying pan and stir in the shallot. Sauté for 2 minutes or until softened. Stir in 30g/1oz of the flour and cook for 1 minute. Remove from the heat and gradually beat in the milk. Return to the heat and cook until thickened.

2 Stir in the nuts, breadcrumbs, parsley, thyme and half the egg. Season to taste, and mix to form a thick paste. Add extra breadcrumbs if the paste is too thin, and chill well.

3 Divide into 8 and shape each portion into an oval cutlet, with lightly floured hands. Dip each oval in the remaining egg, then coat in dry breadcrumbs. Shallow fry for 3 minutes on each side until golden.

4 Meanwhile, melt the remaining fat in a frying pan and fry the onion until beginning to soften. Add the peppers and cook for 3-4 minutes.

5 Stir in the remaining flour, then gradually add the lemon juice and stock, and cook until thickened slightly. Add the capers and season with cayenne, salt and pepper.

6 Arrange the salpicon on 4 plates and place the cutlets on top. Garnish with watercress.

Cook's Notes

TIME
Preparation takes about 25 minutes, plus chilling. Cooking time is about 15 minutes.

VEGETARIAN SUITABILITY
This recipe is suitable for lacto-vegetarians only.

TEN VARIETIES OF BEAUTY

SERVES 4

The ten varieties refers to the selection of vegetable in this exotic
Chinese dish, which is simplicity itself to make.

INGREDIENTS

10 dried Shiitake mushrooms
2 carrots, peeled
60ml/4 tbsps vegetable oil
3 sticks celery, trimmed and sliced diagonally
90g/3oz mange tout peas
8 baby corn cobs, halved lengthways
1 red pepper, seeded and sliced
4 spring onions, sliced
60g/2oz bean sprouts
10 water chestnuts, sliced
60g/2oz can sliced bamboo shoots, drained
280ml/½ pint vegetable stock
2 tbsps cornflour
3 tbsps light soy sauce
1 tsp sesame oil

1 Place the mushrooms in a bowl and add boiling water to cover. Leave to stand for 30 minutes.
2 Drain the mushrooms, remove and discard the stalks.
3 Cut the carrots into ribbons using a potato peeler.
3 Heat the oil in a wok or large frying pan and fry the celery, mange tout peas and baby corn for 3 minutes.
4 Add the red pepper and carrots and stir fry for 2 minutes.
5 Stir in the remaining vegetables and stir fry for 3-4 minutes or until all the vegetables are cooked but still crisp.
6 Add the stock to the pan. Combine the cornflour, soy sauce and sesame oil and stir into the pan.
7 Cook, stirring constantly, until sauce thickens. Serve immediately.

Cook's Notes

TIME
Preparation takes about 15 minutes, plus soaking. Cooking time is about 15 minutes.

VEGETARIAN SUITABILITY
This recipe is suitable for vegans.

SERVING IDEA
Serve with boiled rice.

PASTA SPIRALS WITH WALNUTS AND STILTON

SERVES 4

This classic combination of walnuts and Stilton creates an unusual but delicious Italian-style meal.

INGREDIENTS

450g/1lb pasta spirals
280ml/½ pint double cream
450g/1lb vegetarian Stilton cheese
120g/4oz walnut halves
Salt and freshly ground black pepper
4 sprigs fresh thyme, to garnish
2 ripe figs, to garnish

Step 4 *Rinse the cooked pasta with boiling water.*

1 Cook the pasta in plenty of lightly salted, boiling water for 10 minutes or as directed on the packet.
2 Pour the cream into a saucepan and bring to the boil. Boil rapidly for 3 minutes, then crumble in the Stilton cheese and stir until cheese melts.
3 Stir in the walnut halves and season with pepper.

4 When the pasta is cooked, drain well, rinse with boiling water and return to the pan.
5 Pour the cream and cheese sauce onto the pasta and toss well.
6 Serve each plate garnished with sprigs of thyme and ½ a ripe fig.

Cook's Notes

TIME
Preparation takes about 5 minutes, cooking time is about 20 minutes.

VEGETARIAN SUITABILITY
This recipe is suitable for lacto-vegetarians only.

COOK'S TIP
The walnut sauce, or either of the variations, make a superb fondue sauce into which can be dipped crusty bread or fresh vegetables.

VARIATION
Use hazelnuts and vegetarian Cheshire cheese or peanuts and vegetarian Cheddar cheese, as interesting variations for the sauce.

MUSHROOMS FLORENTINE

SERVES 4

This delicious way of serving large mushrooms is suitable for informal entertaining or for a substantial supper or lunch dish.

INGREDIENTS

150g/5oz butter or vegetable margarine

2 shallots, peeled and finely chopped

900g/2lbs spinach, stalks removed, washed and roughly shredded

4 tomatoes, skinned, seeded and chopped

Salt and freshly ground black pepper

Pinch of nutmeg

450g/1lb open cap mushrooms

45g/1½oz plain flour

½ tsp dry mustard

Pinch of cayenne pepper

570ml/1 pint milk

225g/8oz vegetarian Cheddar cheese, grated

Paprika, to garnish

1 Melt 30g/1oz of the butter or margarine in a large pan and fry the shallots until softened.

2 Add the spinach with just the water that is left clinging to the leaves, cover, and cook for 5 minutes or until wilted.

3 Add the tomatoes, seasoning and nutmeg and stir to combine well.

4 Spread the spinach mixture in a shallow flameproof dish and keep warm.

5 Melt the remaining butter or margarine in a large frying pan and sauté the mushrooms for 6 minutes or until just soft. Remove with a draining spoon and arrange on the spinach.

6 Stir the flour into the pan that had the mushrooms in it, and cook for 1 minute.

7 Remove from the heat, and gradually add the milk, stirring after each addition.

8 Return to the heat and cook, stirring, until thickened.

9 Stir in 150g/6oz of the cheese and cook until cheese melts. Season with salt, pepper and nutmeg.

10 Spoon the sauce over the mushrooms and sprinkle with the remaining cheese.

11 Flash under a preheated grill to melt the cheese. Serve sprinkled with a little paprika.

Cook's Notes

TIME
Preparation takes about 20 minutes, cooking time is about 20 minutes.

VEGETARIAN SUITABILITY
This recipe is suitable for lacto-vegetarians only.

VARIATION
Wild mushrooms are now easily available and make a sophisticated alternative to the cap mushrooms used in this recipe.

SWEET & SOUR NUGGETS

SERVES 4

These delicious almond nuggets are accompanied with a sweet and sour sauce.

INGREDIENTS

30g/1oz butter or vegetable margarine
1 shallot, peeled and finely chopped
30g/1oz plain flour
140ml/¼ pint milk
60g/2oz ground almonds
60g/2oz water chestnuts
1 tsp each of chopped fresh parsley and ground ginger
1 free-range egg, beaten
Salt and freshly ground black pepper
Dry breadcrumbs and sesame seeds, to coat

Oil for shallow frying
60g/2oz light muscovado sugar
60ml/4 tbsps white wine vinegar
2 tbsps each of tomato ketchup and soy sauce
226g/8oz can pineapple chunks, in natural juice
30g/1oz cornflour
1 green pepper, seeded and sliced
2 spring onions, trimmed and sliced
120g/4oz can bamboo shoots, drained
225g/8oz bean sprouts

1 Melt the butter or margarine in a frying pan and fry the shallot for 2 minutes or until softened. Stir in the flour and cook for 1 minute. Remove from the heat and gradually beat in the milk. Return to the heat and cook until thickened.
2 Stir in the almonds, water chestnuts, parsley, ginger and half the egg. Season to taste and mix to form a thick paste. Chill well.
3 Divide into 16 rounds, with lightly floured hands. Dip in the remaining egg and coat in a mixture of dry breadcrumbs and sesame seeds. Shallow fry for 3 minutes each side until golden.
4 Meanwhile, mix together the sugar, vinegar,

ketchup and soy sauce.
5 Drain the juice from the pineapple and add to the soy sauce mixture. Reserve the chunks.
6 Mix a little of the soy sauce mixture with the cornflour and heat the remainder in a small pan until just boiling. Spoon a little of the hot sauce onto the cornflour mixture then return to the pan and cook until thickened.
7 Add the pepper, spring onions, bamboo shoots and pineapple chunks. Simmer for 5 minutes.
8 Arrange the bean spouts on plates with the nuggets on top. Pour a little sauce over and serve the remainder separately.

Cook's Notes

TIME
Preparation takes about 25 minutes, plus chilling. Cooking time is about 20 minutes.

VEGETARIAN SUITABILITY
This recipe is suitable for lacto-vegetarians only.

BEANS BOURGUIGNONNE

SERVES 4

Rich and flavoursome, this vegetarian adaption of the traditional French dish makes a luxurious main course when entertaining.

INGREDIENTS

225g/8oz borlotti or red kidney beans, soaked overnight

1 bay leaf

60ml/4 tbsps olive or vegetable oil

225g/8oz shallots or baby onions, peeled

1 clove garlic, crushed

4 carrots, peeled and cut into 2.5cm/1-inch chunks

225g/8oz button mushrooms

140ml/¼ pint vegetable stock

280ml/½ pint red wine

1 tsp chopped fresh thyme

2 tsps chopped fresh parsley

Salt and freshly ground black pepper

4 slices wholemeal bread, crusts removed

30g/1oz butter or vegetable margarine

Chopped parsley, to garnish

1 Drain the soaked beans and place in a saucepan with the bay leaf and enough water to cover by 2.5cm/1 inch and bring to the boil. Boil rapidly for 10 minutes. Reduce the heat and cook for 2-3 hours or until the beans are very soft. Drain.

2 Preheat the oven to 190°C/375°F/Gas Mark 5.

3 Heat half the oil in a frying pan and fry the shallots or onions, garlic and carrots for 5 minutes.

4 Stir in the mushrooms and fry for 3-4 minutes. Transfer to an ovenproof casserole.

5 Put the stock and wine in a pan and bring to the boil. Boil rapidly for 2-3 minutes, then pour over the vegetables.

6 Stir the beans and herbs into the casserole and season well.

7 Cook in the oven for 40 minutes.

8 Just before the end of the cooking time, cut the bread into triangles. Heat the remaining oil with the butter or margarine and fry the bread until golden.

9 Serve the casserole garnished with the bread triangles and a sprinkling of chopped fresh parsley.

Cook's Notes

TIME
Preparation takes about 25 minutes, plus overnight soaking. Cooking time is about 3½ hours.

VEGETARIAN SUITABILITY
This recipe is suitable for vegans, if bread garnish is fried in oil and dairy-free margarine.

CHINESE BLACK BEAN CASSEROLE

SERVES 4

Black beans are a traditional Chinese delicacy. They are easily available at Oriental food shops or delicatessens.

INGREDIENTS

450g/1lb Chinese black beans, soaked overnight

1 small piece root ginger, grated

1 whole star anise

1 clove garlic, crushed

2 tsps five-spice powder

6-8 sticks celery, trimmed and thickly sliced

90ml/6 tbsps sherry

1 tbsp soy sauce

1 tsp sesame oil

140ml/¼ pint vegetable stock

120g/4oz can water chestnuts, sliced

120g/4oz bean sprouts

4 spring onions, sliced

1 Drain the soaked beans and place in a saucepan with the root ginger, star anise, garlic and five-spice powder.

2 Add enough water to cover by 2.5cm/1 inch, bring to the boil and boil rapidly for 10 minutes. Reduce the heat and cook for 2 hours or until the beans are very soft. Drain.

3 Return the beans to the pan and add the celery, sherry, soy sauce, sesame oil and stock. Cook gently for about 20 minutes or until most of the liquid has been absorbed.

4 Add the water chestnuts and cook until heated through.

5 Mix together the bean sprouts and spring onions and scatter over the top of the casserole just before serving.

Cook's Notes

TIME
Preparation takes about 20 minutes, plus overnight soaking. Cooking time is about 2½ hours.

VEGETARIAN SUITABILITY
This recipe is suitable for vegans.

SERVING IDEA
Serve with vegetable fried rice or boiled brown rice.

VEGETABLE COUSCOUS

SERVES 4

Couscous is a popular dish in North Africa, where it is often cooked by steaming over an accompanying stew.

INGREDIENTS

2 tbsps vegetable oil

3 cloves garlic, crushed

2 onions, peeled and sliced

1 large potato, peeled and diced

4 carrots, peeled and sliced

2 small turnips, peeled and diced

1 green pepper, seeded and sliced

1 tsp each, ground cumin, coriander, turmeric and chilli powder

400g/14oz can chickpeas, drained

570ml/1 pint vegetable stock

225g/8oz courgettes, trimmed and sliced

60g/2oz raisins or sultanas

60g/2oz no-soak dried apricots, chopped

Salt and freshly ground black pepper

450g/1lb couscous

2 tbsps natural yogurt (optional)

1 Heat the oil in a large saucepan and fry the garlic and onions until beginning to soften.

Step 4 *Allow the couscous and boiling water to stand for 15 minutes until the grain has swollen and absorbed most of the liquid.*

2 Add the potato, carrots, turnips and green pepper and sauté for 5 minutes.

3 Stir in the spices and cook for 1 minute. Add the chickpeas, stock, courgettes, raisins or sultanas and apricots. Season with salt and pepper. Bring gently to the boil and simmer for 30 minutes.

4 Meanwhile, place the couscous in a large bowl and pour boiling water over the couscous. Allow to stand for 15 minutes, then place in a steamer lined with muslin and steam for 15 minutes.

5 Pile the couscous onto a serving plate and serve the vegetables on top. Garnish with a little yogurt if wished.

Cook's Notes

TIME
Preparation takes about 20 minutes, cooking time is about 40 minutes.

VEGETARIAN SUITABILITY
This recipe is suitable for vegans if served without the yogurt garnish.

PREPARATION
As is traditional the couscous can be placed in a steamer and steamed on top of the vegetables if wished.

MUSHROOM CROQUETTES

SERVES 4

These tasty croquettes are served with a lightly spiced cream sauce.

INGREDIENTS

45g/1½oz butter or vegetable margarine

2 shallots, peeled and finely chopped

120g/4oz mushrooms, finely chopped

45g/1½oz plain flour

140ml/¼ pint milk

90g/3oz fresh breadcrumbs

1 tsp each chopped fresh parsley and thyme

1 free-range egg, beaten

Salt and freshly ground black pepper

Dry breadcrumbs for coating

Oil for shallow frying

2 tbsps dry vermouth or white wine

280ml/½ pint double cream

2 tbsps green peppercorns in brine, drained

½ red pepper, seeded and diced

1 Melt half the butter or margarine in a frying pan and stir in 1 shallot and the mushrooms. Sauté for 5 minutes or until softened.

2 Stir in 30g/1oz flour and cook for 1 minute. Remove from the heat and gradually beat in the milk. Return to the heat and cook until thickened.

3 Stir in the breadcrumbs, parsley, thyme and half the egg. Season and mix to form a thick paste. Add extra breadcrumbs if it is too thin, and chill well.

4 Divide into 12 and shape into small ovals with lightly floured hands. Dip in the remaining egg and coat in dry breadcrumbs. Shallow fry for 3 minutes on each side until golden.

5 Meanwhile, heat the remaining fat and shallot in a pan until softened.

6 Stir in the remaining flour, whisk in the vermouth or wine and cream. Season to taste. Cook until thickened slightly. Stir in the peppercorns and red pepper, cook for 1 minute. Serve with a little sauce poured over them.

Cook's Notes

TIME
Preparation takes about 30 minutes, plus chilling. Cooking time is about 10 minutes.

VEGETARIAN SUITABILITY
This recipe is suitable for lacto-vegetarians.

SERVING IDEA
Serve with a watercress and orange salad.

VEGETABLES MORNAY

SERVES 4

This simple but elegant dish will add a touch of class to your entertaining.

INGREDIENTS

225g/8oz new potatoes, scrubbed
3 carrots, peeled and cut into thin sticks
2 parsnips, peeled and cut into thin sticks
120g/4oz mange tout peas
90g/3oz butter or vegetable margarine
120g/4oz button mushrooms
1 tsp unrefined brown sugar or molasses
225g/8oz shallots or baby onions, peeled
45g/1½ oz plain flour
1 tsp dry mustard
Pinch of cayenne pepper
570ml/1 pint milk
120g/4oz vegetarian Cheddar cheese, finely grated
Salt and freshly ground black pepper
Ground nutmeg, to garnish

1 Cook the potatoes, carrots, parsnips and mange tout peas separately in lightly salted, boiling water until tender, drain and keep warm.
2 Melt half the butter or margarine in a small frying pan and sauté the mushrooms for 4 minutes or until cooked. Remove with a draining spoon and keep warm.
3 Add the sugar to the pan, stir until dissolved, add the onions and cook over a low heat for about 5 minutes, tossing frequently until soft. Remove and keep warm.
4 In a small saucepan, melt the remaining fat and stir in the flour, mustard and cayenne pepper. Cook gently for 1 minute.
5 Remove from the heat and gradually add the milk. Return to the heat and cook gently, stirring constantly, until the sauce thickens.
6 Stir in the cheese and cook until the cheese melts. Season with salt and pepper.
7 Arrange the cooked vegetables on a serving plate and pour over a little of the sauce. Sprinkle with nutmeg.
8 Serve the remaining sauce separately.

Cook's Notes

TIME
Preparation takes about 20 minutes, cooking time is about 10 minutes.

VEGETARIAN SUITABILITY
This recipe is suitable for lacto-vegetarians only.

AUBERGINE ROLLS

SERVES 4

This colourful and tasty dish is ideal for informal entertaining.

INGREDIENTS

2 large aubergines
Salt
2 tbsps vegetable oil
1 onion, peeled and chopped
1 clove garlic, crushed
454g/1lb can tomatoes
2 tbsps tomato purée
Pinch of unrefined sugar
Pinch of dried oregano
1 bay leaf
2 sprigs fresh parsley
Salt and freshly ground black pepper
About 3 tbsps olive oil
225g/8oz vegetarian Cheshire cheese, grated
120g/4oz black olives, pitted and chopped
175g/6oz vegetarian Cheddar cheese, grated
60g/2oz pine nuts
1 tbsp white wine
1 tsp chopped fresh parsley
1 tsp chopped fresh basil
Pinch of nutmeg

1 Preheat the oven to 180°C/350°F/Gas Mark 4.
2 Heat the vegetable oil and fry the onion and garlic until softened, stir in the tomatoes, tomato purée, sugar, herbs and seasoning. Bring to the boil and simmer gently for 10 minutes.
3 Remove and discard the bay leaf and parsley. Blend the sauce thoroughly in a liquidiser or food processor, then push through a fine sieve.
4 Heat a little of the olive oil in a frying pan and fry the aubergine slices, in batches, for 1 minute on each side, adding more oil if necessary. Remove and drain on kitchen paper.
5 Put the Cheshire cheese, olives, 60g/2oz of the Cheddar cheese, the pine nuts, white wine, herbs, nutmeg and a little seasoning into a bowl and mix to combine well.
6 Spoon about half of the tomato sauce into a shallow ovenproof dish.
7 Put equal amounts of cheese filling onto one half of each of the aubergine slices, fold the other half of each slice over the filling and arrange the rolls in the ovenproof dish.
8 Spoon the remaining sauce over the aubergine rolls and sprinkle with the remaining cheese.
9 Cover with foil and bake for 20-25 minutes or until piping hot and the cheese has melted.

Cook's Notes

TIME
Preparation takes about 30 minutes, plus 30 minutes standing. Cooking time is about 40 minutes.

VEGETARIAN SUITABILITY
This recipe is suitable for lacto-vegetarians only.

TRI-COLOURED TAGLIATELLE AND VEGETABLES

SERVES 4

A delicious Italian dish that is ideal for an informal supper party.

INGREDIENTS

8oz/225g tri-coloured tagliatelle (mixture of tomato, spinach and egg pasta)

60g/2oz butter or vegetable margarine

1 large onion, peeled and sliced

225g/8oz broccoli florets

2 red peppers, seeded and sliced

2 cloves garlic, crushed

2 tsps chopped fresh rosemary

90g/3oz vegetarian Cheddar cheese, finely grated

Salt and freshly ground black pepper

1 Cook the pasta in plenty of lightly salted, boiling water for 10 minutes or as directed on the packet.

2 Meanwhile, melt half the butter or margarine in a frying pan, sauté the onion for 4 minutes, then add the broccoli and peppers and continue to cook for 5 minutes or until all the vegetables are tender.

3 In a separate saucepan place the garlic, rosemary and remaining fat and heat gently for a few minutes until the fat melts and the flavours combine.

4 When the pasta is cooked, drain well and return to the pan. Strain the garlic mixture through a sieve on to the pasta – this gives a very subtle hint of garlic and rosemary to the pasta.

5 Add the cooked vegetables and cheese.

6 Season to taste and toss well before serving.

Cook's Notes

TIME
Preparation takes about 10 minutes, cooking time is about 15 minutes.

VEGETARIAN SUITABILITY
This recipe is suitable for lacto-vegetarians only.

VARIATION
Use fresh pasta and any combination of vegetables in this recipe.

CURRIED CASHEW NUTS

SERVES 4

The highly nutritious curry is simple to prepare and has a delicious flavour.

INGREDIENTS

2 tbsps vegetable oil

1 tbsp white mustard seeds

1 tsp ground cumin

1 tsp ground coriander

1 tsp garam masala

1 large onion, peeled and chopped

1 green pepper, seeded and sliced

120g/4oz cashew nuts, chopped

60g/2oz raisins

450ml/16 fl oz tomato juice

225g/8oz bean sprouts

Cucumber slices and coriander leaves, to garnish

1 Heat the oil in a large frying pan and fry the mustard seeds and spices for 30 seconds.

2 Add the onion and pepper and fry for a few minutes, or until just beginning to soften.

3 Add the nuts, raisins and tomato juice, stirring well.

4 Bring gently to a simmering point and simmer for 10 minutes.

5 Add the bean sprouts and simmer for a further 5 minutes, or until sauce has thickened.

6 Serve the curry garnished with cucumber slices and coriander leaves.

Cook's Notes

TIME
Preparation takes about 15 minutes, cooking time is about 25 minutes.

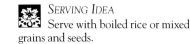

VEGETARIAN SUITABILITY
This recipe is suitable for vegans.

SERVING IDEA
Serve with boiled rice or mixed grains and seeds.

HAZELNUT ESCALOPES WITH PEAR SAUCE

SERVES 4

These delicious escalopes, complemented perfectly by the pear brandy sauce, create real style when entertaining.

INGREDIENTS

30g/1oz butter or vegetable margarine
1 shallot, peeled and finely chopped
30g/1oz plain flour
140ml/¼ pint milk
120g/4oz lightly toasted hazelnuts, ground
60g/2oz fresh breadcrumbs
1 tsp each of chopped fresh parsley and thyme
1 free-range egg, beaten
Salt and freshly ground black pepper
Dry breadcrumbs, to coat
Oil for shallow frying
280ml/½ pint double cream
1 tbsp Calvados or brandy
60g/2oz vegetarian Cheddar cheese, grated
4 small ripe pears, halved and cored
Lemon juice
Fresh sage leaves, to garnish

1 Melt the butter or margarine in a frying pan and fry the shallot for 2 minutes or until softened.

2 Stir in the flour and cook for 1 minute. Remove from the heat and gradually beat in the milk.

3 Return to the heat and cook until thickened.

4 Stir in the hazelnuts, breadcrumbs, parsley, thyme and half the egg. Season to taste, and mix to form a thick paste. Add extra breadcrumbs if the paste is too thin, and chill well.

5 Divide the mixture into 8 and shape each piece into a round escalope with lightly floured hands.

6 Dip each escalope in the remaining egg and coat in dry breadcrumbs.

7 Shallow fry the escalopes each side for 3 minutes or until golden.

8 Meanwhile, boil the cream and brandy in a small saucepan for a few minutes or until the mixture thickens slightly.

9 Stir in the cheese, season to taste and cook until cheese melts.

10 Spoon the sauce onto 4 serving plates. Brush the cut side of the pear with lemon juice and arrange on the plate with a sprig of sage. Place 2 escalopes on each plate and serve immediately.

Cook's Notes

TIME
Preparation takes about 25 minutes, plus chilling. Cooking time is about 15 minutes.

VEGETARIAN SUITABILITY
This recipe is suitable for lacto vegetarians only.

SERVING IDEA
Serve with creamed potatoes and steamed broccoli or courgettes.

SESAME STIR-FRY

<u>SERVES 4</u>

This recipe can be prepared in advance and cooked quickly for a convenient Oriental meal.

INGREDIENTS

2 tbsps vegetable oil

½ tsp grated ginger root

15g/½ oz sesame seeds

60g/2oz mange tout peas

1 stick celery, sliced

2 baby corn cobs, cut in half lengthways

60g/2oz water chestnuts, thinly sliced

30g/1oz mushrooms, thinly sliced

2 spring onions, sliced diagonally

½ red pepper, seeded and sliced

120g/4oz Chinese leaves, washed and shredded

120g/4oz bean sprouts

1 tbsp cornflour

2 tbsps soy sauce

1 tbsp sherry

½ tsp sesame oil

60ml/4 tbsps water

1 Heat the oil in a wok or large frying pan and fry the ginger and sesame seeds for 1 minute.

2 Add the mange tout peas, celery, baby corn, water chestnuts, mushrooms, spring onions and pepper. Stir-fry for 5 minutes or until the vegetables are beginning to soften slightly.

3 Add the Chinese leaves and bean sprouts and toss over the heat for 1-2 minutes.

4 Combine the remaining ingredients in a small bowl, then add to the pan.

5 Continue cooking until sauce thickens slightly and serve immediately.

Cook's Notes

TIME
Preparation takes about 15 minutes, cooking time is about 10 minutes.

VEGETARIAN SUITABILITY
This recipe is suitable for vegans.

VARIATION
Use any combination of vegetables according to what you have at hand.

CURRIED LENTILS

SERVES 4

This curry does take a while to prepare, but is worth the effort.

INGREDIENTS

225g/8oz brown lentils
60ml/4 tbsps vegetable oil
1 large onion, peeled and finely chopped
1 clove garlic, crushed
1 red or green chilli, seeded and finely chopped
1 tsp each ground cumin, coriander and turmeric
½ tsp each ground cinnamon and nutmeg
570ml/1 pint vegetable stock
60g/2oz blanched almonds
Salt and freshly ground black pepper
30g/1oz vegetable margarine or oil
2 slightly under-ripe bananas, peeled and sliced

1 tbsp unrefined dark brown sugar
2 tbsps lemon juice
Pinch each of nutmeg, cinnamon and garam masala
2 dessert apples, cored and chopped
60g/2oz raisins
120g/4oz cucumber, finely chopped
60ml/4 tbsps mango chutney
2 large tomatoes, skinned and chopped
½ green pepper, seeded and finely chopped
4 spring onions, trimmed and sliced
2 tsps walnut oil
Pinch cayenne pepper
Fresh coriander leaves and desiccated coconut, to garnish

1 Rinse the lentils under running water and set aside.
2 Heat the oil in a saucepan and fry the onion, garlic and chilli for 3-4 minutes, or until beginning to soften. Stir in the spices and fry for 1 minute.
3 Add the lentils and stock and bring to the boil, cover and cook for 45 minutes or until lentils are soft and most of the liquid has been absorbed. If the lentils are soft but there is a lot of liquid remaining, simmer uncovered for a further 10 minutes to evaporate the liquid. Stir in the almonds. Season to taste. Cover and keep warm.

4 To make the accompaniments, melt the margarine or oil and cook the banana for 1 minute. Sprinkle with sugar, half the lemon juice, the nutmeg, cinnamon and garam masala. Stir well and transfer to a serving dish.
5 Mix the apple with the raisins, cucumber and chutney and transfer to a serving dish.
6 Mix together the tomatoes, green pepper, spring onions, remaining lemon juice, walnut oil and cayenne. Season and transfer to a serving dish.
7 Serve the curry garnished with coriander leaves, coconut and the accompaniments.

Cook's Notes

TIME
Preparation takes about 50 minutes, cooking time is about 40 minutes.

VEGETARIAN SUITABILITY
This recipe is suitable for vegans if dairy-free margarine is used.

JAPANESE STEAMER

<u>SERVES 4</u>

The Japanese are renowned for their elegant cuisine, and this simple recipe is no exception. Serve for a delicious Oriental style meal.

INGREDIENTS

120g/4oz buckwheat noodles
16 dried shiitake mushrooms, soaked overnight
120g/4oz button mushrooms
8 baby corn, sliced lengthways
1 small daikon (mooli) radish, sliced
340g/12oz tofu, drained
1 packet dried sea spinach, soaked for 1 hour
140ml/¼ pint Japanese soy sauce
Small piece root ginger, peeled and grated
60ml/4 tbsps vegetable stock
1 tbsp sherry
1 tsp cornflour
1 lemon, thinly sliced
1 small bunch fresh chives

Step 4 Cut the drained tofu into 1.25cm/½-inch chunks.

1 Prepare the ingredients as directed below so that they are all cooked at the same time.
2 Cook the noodles in plenty of lightly salted, boiling water for 10 minutes.
3 Remove the stems from the shiitake mushrooms and discard. Steam the mushroom caps, button mushrooms, baby corn, and diakon for 5-10 minutes.
4 Cut the tofu into chunks and steam with the sea spinach for 2 minutes.
5 Make the sauce by heating the soy sauce, ginger and vegetable stock in a small pan until simmering.
6 Blend the sherry and cornflour together, add to the pan and cook until thickened.
7 Drain the noodles and arrange along with the steamed vegetables on serving plates.
8 Pour a little of the sauce over each and serve remaining sauce separately. Garnish with lemon slices and chives.

Cook's Notes

TIME
Preparation takes about 30 minutes, plus overnight soaking. Cooking time is about 15 minutes.

VEGETARIAN SUITABILITY
This recipe is suitable for vegans.

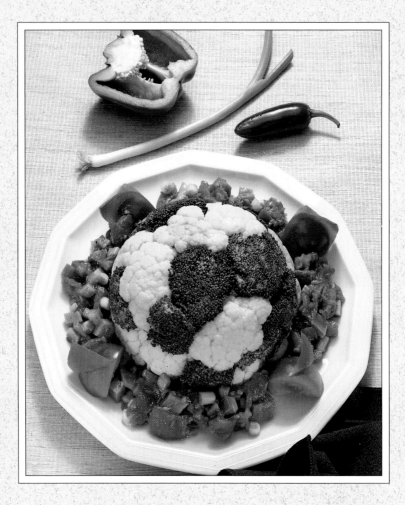

Chapter 6
SIDE DISHES

POMMES NOISETTES

SERVES 4-6

These delicious cheesy potato balls will complement any meal, whether a sophisticated dinner party or a homely family meal.

INGREDIENTS

450g/1lb potatoes, peeled and cut into chunks
30g/1oz butter or vegetable margarine
Salt and freshly ground black pepper
60g/2oz vegetarian Gruyère or Edam cheese, finely grated
60g/2oz ground hazelnuts
Oil for shallow frying
Fresh parsley or watercress sprigs, to garnish

1 Cook the potatoes until tender and mash well.
2 Add the butter or margarine, seasoning and cheese, and fork through until well combined.
3 Refrigerate until completely cold.

Step 4 *Shape spoonfuls of the chilled mashed potato into 2.5cm/1-inch diameter balls.*

4 Shape spoonfuls of the mashed potatoes into 2.5cm/1-inch balls.
5 Spread the nuts on a plate and roll the potato balls in the nuts, making sure they are well coated.
6 Heat the oil in a frying pan and fry the potato until golden, turning frequently.
7 Serve garnished with parsley or watercress.

Cook's Notes

TIME
Preparation takes about 15 minutes, plus chilling. Cooking time is about 30 minutes.

SERVING IDEA
Serve with grills, salads or roasts.

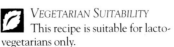
VEGETARIAN SUITABILITY
This recipe is suitable for lacto-vegetarians only.

PREPARATION
The noisettes can be prepared up to 24 hours in advance.

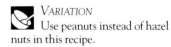
VARIATION
Use peanuts instead of hazel nuts in this recipe.

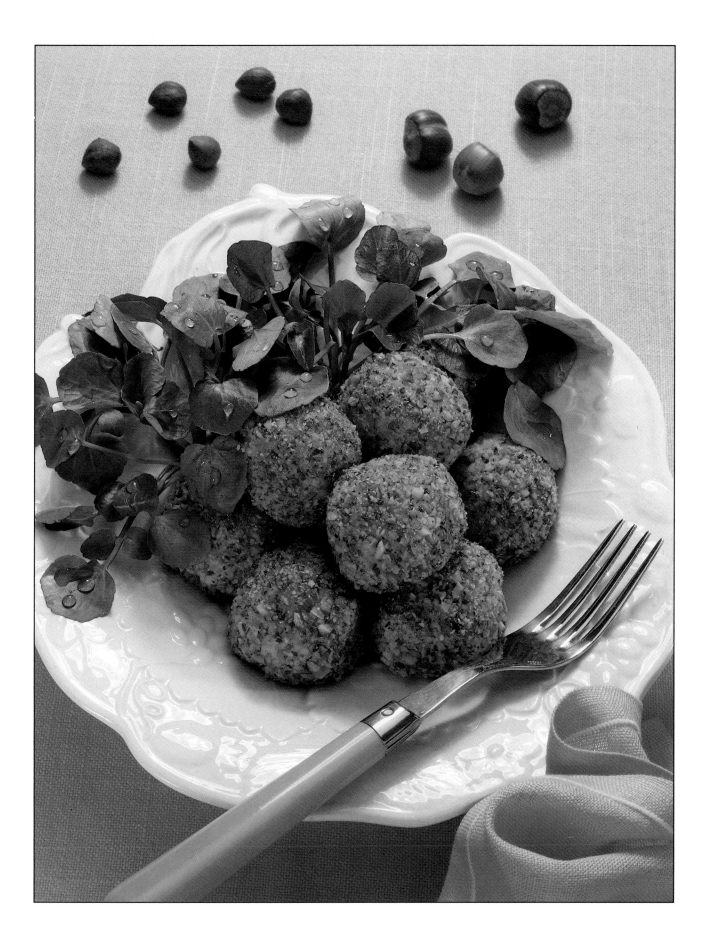

BRUSSELS SPROUTS WITH HAZELNUTS

SERVES 4

This is a delicious variation to Brussels sprouts with chestnuts and will soon become a firm favourite.

INGREDIENTS

450g/1lb Brussels sprouts, trimmed
30g/1oz butter or vegetable margarine
60g/2oz hazelnuts
Salt and freshly ground black pepper

1 Cut a cross in the stalks of any large sprouts. Cook in lightly salted boiling water for 10-15 minutes or until tender.

2 Just before the sprouts are cooked, melt the butter or margarine in a frying pan and fry the hazelnuts, stirring frequently, until browned.
3 When the sprouts are cooked, drain well and return to the pan. Add the hazelnuts and toss well.
4 Transfer to a serving dish and serve with a good sprinkling of black pepper.

Cook's Notes

TIME
Preparation takes about 10 minutes, cooking time is about 15 minutes.

VEGETARIAN SUITABILITY
This recipe is suitable for vegans if a non-dairy margarine is used.

SERVING IDEA
Serve with grills and nut roasts.

VARIATION
Use chestnuts, almonds or peanuts instead of hazelnuts in this recipe.

STUFFED TOMATOES

SERVES 4

These delicious filled tomatoes are an excellent vegetable accompaniment, but could also be served as a starter, garnished with a little salad.

INGREDIENTS

4 beefsteak tomatoes
2 tbsps oil
1 shallot, peeled and finely chopped
1 clove garlic, crushed
225g/8oz button mushrooms, finely chopped
1 tbsp white wine
45g/1½oz fresh breadcrumbs
1 tsp Dijon mustard
1 tsp chopped fresh parsley
1 tsp chopped fresh oregano
¼ tsp chopped fresh thyme
Salt and freshly ground black pepper
Sprigs of parsley, to garnish

1 Preheat the oven to 170°C/325°F/Gas Mark 3.
2 Skin the tomatoes if wished. To do this, plunge them into boiling water for a few seconds and then into cold water, to loosen the skins. Now carefully peel away the skin.
3 Cut the tops from the tomatoes and carefully

Step 3 Sta... the tomatoes u... ... drain.

scoop out the flesh. Stand the tomatoes upside down to drain.
4 Strain the tomato flesh through a sieve to reserve as much juice as possible.
5 Heat the oil in a frying pan and fry the shallot and garlic until soft.
6 Add the mushrooms and wine and cook for 5 minutes or until softened.
7 Remove from the heat and add the breadcrumbs, mustard, herbs, seasoning and reserved tomato juice, mixing well.
8 Pile the filling into the tomato shells and arrange in a oven-proof dish. Place tops on the tomatoes and bake for 20 minutes.
9 Serve hot, garnished with parsley sprigs.

Cook's Notes

TIME
Preparation takes about 20 minutes, cooking time is about 25 minutes.

VEGETARIAN SUITABILITY
This recipe is suitable for Vegans.

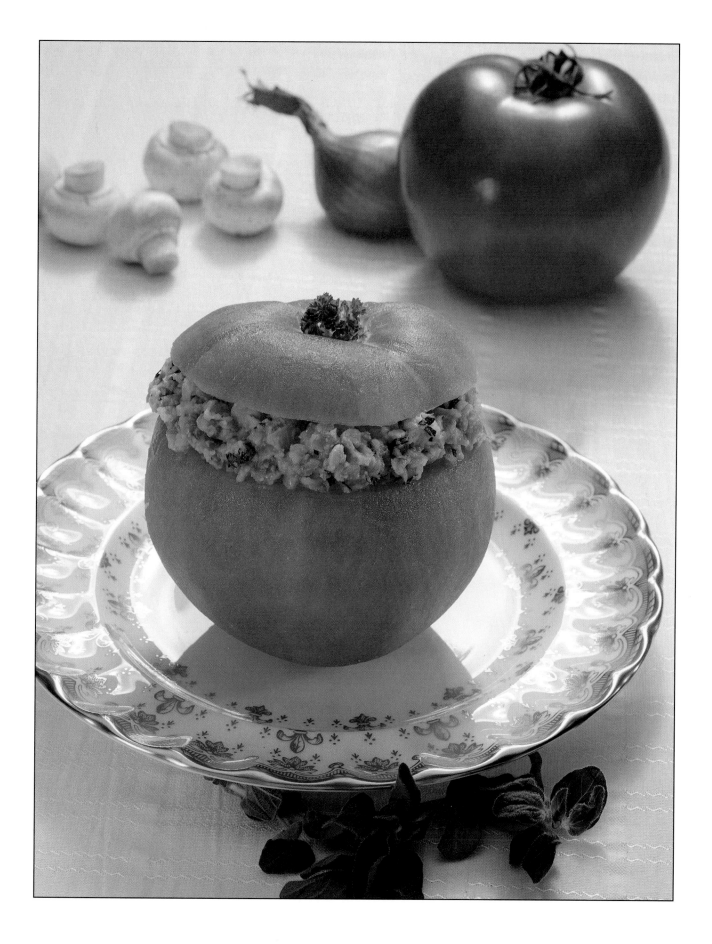

SPINACH WITH BLUE CHEESE AND WALNUTS

SERVES 4

This hot salad is an ideal accompaniment to a rich meal.

INGREDIENTS

900g/2lbs spinach, washed
30g/1oz butter or vegetable margarine
Pinch of nutmeg
Salt and freshly ground black pepper
120g/4oz walnuts, roughly chopped
120g/4oz vegetarian blue cheese, crumbled

Step 1 *Remove any tough leaves from the spinach using a sharp knife.*

1 Remove any tough leaves from the spinach and place the leaves in a saucepan with just the water left clinging to them after washing.
2 Cook over a low heat for 5-10 minutes, until the spinach wilts.
3 Put the spinach onto a plate and press a second plate firmly on top to remove excess water.

4 Melt the butter or margarine in the pan and stir in the spinach along with the nutmeg and seasoning. Stir well to coat evenly.
5 Quickly stir in the walnuts and cheese, tossing the ingredients together lightly.
6 Serve quickly before the cheese melts too much.

Cook's Notes

 TIME
Preparation takes about 15 minutes, cooking time is about 10 minutes.

VEGETARIAN SUITABILITY
This recipe is suitable for lacto-vegetarians only. See variation for vegan alternative.

SERVING IDEA
Serve with nut roasts, vegetable cutlets or pâtés.

VARIATION
Use diced tofu instead of cheese in this recipe for a vegan alternative.

Broccoli and Cauliflower Mould

Serves 4-6

Although this dish takes a little while to prepare, it will make a spectacular addition to your dinner table.

INGREDIENTS

1 small cauliflower
225g/8oz broccoli
3 tbsps walnut oil
1 tbsp white wine vinegar
1 tsp mustard powder
½ clove garlic, crushed
Salt and freshly ground black pepper
1 tbsp olive oil
1 green chilli, seeded and finely chopped
5 tomatoes, skinned, seeded and chopped
1 green pepper, seeded and finely chopped
1 tsp ground cumin
4 spring onions, finely chopped
Tomato quarters, to garnish

1 Divide the cauliflower into florets and discard the thick stalks. Trim the broccoli to within 5cm/2 inches of the florets.
2 Bring a saucepan of water to the boil, add the cauliflower and cook for 5 minutes. Add the broccoli and cook a further 10 minutes, drain well.
3 Combine the walnut oil, vinegar, mustard, garlic, salt and pepper in a small bowl and whisk with a fork.
4 Pour the dressing over the warm vegetables and toss to coat well, taking care not to break them up.
5 Carefully arrange the cauliflower and broccoli in a deep-sided 570ml/1-pint bowl, alternating the 2 vegetables and pressing them together lightly to push them firmly into the bowl shape.
6 Cover with a plate and weight slightly. Leave to cool, before refrigerating it ready for serving.
7 Heat the olive oil in a small pan and fry the chilli for 2-3 minutes, add the tomatoes, pepper, cumin and spring onions. Cook for 5 minutes.
8 Season with salt and pepper, allow to cool, then refrigerate well before serving.
9 To serve, carefully turn out the cauliflower mould on to a serving plate and spoon the tomato salsa around the base. Garnish with tomato quarters.

--- *Cook's Notes* ---

TIME
Preparation takes about 20 minutes, plus chilling. Cooking time is about 20 minutes.

VEGETARIAN SUITABILITY
This recipe is suitable for vegans.

COURGETTE ROLLS

SERVES 4

These artistic little vegetable rolls of are an impressive way of serving an accompaniment to a sophisticated meal.

INGREDIENTS

2 carrots, peeled and cut into thin sticks
2 green peppers, seeded and cut into strips
4 spring onions, trimmed
Salt and freshly ground black pepper
1 tsp chopped fresh basil or thyme
2 large courgettes
Juice of 1 lemon
Bunch of fresh chives
30g/1oz butter or vegetable margarine
2 tbsps vegetable oil

1 Cook the carrots and green peppers for 5 minutes in boiling water until just softened.
2 Drain well and place in a mixing bowl.
3 Shred the spring onions lengthways and add to the carrots and pepper.
4 Season the vegetables, add the chopped herbs and toss together thoroughly.
5 Trim the courgettes and carefully cut

Step 6 *Arrange bundles of carrots, peppers and spring onion across the strips of courgette.*

lengthways into very thin slices. Sprinkle with lemon juice.
6 Lay out the courgette strips on the work surface and arrange bundles of the vegetables in piles across them.
7 Carefully roll up the courgette strips around the vegetables. Secure them by tying at each end with chives.
8 Melt the butter or margarine with the oil in a frying pan and sauté the vegetable bundles for 10 minutes, turning frequently until the courgettes are cooked and the vegetables are hot.

Cook's Notes

TIME
Preparation takes about 20 minutes, cooking time is about 20 minutes.

VEGETARIAN SUITABILITY
This recipe is suitable for lacto-vegetarians only. See variation of vegan alternative.

PREPARATION
The bundles can be prepared in advance but cover closely to prevent them drying out.

VARIATION
For vegans, omit the butter or margarine and add an extra 2 tbsps oil. Use green beans and red peppers for a tasty variation.

LEEKS PROVENÇALE

SERVES 4

This classic method of serving vegetables is exceptionally well suited to leeks as the flavours combine so well.

INGREDIENTS

6 leeks, washed and trimmed

1 tbsp olive oil

2 cloves garlic, crushed

4 tomatoes, skinned, seeded and chopped

1 tsp dried thyme

2 tbsps chopped fresh parsley

60ml/4 tbsps dry white wine

Salt and freshly ground black pepper

Sprigs of fresh parsley, to garnish

1 Cut the leeks into 5cm/2-inch pieces.

2 Cook the leeks for 10-15 minutes in lightly salted boiling water, until tender.

3 Heat the oil in a small saucepan and fry the garlic until softened but not beginning to brown.

4 Stir in the tomatoes, herbs and wine and simmer gently for 10 minutes or until the tomatoes are softened.

5 Season the tomato mixture with salt and pepper.

6 When the leeks are cooked, drain well and place in a serving dish. Spoon the tomato mixture into the dish and turn the leeks in the sauce to coat.

7 Serve garnished with a sprig of parsley.

Cook's Notes

TIME
Preparation takes about 10 minutes, cooking time is about 25 minutes.

VEGETARIAN SUITABILITY
This recipe is suitable for vegans.

SERVING IDEA
Serve with any vegetarian meal.

SWEET AND SOUR CABBAGE WITH APPLE

SERVES 4

This tasty side dish adds a splash of colour as well as a lively flavour which will enhance any meal.

INGREDIENTS

1.4kg/3lbs red cabbage
1 onion, peeled and chopped
1 cooking apple, peeled, cored and chopped
60g/2oz light muscovado sugar
¼ tsp ground mixed spice
Salt and freshly ground black pepper
140ml/½ pint vegetable stock
2 tbsps red wine vinegar
1 tbsp walnut oil
1 dessert apple, cored and chopped
2 tsps chopped fresh parsley

Step 1 *Shred the cabbage into thin strips with a sharp knife.*

1 Quarter, core and shred the cabbage and layer in a large saucepan with the onion and cooking apple.
2 Sprinkle with the sugar and mixed spice. Season with salt and pepper.

3 Add the stock and vinegar and stir to mix the ingredients well.
4 Cover and cook gently for 45 minutes, stirring occasionally.
5 Just before the end of the cooking time, heat the oil in a frying pan and sauté the dessert apple for 2-3 minutes until just soft. Remove from the heat and stir in the parsley.
6 Transfer the cabbage to a serving dish and garnish with the apple and parsley mixture.

Cook's Notes

TIME
Preparation takes about 20 minutes, cooking time is about 45 minutes.

VEGETARIAN SUITABILITY
This recipe is suitable for vegans.

RED HOT SLAW

<u>SERVES 4</u>

This spicy variation of coleslaw makes a delicious and less usual salad that is ideal with highly flavoured dishes.

INGREDIENTS

450g/1lb red cabbage, cored and shredded

2 red onions, peeled and sliced

1 small white daikon (mooli) radish, peeled and grated

60ml/4 tbsps mayonnaise

60ml/4 tbsps natural yogurt

2 tsps grated horseradish

½ tsp aniseed, (ground anise)

½ tsp chilli powder

1 Combine the cabbage, onions and daikon radish in a large bowl and toss until well combined.

2 In a small bowl mix together the mayonnaise, yogurt, horseradish, aniseed and chilli powder.

Step 3 *Pour the mayonnaise dressing over the cabbage mixture and toss until well coated.*

3 Pour the mayonnaise dressing over the cabbage mixture and toss until well coated. Chill until ready to serve.

4 Alternatively, serve the cabbage with a little of the dressing drizzled over the top and the remaining dressing served separately.

Cook's Notes

TIME
Preparation takes about 10 minutes.

VEGETARIAN SUITABILITY
This recipe is suitable for lacto-vegetarians only.

VARIATION
Grate an unpeeled dessert apple into the slaw for a slightly sweetened variation.

COOK'S TIP
Diakon (Mooli) radishes are long white Asian radishes and can be found at delicatessens or ethnic food shops.

BRAISED FENNEL

SERVES 4

The aromatic, aniseed flavour of fennel makes it an ideal accompaniment to many richer casseroles and vegetable bakes.

INGREDIENTS

2 large bulbs of fennel
2 tsps chopped fresh lovage
120ml/4 floz vegetable stock
2 tbsps sherry
½ tsp celery seeds or celery seasoning

1 With a sharp knife cut away the thick root end of the fennel bulbs.
2 Trim away the upper stalks and reserve a little of the green top for a garnish.
3 Thickly slice the fennel, separating the strips from each other as you cut.
4 Place the fennel, lovage, stock and sherry in a saucepan and bring gently to the boil.
5 Reduce the heat and simmer gently for about 15 minutes or until the fennel is tender.
6 Drain and transfer to a warm serving dish.

Step 1 *With a sharp knife cut away the thick root end of the fennel bulbs.*

Step 2 *Trim away the upper stalks and leafy parts.*

Sprinkle with celery seeds or seasoning and garnish with fennel tops.

Cook's Notes

TIME
Preparation takes about 10 minutes, cooking time is about 15 minutes.

VEGETARIAN SUITABILITY
This recipe is suitable for vegans.

COOK'S TIP
If lovage is unavailable, use some of the leafy fennel tops, chopped, instead.

VARIATION
Add 1 peeled, cored and thinly sliced cooking apple to the fennel for a delicious variation.

WILD RICE PILAU

SERVES 4

*Although expensive, a little wild rice goes a long way when mixed with
long grain rice and really does add a special flavour and texture to a dish.*

INGREDIENTS

175g/6oz long grain rice

60g/2oz wild rice

2 tbsps vegetable oil

1 piece cassia bark or ½ stick cinnamon

4 black or green cardamom pods, crushed

8 cloves

4 black peppercorns

1 piece star anise

570ml/1 pint vegetable stock

60ml/4 tbsps dry white wine

60g/2oz flaked almonds

60g/2oz raisins

1 Place the rices in two separate sieves and rinse
thoroughly under running water, drain each well.
2 Heat half the oil in a saucepan and fry the spices
for 1 minute. Stir in the wild rice and cook for 1
minute, stirring constantly. Add the stock and
wine and bring to the boil. Stir, cover and simmer
for 30 minutes.

Step 1 *Rinse the rice
under cold running water
to remove dust and excess
starch from the grains.*

3 Just before the 30 minutes is up, heat the
remaining oil in a frying pan, add the long grain
rice and cook, stirring, for 1 minute.
4 Add some of the hot liquid from the wild rice to
the frying pan and stir in. Pour the long grain rice
and liquid into the wild rice and stir well.
5 Cover the pan and simmer for a further 20-30
minutes, or until the rice is tender and most of the
liquid has been absorbed. If the rice is still hard
when most of the liquid has been absorbed, add a
little water.
6 Stir the remaining ingredients into the pan and
allow to stand covered for 5 minutes, until the
liquid is completely absorbed.
7 Fluff up the rice with a fork before serving.

Cook's Notes

TIME
Preparation takes about 5
minutes, cooking time is about 1 hour.

VEGETARIAN SUITABILITY
This recipe is suitable for
vegans.

SERVING IDEA
Serve with vegetarian curries,
casseroles or salads.

VARIATION
Add some cooked chopped
mixed vegetable instead of the nuts
and raisins.

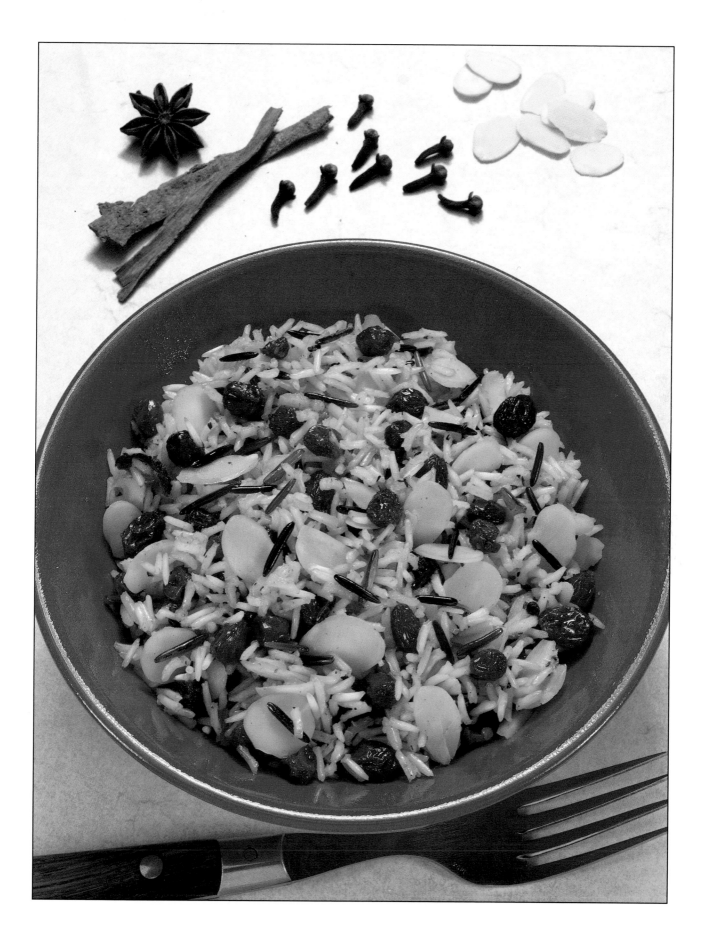

GREEN BEANS WITH MUSTARD SAUCE

SERVES 4

French beans, cooked until tender-crisp and coated with a piquante sauce make a delicious side dish to a nut roast.

INGREDIENTS

450g/1lb green beans
140ml/¼ pint vegetable stock
Approximately 140ml/¼ pint milk
30g/1oz butter or vegetable margarine
30g/1oz plain flour
1 tsp dry mustard
Salt and ground white pepper
Snipped chives, to garnish

1 Trim the beans and cut them into 5cm/2-inch lengths.

2 Bring the stock to the boil, add the beans, and simmer gently for 10 minutes or until tender-crisp.
3 Drain, reserving the cooking liquid. Transfer the beans to a serving dish and keep warm.
4 Make the liquid up to 280ml/½ pint with milk.
5 Melt the butter or margarine and stir in the flour and mustard. Cook for 1 minute.
6 Remove from the heat and gradually add the stock and milk, stirring well.
7 Return to the heat and cook until sauce thickens, stirring continuously. Season well.
8 Pour the sauce over the beans and garnish with snipped chives.

Step 1 *Trim the beans at either end, before cutting into 5cm/2-inch lengths.*

Step 3 *Drain the cooked beans, reserving the cooking liquid.*

Cook's Notes

TIME
Preparation takes about 10 minutes, cooking time is about 15 minutes.

VEGETARIAN SUITABILITY
This recipe is suitable for lacto-vegetarians only.

Chapter 7
DESSERTS

CRÈPES SUZETTE

SERVES 4

*A spectacular end to a dinner party meal, most of the preparation can
be done well in advance.*

INGREDIENTS

120g/4oz plain flour

¼ tsp ground nutmeg

2 free-range eggs

2 tsps vegetable oil

280ml/½ pint milk

Oil for frying

60g/2oz butter or vegetable margarine

Grated rind of 1 orange

60g/2oz unrefined caster sugar

225ml/8 fl oz fresh orange juice

2 tbsps orange-flavoured liqueur

2 tbsps brandy

Orange slices, to decorate

1 Sift the flour and nutmeg into a mixing bowl and make a well in the centre.

2 Drop the eggs, oil and a little of the milk into the well. Using a wooden spoon beat well, slowly incorporating the flour until you have a smooth paste.

3 Gradually beat in the remaining milk, then allow to stand for 20 minutes.

4 Heat a little oil in a 20.5cm/8-inch heavy based frying pan. Pour off the excess.

5 Spoon about 3 tbsps of the batter into the pan and tilt the pan so that the batter coats the base.

6 Cook for about 1 minute until the underside is golden, then flip or turn over and cook the other side.

7 Slide the pancake out of the pan and set aside. Repeat until all the batter has been used, stacking the pancakes on top of each other. Cover to prevent them from drying out.

8 Melt the butter or margarine in a frying pan, and stir in the orange rind, sugar and juice. Cook, stirring, until the sugar dissolves.

9 Add the orange liqueur and allow to boil gently for a few minutes until the liquid has reduced slightly.

10 Fold the pancakes into triangles and add to the pan. Cook gently to warm the pancakes through.

11 Heat the brandy in a small pan. Set alight and pour over the pancakes. Serve when the flames have died down. Decorate with orange slices.

Cook's Notes

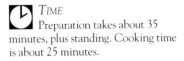

TIME
Preparation takes about 35 minutes, plus standing. Cooking time is about 25 minutes.

VEGETARIAN SUITABILITY
This recipe is suitable for lacto-vegetarians only.

FREEZING
Freeze the pancakes, well wrapped, for up to 6 months. Allow to defrost before using.

APPLEMINT PUDDING

SERVES 4-6

Applemint is a type of mint that is particularly well suited to this recipe.

INGREDIENTS

225g/8oz cooking apples, peeled cored and sliced

Small knob butter or vegetable margarine

120g/4oz unrefined caster sugar

1 tbsp chopped fresh applemint

90g/3oz butter or vegetable margarine

2 free-range eggs

120g/4oz self-raising flour

3 tbsps milk

1 Place the apples, knob of butter and 30g/1oz of the sugar in a small saucepan and cook gently until the apples soften and go mushy. Break up with the back of a spoon as the apple cooks.

2 Stir in 1 tsp of the applemint. Spoon into a 1150ml/2-pint pudding basin.

3 Place the fat in a mixing bowl with the rest of the sugar and beat until pale and creamy. Gradually add the eggs, beating well after each addition.

4 Fold in the flour, remaining mint and milk. Spoon the mixture over the purée in the basin.

5 Cover with a piece of greased, greaseproof paper and foil pleated across the centre to allow the pudding room to expand. Secure string tightly

Step 3 *Beat together the butter of margarine and caster sugar until light and creamy.*

around the basin to hold the foil and paper in place.

6 Steam in a double boiler for 1½-2 hours over boiling water. Top up the level of boiling water when necesssary.

7 Serve the pudding turned out onto a hot plate.

Step 4 *Fold in the remaining applemint into the cake mixture with a metal spoon.*

Cook's Notes

TIME
Preparation takes about 15 minutes, cooking time is about 1½-2 hours.

VEGETARIAN SUITABILITY
This recipe is suitable for lacto-vegetarians only.

SERVING IDEA
Serve with fresh cream or ice-cream.

SWEET FRUIT PILAU

<u>SERVES 6</u>

Fragrantly spiced and served with fresh fruit, this unusual dessert is a delicious way of serving rice.

INGREDIENTS

60g/2oz butter or vegetable margarine
30g/1oz cashew nuts
30g/1oz flaked almonds
9 cardamom pods, lightly crushed
4 cloves
½ tsp ground nutmeg
225g/8oz pudding rice
570ml/1 pint milk
120g/4oz unrefined caster sugar
Freshly grated rind of 1 orange
Few drops of orange flower water
60g/2oz black sesame seeds
1 small mango, peeled, stoned and sliced
60g/2oz seedless white grapes
1 orange, peeled and segmented
1 kiwi fruit, peeled and sliced

1 Melt the butter or margarine in a saucepan and sauté the nuts until beginning to brown. Stir in the spices and cook for 30 seconds, stirring constantly.
2 Stir in the rice, milk, sugar, orange rind and orange flower water.
3 Heat, gently stirring, until sugar dissolves. Bring the mixture up to simmering point.
4 Cook over a low heat for about 20 minutes or until the rice is tender and most of the liquid has been absorbed, stirring occasionally. Take care not to let the milk boil over.
5 If the rice is not tender when the milk has been absorbed add a little extra.
6 Stir in the sesame seeds and stand, covered, for 5 minutes. The milk will then have been fully absorbed.
7 Spoon the rice into a serving dish and decorate with the prepared fruit.

Cook's Notes

TIME
Preparation takes about 20 minutes, cooking time is about 20 minutes.

VEGETARIAN SUITABILITY
This recipe is suitable for lacto-vegetarians only.

SERVING IDEA
Serve with sponge biscuits.

VARIATION
Use any fresh fruit of your choice in place of that suggested in the recipe.

POACHED PEARS WITH RASPBERRY COULIS

SERVES 4

This simple-to-prepare dessert is superb when lightly perfumed with the fragrance of fresh hyssop, but you can use cinnamon instead.

INGREDIENTS

280ml/½ pint water
60ml/4 tbsps clear honey
1 tbsp lemon juice
2 sprigs fresh hyssop or 1 stick cinnamon
4 pears with stalks
225g/8oz raspberries
1 tsp chopped fresh hyssop
Sprigs fresh hyssop to decorate (optional)

Step 2 *Keeping the split stalks intact, carefully remove the cores from the pears using a grapefruit knife.*

1 Place the water and honey in a large saucepan or frying pan and heat until honey dissolves. Stir in the lemon juice and hyssop or cinnamon stick.

2 Peel the pears and carefully cut them in half lengthways with a sharp knife, splitting the stalk if possible.

3 Keep the stalks intact if possible, and remove the core with a grapefruit knife or teaspoon.

4 Put the pears in the syrup and bring gently to the boil.

5 Cover, reduce the heat, and simmer gently until the pears are tender. Chill until required.

6 Meanwhile, purée the raspberries and chopped hyssop in a food processor or liquidiser and push through a sieve to remove the seeds.

7 Sweeten the raspberry coulis with a little of the honey syrup if wished.

8 Arrange the pears on serving plates and pour a little raspberry coulis over each.

9 Decorate with sprigs of hyssop, if wished, and serve the remaining sauce separately.

Cook's Notes

TIME
Preparation takes about 20 minutes, plus chilling. Cooking time is about 10 minutes.

VEGETARIAN SUITABILITY
This recipe is suitable for vegans.

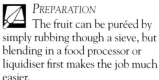

PREPARATION
The fruit can be puréed by simply rubbing though a sieve, but blending in a food processor or liquidiser first makes the job much easier.

TREASURE RICE

SERVES 4-6

*This is a traditional Chinese dessert which can be served either
hot or cold.*

INGREDIENTS

225g/8oz pudding rice

225g/8oz unrefined caster sugar

850ml/1½ pints water

175g/5oz red bean paste

1 tbsp candied lotus seeds (optional)

30g/1oz blanched almonds

4 red glacé cherries

4 green glacé cherries

2 rings glacé pineapple

2-3 pitted dates

4 glacé apricots

1 Put the rice in a saucepan with the sugar and water and bring gently to the boil. Reduce the heat and simmer gently for 20 minutes or until rice is tender, stirring occasionally, until the liquid has been absorbed.

2 Spread half the cooked rice in a hot shallow serving dish, then carefully spread the red bean paste over the rice layer, taking care not to dislodge the rice.

3 Spoon the remaining rice over the bean paste.

4 Cut the fruit into pieces and arrange decoratively over the rice before serving.

5 If the rice begins to get cold you can cover with foil and heat through in a warm oven.

Cook's Notes

TIME
Preparation takes about 25 minutes, cooking time is about 20 minutes.

SERVING IDEA
Glaze the dessert with a sugar syrup if liked.

VEGETARIAN SUITABILITY
This recipe is suitable for vegans.

VARIATION
Use any combination of glacé fruits to decorate this dessert.

PREPARATION
Chinese desserts are very sweet. The sugar in this recipe can be halved if preferred.

APRICOT PUDDING

SERVES 4-6

*Served with a rich fruity sauce, this steamed sponge pudding is just right
for chilly winter days.*

INGREDIENTS

411g/14½oz can apricots in natural juice
90g/3oz butter or vegetable margarine
90g/3oz unrefined caster sugar
2 free-range eggs
120g/4oz self-raising flour
2 tbsps milk
Few drops almond essence
Juice of ½ lemon
1 tbsp cornflour

1 Drain the apricots, reserving half of the juice.
2 Chop half of the drained apricots and set them aside for use in the sponge.
3 Place the butter or margarine in a mixing bowl with the caster sugar and beat until pale and creamy.
4 Gradually add the eggs, beating well after each addition.
5 Fold in the flour, milk, almond essence and chopped apricots. Spoon the cake mixture into a greased 570ml/1-pint pudding basin.

Step 3 Beat the butter or margarine and sugar together until pale and creamy.

6 Cover with a piece of greased greaseproof paper and foil, pleated across the centre to allow the pudding space to expand. Tie down with string to secure well.
7 Steam in a double boiler over boiling water for 1½-2 hours. Top up the level of boiling water when necessary.
8 Meanwhile make the sauce. Purée the remaining apricots and juice in a liquidiser or food processor. Transfer to a small saucepan.
9 Mix the lemon juice and cornflour together then add to the apricot purée. Cook gently until sauce thickens.
10 Serve the pudding turned out onto a hot serving plate, with the hot apricot sauce poured over the top.

Cook's Notes

⏰ TIME
Preparation takes about 15 minutes, cooking time is about 1½ to 2 ½ hours.

🌿 VEGETARIAN SUITABILITY
This recipe is suitable for lacto-vegetarians only.

◼ VARIATION
Use any other favourite canned fruit in place of the apricots in this recipe.

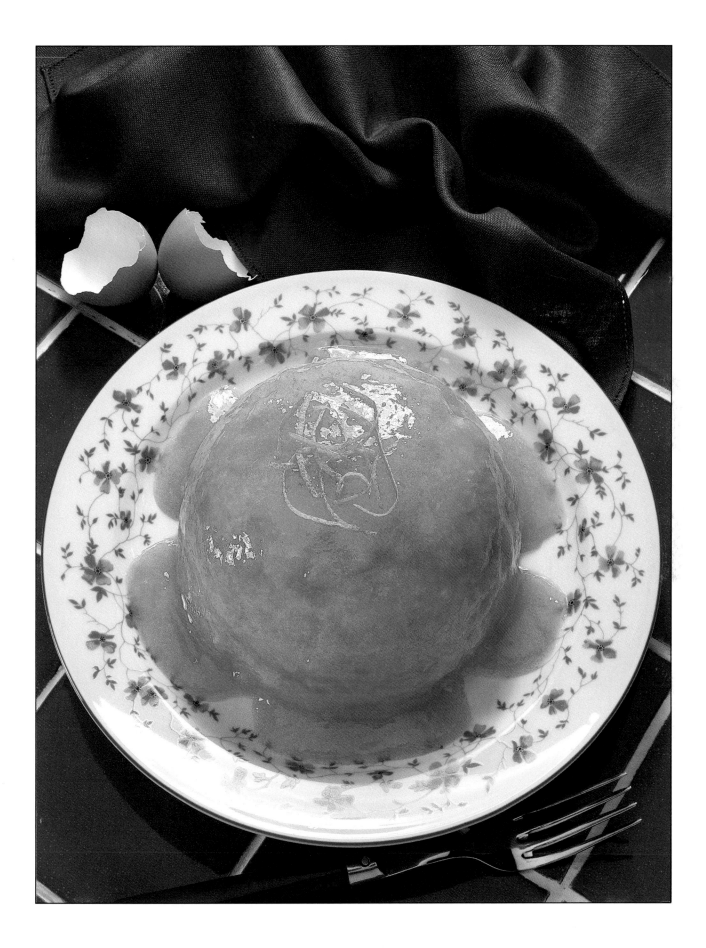

BROWN BREAD CRUMBLE

SERVES 4

The unusual crumble topping on this dessert is simple to make, high in fibre and very tasty.

INGREDIENTS

225g/8oz cooking apples, cored and sliced

225g/8oz raspberries

90g/3oz fresh wholemeal breadcrumbs

90g/3oz rolled oats

60g/2oz light muscovado sugar

1 tsp ground cinnamon

½ tsp ground cardamom

60g/2oz butter or vegetable margarine

Step 3 *Mix together the breadcrumbs, oats, sugar and spices.*

Step 4 *Rub the butter or margarine into the breadcrumb mixture with the fingertips.*

1 Preheat the oven to 190°C/375°F/Gas Mark 5.

2 Arrange the apple slices in a pie dish and scatter the raspberries over the top.

3 Put the breadcrumbs, oats, sugar and spices in a large bowl. Mix together well to distribute the spices evenly.

4 Add the butter or margarine and rub into the mixture until well blended.

5 Spoon the topping over the prepared fruit and smooth the top with a spoon.

6 Bake for 20-25 minutes and serve.

 *Cook's Notes*

 TIME
Preparation takes about 15 minutes, cooking time is about 20 minutes.

VEGETARIAN SUITABILITY
This recipe is suitable for vegans if a suitable margarine is used.

 FREEZING
The crumble can be frozen for up to 2 months.

SERVING IDEA
Serve hot or cold with fresh cream (for lacto-vegetarians).

VARIATION
Use the topping over any variety of prepared fruit.

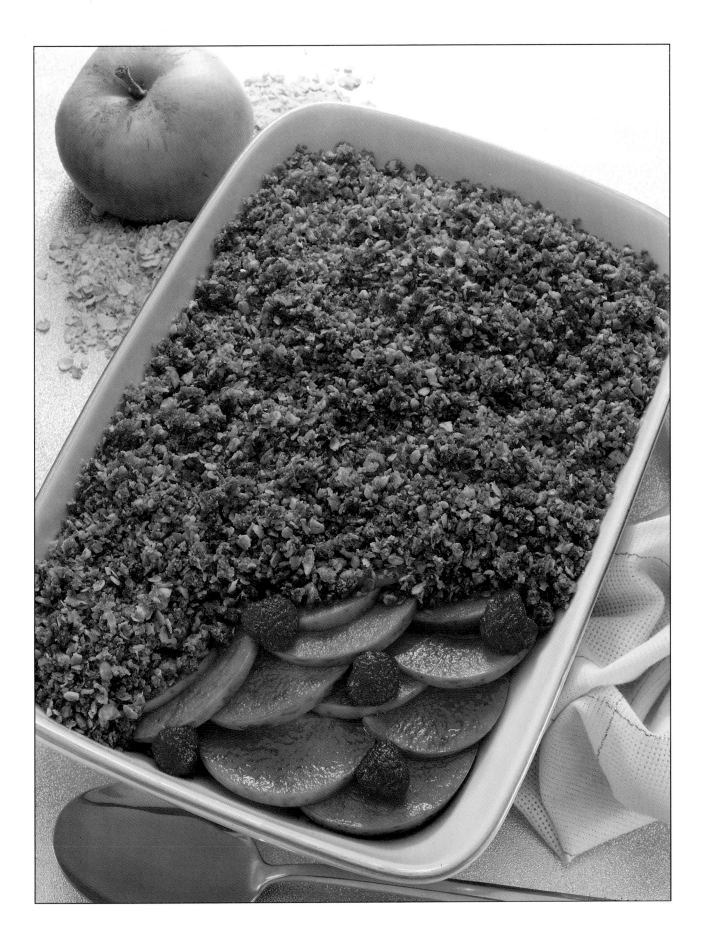

BAKED CARROT CUSTARD

SERVES 4

The natural sweetness of carrots makes them an ideal ingredient in desserts.

INGREDIENTS

450g/1lb carrots, peeled
140ml/¼ pint water
120g/4oz pitted dates, finely chopped
1 tsp ground cinnamon
½ tsp ground nutmeg
¼ tsp ground ginger
¼ tsp ground cloves
3 free-range eggs, beaten
60g/2oz pistachio nuts, chopped
420ml/¾ pint milk
Pistachio nuts to decorate

1 Preheat the oven to 160°C/325°F/Gas Mark 3.
2 Using the coarse side of a grater, grate the carrots.
3 Place the carrots in a saucepan, add the water and simmer gently for 5 minutes or until soft.
4 Add the dates and cook for a further 3 minutes.

5 Place the carrot mixture into a liquidiser or food processor and blend to make a fine purée.
6 Transfer to a large mixing bowl. Stir in the spices, then beat in the eggs and pistachios.
7 Heat the milk until almost boiling, then beat into the carrot mixture.
8 Transfer to a shallow, ovenproof serving dish.
9 Bake for 40-45 minutes or until set.
10 Allow to cool slightly and serve warm, or chill completely before serving. Decorate with extra pistachio nuts.

Step 9 *Bake the custard until the centre is just set and the outer edges are firm.*

Cook's Notes

TIME
Preparation takes about 15 minutes, cooking time is about 40-50 minutes.

VEGETARIAN SUITABILITY
This recipe is suitable for lacto-vegetarians only.

PREPARATION
Save time by using the grating attachment for the food processor to grate the carrots.

ALMOND SAVARIN

SERVES 8

Savarins make ideal centre-pieces for cold tables or buffets, and this recipe is ideal for such an occasion as it can be made well in advance and frozen until required.

INGREDIENTS

225g/8oz plain flour
Pinch of salt
2 tsps unrefined caster sugar
1 tbsp dried yeast
175ml/6 fl oz lukewarm milk
90g/3oz butter or vegetable margarine
4 free-range eggs, beaten
30g/1oz flaked almonds
140ml/¼ pint water
90g/3oz unrefined granulated sugar
90ml/6 tbsps Amaretto liqueur
Fresh fruit and whipped cream, to serve

1 Preheat the oven to 200°C/400°F/Gas Mark 6.
2 Sift the flour and salt into a large bowl and make a well in the centre.
3 Stir the caster sugar and yeast into the warm milk. Pour the yeast mixture into the well and carefully sprinkle a little flour over the top.
4 Leave the bowl in a warm place for about 30 minutes, or until the yeast has become very frothy.
5 Carefully mix the flour into the yeast mixture to form a batter, mixing from the centre and gradually incorporating the flour, a little at a time, from the edges.
6 Soften the butter or margarine, beat into the yeast and flour batter along with the eggs and mix well until it is shiny and elastic, but still very soft.
7 Thoroughly grease a 20.5cm/8-inch ring or savarin tin and sprinkle the almonds into the tin. Spoon in the batter.
8 Cover with a piece of oiled cling film and leave in a warm place for 30-40 minutes or until the mixture has almost doubled in volume.
9 Bake for about 40 minutes, or until well risen and golden brown. Cool in the tin for a few minutes, then turn out and transfer to a wire rack to cool completely.
10 Heat the sugar and water together until the sugar dissolves, then stir in the Amaretto. Place the savarin on the rack over a tray, and prick the top several times with a skewer. Spoon the syrup over the savarin, collect any from the tray and spoon over again, repeat until all the syrup has been absorbed.
11 Serve with fresh fruit and whipped cream.

Cook's Notes

TIME
Preparation takes about 1 hour, plus proving. Cooking time is about 20 minutes.

VEGETARIAN SUITABILITY
This recipe is suitable for vegans if a suitable margarine is used. (Do not serve to vegans with cream.)

FREEZING
The savarin can be frozen for up to 2 months after the syrup has been soaked into it.

BAKED MANGO AND RICE

SERVES 4-6

An exotic variation of traditional rice pudding, this recipe demonstrates a delicious way of using mangoes.

INGREDIENTS

2 large ripe mangoes
Juice of 1 lime
225g/8oz pudding rice
850ml/1½ pints water
60g/2oz unrefined caster sugar
411g/14½oz can evaporated milk
Pinch of ground nutmeg
Pinch of ground cinnamon

Step 1 *If you cannot separate the mango halves from the stone, peel the fruit and chop the flesh away.*

1 Cut off the rounded sides of both mangoes lengthways, either side of the large flat central stone.
2 Cut 1 mango section into slices and reserve for decoration. Carefully scoop the flesh from the inside of the skin of the remaining 3 sections.
3 Put the mango flesh and lime juice into a liquidiser or food processor and purée.
4 Place the rice in a saucepan with the water and sugar. Bring to the boil, reduce the heat and simmer for 10-15 minutes or until the rice is tender and most of the liquid has been absorbed.
5 Stir in the evaporated milk and spices and continue cooking for 5-10 minutes, stirring occasionally until mixture is thick and creamy.
6 If serving hot, heat the mango purée to warm through.
7 Put a layer of the rice into a glass serving dish and cover with a layer of the mango purée.
8 Repeat until all the rice and mango has been used.
9 Serve hot or cold decorated with the reserved mango slices.

Cook's Notes

 TIME
Preparation takes about 20 minutes, cooking time is about 15-25 minutes.

VEGETARIAN SUITABILITY
This recipe is suitable for lacto-vegetarians only.

 SERVING IDEA
Serve with crisp dessert biscuits.

 PREPARATION
If you do not have a liquidiser or food processor, the fruit purée can be made by rubbing the mango flesh through a sieve.

JAMAICAN MOUSSE CAKE

SERVES 6-8

This delectable chocolate mousse cake is sure to tempt even the most strong-willed dieter, so be warned!

INGREDIENTS

175g/6oz plain chocolate

3 tbsps dark rum

280ml/½ pint double cream

2 large bananas, peeled and mashed until smooth

15g/½oz light muscovado sugar

1 tbsp strong black coffee

3 free-range eggs, separated

Chocolate curls, to decorate

Step 5 *Fold the whisked egg whites into the chocolate and banana mixture.*

1 Break the chocolate into cubes and place in a bowl, or in the top of a double boiler.

2 Melt the chocolate mixture over hot water, and stir in the rum and half of the cream, beating thoroughly until smooth.

3 Put the mashed bananas, sugar and coffee in a large mixing bowl and beat until well combined.

4 Add the egg yolks and beat well. Continue beating, and then add the chocolate mixture.

5 Whisk the egg whites until they are stiff and form peaks, and fold into the banana mixture.

6 Spoon the mixture into a lightly greased 20.5cm/8-inch spring-form or loose-bottomed cake tin. Chill for at least 2 hours or until completely set and firm.

7 Loosen the sides of the cake with a warm knife, then remove the sides of the cake tin.

8 Carefully slide the cake off the base of the tin onto a serving plate.

9 Whip the remaining cream and decorate with swirls of whipped cream and chocolate curls.

Cook's Notes

TIME
Preparation takes about 30 minutes, plus chilling.

VEGETARIAN SUITABILITY
This recipe is suitable for lacto-vegetarians only

VARIATION
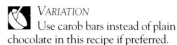
Use carob bars instead of plain chocolate in this recipe if preferred.

PINEAPPLE UPSIDE-DOWN CAKE

<u>SERVES 6</u>

A popular dessert, especially with children.

INGREDIENTS

150g/5oz butter or vegetable margarine

30g/1oz light muscovado sugar

225g/8oz canned pineapple rings, drained well

6 maraschino or glacé cherries

30g/1oz walnut halves

120g/4oz unrefined caster sugar

2 free-range eggs, beaten

120g/4oz self-rasing flour

1 Preheat the oven to 190°C/375°F/Gas Mark 5.

2 Melt 30g/1oz of the butter or margarine in a pan and pour into a lightly greased 20.5cm/8-inch sandwich tin.

3 Sprinkle the muscovado sugar over the base of the tin.

4 Cut the pineapple rings in half and arrange on top of the sugar around the edges of the tin.

5 Cut the cherries in half, arrange in a circle next to the pineapple and finally arrange the walnut halves in the centre.

6 Place the remaining fat in a mixing bowl with the caster sugar and beat until pale and creamy.

7 Gradually add the eggs, beating well after each addition.

8 Fold in the flour, carefully spoon the cake mixture over the arranged fruit and level the top.

9 Bake for 30 minutes or until springy to the touch.

10 Cool slightly in the tin then turn out and serve hot with a custard sauce or allow to cool completely.

Cook's Notes

TIME
Preparation takes about 20 minutes, cooking time is about 30 minutes.

VEGETARIAN SUITABILITY
This recipe is suitable for lacto-vegetarians only.

PLUM AND GINGER CRISP

SERVES 4-6

Plums and ginger biscuits complement each other beautifully in this simple dish.

INGREDIENTS

450g/1lb dessert plums
60g/2oz light muscovado sugar
3 tbsps orange juice
75g/2½oz unsalted butter or vegetable margarine
225g/8oz ginger biscuits, crushed
60g/2oz flaked almonds

1 Preheat the oven to 180°C/350°F/Gas Mark 4.
2 Wash and halve the plums and remove the stones.
3 Place the plums, sugar and orange juice in a pie dish.
4 Melt the butter or margarine and stir in the crushed biscuits and almonds. Mix well to coat all the crumbs.
5 Sprinkle the biscuit topping over the fruit and level the top.

Step 2 *Halve the washed plums and remove the stones with a sharp knife.*

Step 5 *Sprinkle the biscuit topping over the plums and level the top before baking.*

6 Bake for 25 minutes, cover with foil if the topping begins to brown too much.

Cook's Notes

TIME
Preparation takes about 15 minutes, cooking time is about 25 minutes.

VEGETARIAN SUITABILITY
This recipe is suitable for vegans if a non-dairy margarine is used and care is taken to use a brand of biscuits that does not include any animal fat.

VARIATION
Use apricots instead of the plums and wholemeal digestive biscuits instead of the ginger biscuits.

CHOCOLATE BRANDY CAKE

SERVES 8

This rich and sumptuous no-cook chocolate cake can be served as a dessert or for a tea time treat.

INGREDIENTS

340g/12oz plain chocolate

120g/4oz unsalted butter or vegetable margarine

2 free-range eggs, beaten

60ml/4 tbsps brandy

225g/8oz digestive sweetmeal biscuits, coarsely crushed

60g/2oz blanched almonds, chopped

140ml/¼ pint double cream, whipped

Candied rose petals, toasted flaked almonds and slivers of angelica, to decorate

1 Break the chocolate into cubes and place in a bowl, or in the top of a double boiler with the butter or margarine.

2 Melt the chocolate mixture over a pan of hot water, stirring occasionally to combine.

3 Beat the eggs a little at a time into the chocolate mixture.

4 Allow the mixture to cool slightly then beat in the brandy, biscuits and chopped almonds.

Step 6 *Spread the chocolate mixture evenly into the cake tin with a round-bladed palette knife.*

5 Lightly grease and base line a 17.5cm/7-inch springform or loose-based cake tin.

6 Pour the cake mixture into the tin and spread out evenly with a round-bladed knife.

7 Chill overnight in the refrigerator to set.

8 Loosen the sides of the cake with a warm knife then remove the sides of the cake tin.

9 Carefully slide the cake off the base of the tin, remove the silicone paper and slide onto a serving plate.

10 Pipe swirls of whipped cream around the edge of the cake and decorate with the rose petals, almonds and angelica.

Cook's Notes

TIME
Preparation takes about 15 minutes, plus overnight chilling.

VEGETARIAN SUITABILITY
This recipe is suitable for lacto-vegetarians only.

VARIATION
Use carob bars instead of plain chocolate in this recipe.

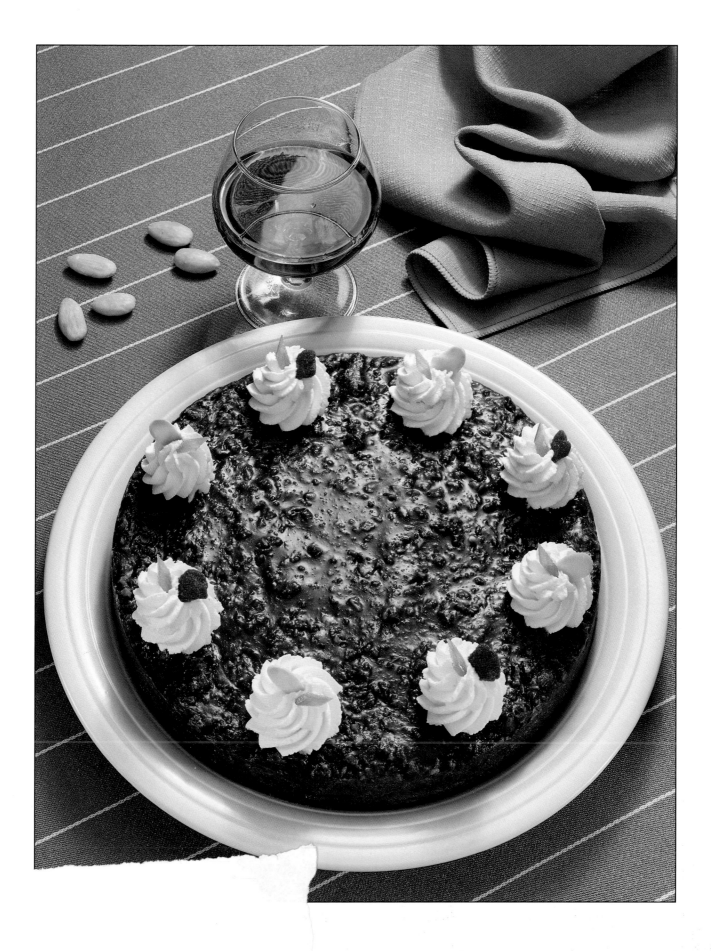

HALVA OF CARROTS AND CASHEWS

<u>SERVES 4-6</u>

Halva is a traditional Indian dessert made from carrots and cream. Do not let the use of vegetables in a dessert put you off trying this rather special recipe, as the results are really delicious.

INGREDIENTS

900g/2lbs carrots, peeled
280ml/½ pint double cream
175g/6oz dark muscovado sugar
2 tbsps clear honey
2 tsps ground coriander
1 tsp ground cinnamon
Pinch saffron
60g/2oz butter or vegetable margarine
60g/2oz raisins
120g/4oz unsalted cashew nuts, chopped
*Candied violets, silver balls or desiccated coconut, to
    decorate*

1 Grate the carrots using the coarse side of a grater.
2 Place the carrot, cream, sugar, honey and spices in a large saucepan. Mix well.
3 Cook over a low heat for 15-20 minutes until the carrots are soft, stirring frequently during the cooking to prevent burning on the bottom.
4 Add the butter or margarine, raisins and nuts, stir well and continue cooking for 10-15 minutes until the mixture has thickened and the carrots are well broken down.
5 Pile onto serving dishes and decorate with candied violets, silver balls or desiccated coconut.

Cook's Notes

TIME
Preparation takes about 15 minutes, cooking time is about 30 minutes.

VEGETARIAN SUITABILITY
This recipe is suitable for lacto-vegetarians only.

SERVING IDEA
Serve with spiced poached apples.

COOK'S TIP
Use the grating attachment on a food processor to reduce the preparation time.

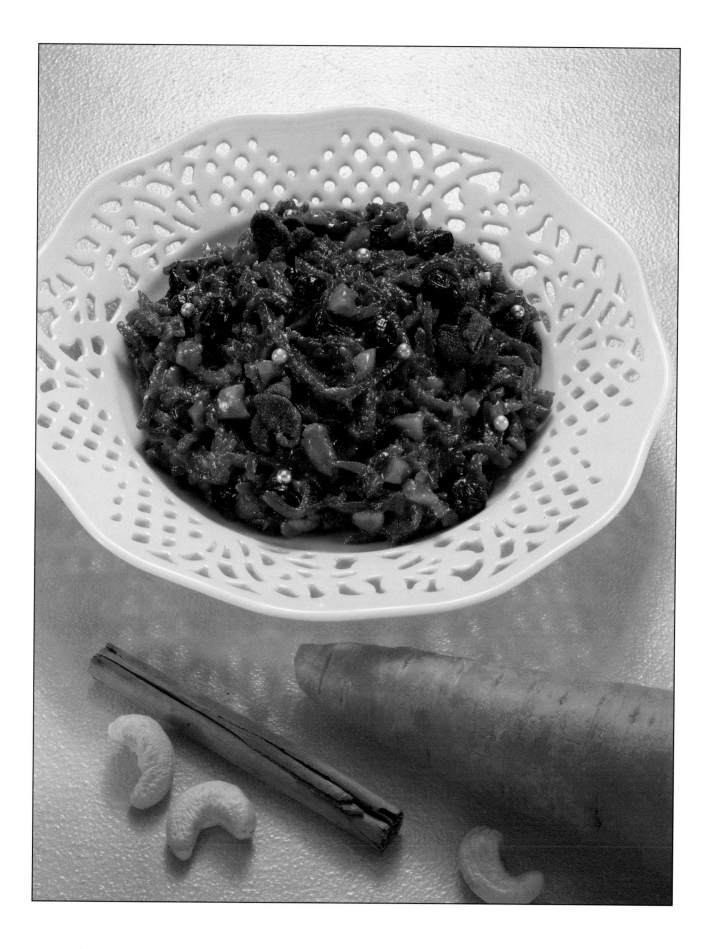

RUM BABAS

MAKES 10-12

Served with a honey syrup, these are a delicious treat.

INGREDIENTS

225g/8oz plain flour
Pinch salt
2 tsps unrefined caster sugar
1 tbsp dried yeast
120ml/4 fl oz lukewarm milk
90g/3oz butter or vegetable margarine
4 free-range eggs, beaten
60g/2oz currants
140ml/¼ pint clear honey
90ml/6 tbsps hot water
3 tbsps rum
Fresh fruit and whipped cream, to serve

Step 6 Add the beaten eggs to the flour and yeast mixture, together with the softened butter or margarine, and then beat the mixture into a shiny, elastic batter.

1 Preheat the oven to 200°C/400°F/Gas Mark 6.
2 Sift the flour and salt into a large bowl and make a well in the centre.
3 Stir the sugar and yeast into the warm milk. Pour the yeast mixture into the well and carefully sprinkle a little flour over the top.
4 Leave the bowl in a warm place for about 30 minutes or until the yeast has become very frothy.
5 Carefully mix the flour into the yeast mixture to form a batter. Mix from the centre and slowly incorporate the flour from the edges.
6 Soften the fat and beat into the batter along with the eggs, mixing well until it is shiny and elastic, but still very soft. Stir in the currants.
7 Half fill 10-12 well oiled ramekins or baba moulds with the mixture.
8 Cover with oiled cling film and leave in a warm place for 30-40 minutes or until the mixture has almost doubled in volume.
9 Bake for 15-20 minutes or until well risen and golden brown. Cool in the tins for a few minutes, then transfer to a wire rack to cool completely.
10 Mix together the honey, water and rum. Place the babas in a shallow dish and spoon the syrup over the babas. Allow to soak in completely.
11 Serve with fresh fruit and whipped cream.

Cook's Notes

TIME
Preparation takes about 1 hour, plus proving. Cooking time is about 20 minutes.

VEGETARIAN SUITABILITY
This recipe is suitable for vegans if a non-dairy margarine is used. (For vegans serve with a cream substitute.)

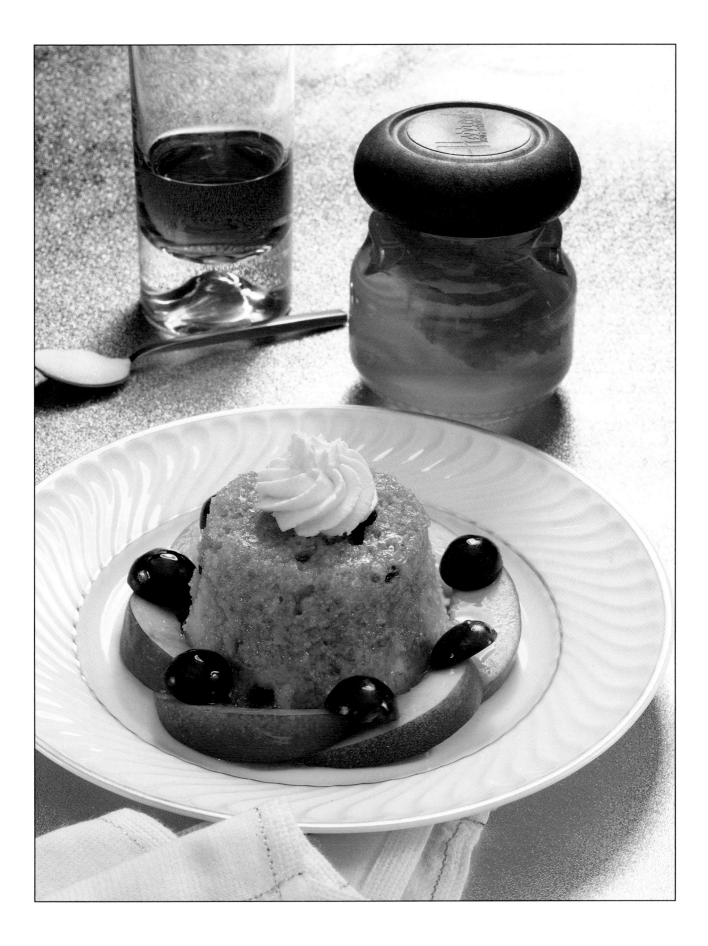

BAKED BANANAS WITH SAUCE A LA POIRE

SERVES 4

*Baked bananas are an established favourite for dessert and served with
this delightful fruity sauce they are particulary delicious.*

INGREDIENTS

2 small oranges
2 ripe pears, peeled and cored
Honey to taste
4 bananas

1 Preheat the oven to 180°C/350°F/Gas Mark 4.
2 Using a potato peeler, pare the rind from one of the oranges, taking care not to include too much white pith.
3 Cut the pared rind into very thin strips with a sharp knife and blanch in boiling water for 2-3 minutes, to soften. Drain and set aside
4 Cut off all the peel and pith from one orange using a sharp knife, then carefully cut out the orange segments from in between the membranes. Squeeze the juice from the other orange.
5 Place the orange juice and pears in a food processor and purée until smooth. Sweeten to taste with honey.
6 Peel the bananas and place in an ovenproof dish and pour the pear purée over the top. Cover, and bake for 15 minutes or until the pears are soft.
7 Decorate with the orange segments and strips of orange rind. Serve immediately.

Cook's Notes

TIME
Preparation takes about 10 minutes, cooking time is about 15 minutes.

PREPARATION
This dessert is best prepared as late as possible to prevent discolouration of the fruit.

VEGETARIAN SUITABILITY
This recipe is suitable for vegans.

SERVING IDEA
Serve with coconut biscuits and some cream (lacto-vegetarians only) if wished.

VARIATION
Use pineapple instead of pears in this recipe, and sprinkle 1 tbsp flaked coconut over the finished dish.

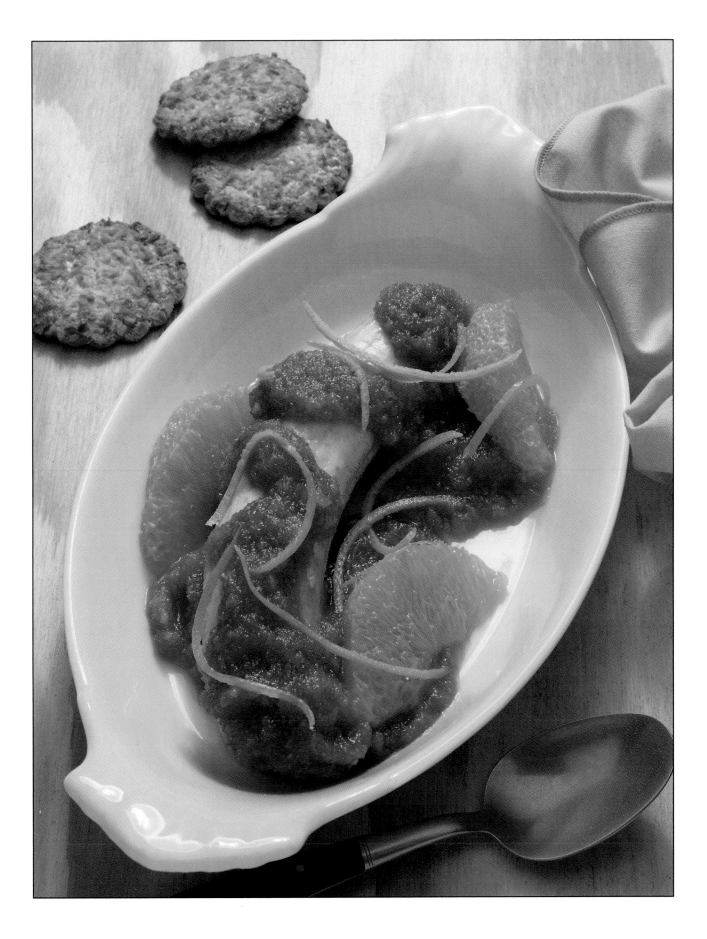

ST CLEMENT'S SORBET

SERVES 6

St.Clement's is possibly the most popular type of sorbet, and it is really quite simple to make your own.

INGREDIENTS

280ml/½ pint water

225g/8oz unrefined granulated sugar

4 lemons

1 tbsp agar agar

570ml/1 pint freshly squeezed orange juice

2 free-range egg whites

Grated orange zest and mint leaves, to decorate

Step 5 *Remove the frozen mixture from the freezer and beat will to break up the ice crystals.*

1 Place the water and sugar in a saucepan, heat gently until the sugar dissolves, bring to the boil and boil for 5 minutes. Remove from the heat and allow to cool completely.

2 Grate the rind from the lemons with a zester and squeeze the juice.

3 Put a little of the lemon juice in a small bowl and sprinkle over the agar agar. Dissolve over hot water.

4 Combine the cooled sugar syrup, lemon rind, juice, dissolved agar agar and orange juice, pour into a shallow freezer-proof container and freeze until slushy.

5 Remove from the freezer and beat well to break up the ice crystals.

6 Whisk the egg whites until they stand in soft peaks and beat into the sorbet mixture. Cover and freeze until required.

7 Serve scooped into serving glasses and decorated with orange zest and mint leaves.

Cook's Notes

TIME
Preparation takes about 30 minutes, plus freezing.

VEGETARIAN SUITABILITY
This recipe is suitable for vegans.

 SERVING IDEA
Spoon the sorbet into hollowed out lemon or orange halves.

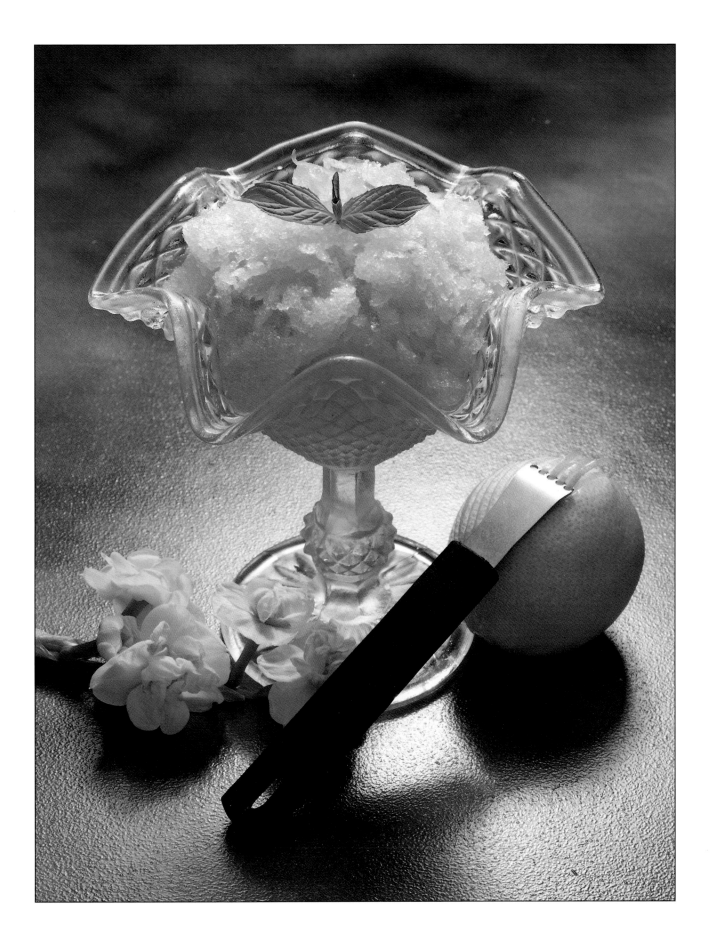

CHOCOLATE ORANGE CHEESECAKE

<u>SERVES 8-10</u>

Chocolate and orange, a favourite combination for many, are combined in this delicious, rich cheesecake.

INGREDIENTS

90g/3oz butter or vegetable margarine, melted
175g/6oz chocolate digestive biscuits, crushed
450g/1lb full-fat cream cheese
120g/4oz unrefined caster sugar
Grated rind and juice of 1 orange
280ml/½ pint Greek style yogurt
1 tbsp agar agar
3 tbsps water
60g/2oz plain chocolate, melted
2 oranges, peeled and segmented

1 Mix together the butter or margarine and biscuits and press into the bottom of an 20.5cm/8-inch loose-bottomed cake tin. Chill.
2 Beat together the cream cheese and sugar and then beat in the orange juice and rind.
3 Fold in the yogurt. Dissolve the agar agar in the water and stir into the mixture.
4 Pile the cheese mixture on top of the base, and level the top. Drizzle about two-thirds of the melted chocolate over the top and swirl a skewer through the mixture to form a marbled effect.
5 Chill until set. Transfer to a serving dish and arrange the orange segments on top. Decorate with the remaining chocolate.

Cook's Notes

TIME
Preparation takes about 30 minutes, plus chilling.

VEGETARIAN SUITABILITY
This recipe is suitable for lacto-vegetarians only.

WHITE AND DARK CHOCOLATE BOMBE

SERVES 6-8

An easy to make delicious white and dark chocolate iced dessert.

INGREDIENTS

280ml/½ pint dark chocolate ice-cream
1 tbsp strong black coffee
570ml/1 pint vanilla ice-cream
120g/4oz white chocolate
60g/2oz ratafia biscuits, coarsely crushed

1 Put a 1150ml/2-pint bombe mould or decorative mould into the freezer to chill.
2 Allow the chocolate ice-cream to stand at room temperature until just softened, but not melted. Beat in the coffee.
3 Coat the base and sides of the chilled mould with the softened ice-cream, leaving a hollow in the centre. Refreeze the ice-cream if it is too soft to stay up the sides.
4 Once the sides are coated, freeze until solid.
5 Allow the vanilla ice-cream to soften slightly at room temperature.
6 Break the chocolate into small cubes and melt in a bowl over a pan of simmering water.

Step 8 *Fill the centre of the dark chocolate ice-cream mould with the white chocolate ice-cream, smoothing the top flat.*

7 Beat the chocolate into the ice-cream, add the crushed biscuits and mix until evenly distributed.
8 Fill the centre of the mould with the white chocolate ice-cream mixture, level the top and then freeze until solid.
9 About 30 minutes before the dessert is to be served, remove the bombe from the freezer and stand in hot water for a few seconds. Upturn the mould onto a serving dish and shake the ice-cream out. Leave to stand in the refrigerator to soften slightly.

Cook's Notes

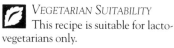

TIME
Preparation takes about 20 minutes, plus standing and freezing.

VEGETARIAN SUITABILITY
This recipe is suitable for lacto-vegetarians only.

WHITE COFFEE CREAMS

<u>SERVES 6-8</u>

*An unusual combination of light coffee flavoured cream and tangy
summer fruits, this dessert is a sure way to create an impressive finale
to any meal.*

INGREDIENTS

8 coffee beans

280ml/½ pint milk

3 free-range eggs

60g/2oz unrefined caster sugar

140ml/¼ pint double cream

225g/8oz blackberries, blackcurrants or raspberries

1 tbsp lemon juice

Icing sugar to taste

Mint sprigs, to decorate

---

1 Preheat the oven to 160°C/325°F/Gas Mark 3.

2 Place the coffee beans and milk in a small pan and bring slowly up to simmering point, simmer for 3 minutes, then remove from the heat and allow to stand for 30 minutes to allow the flavour to infuse.

3 Whisk the eggs and caster sugar together until they are thick, creamy and pale in colour.

4 Strain the flavoured milk onto the egg mixture through a fine sieve. Stir in the cream and whisk to blend well.

5 Pour equal amounts of the egg mixture into 6-8 lightly greased individual ramekin dishes.

6 Place a few sheets of newspaper in a roasting tin and place the ramekin dishes on top. Fill the tin with enough hot water to come about half the way up the dishes.

7 Bake for 25 minutes or until the custards are just set and a knife blade inserted into the centre of the custards comes out clean.

8 Remove the dishes from the water bath and chill completely.

9 Reserve a few well shaped fruits for decoration and push the remaining fruit through a sieve into a small bowl.

10 Stir in the lemon juice and enough icing sugar to sweeten to taste.

11 Carefully loosen the sides of the chilled creams with a round-bladed knife.

12 Invert a small serving plate over the top of each ramekin and turn the cream out, shaking gently to loosen them if necessary.

13 Pour a little fruit sauce around and over each cream. Decorate with the reserved fruit and mint.

Cook's Notes

TIME
Preparation takes about 20 minutes, plus standing and chilling. Cooking time is about 25 minutes.

VEGETARIAN SUITABILITY
This recipe is suitable for lacto-vegetarians only.

VARIATION
Use a vanilla pod instead of the coffee beans in this recipe.

FRUIT SALAD CUPS

<u>SERVES 4</u>

*These attractive cups of warm fresh fruit make a delightful and unusual
ending to a meal.*

INGREDIENTS

2 large oranges

1 small dessert apple

1 slice fresh pineapple

1 banana

A little orange juice

30g/1oz unrefined caster sugar

1 tsp rum

15g/½oz pistachio nuts, skin removed and chopped

Orange zest, to decorate (optional)

Step 3 *Slice the pineapple, peel the slices, remove any brown 'eyes', and then cut into bite-sized wedges.*

1 Cut the oranges in half and, using a grapefruit knife, remove the flesh and membranes, leaving just the white pith and zest to form a shell. Set aside. Reserve as much juice as possible and chop the flesh, discarding tough membranes.

2 Cut the apples into quarters, remove the core but do not peel. Cut each quarter into bite-size pieces.

3 Remove the skin and any brown 'eyes' from the pineapple and cut into bite-size wedges. Peel and slice the banana.

4 Make the reserved juice up to 140ml/¼ pint with extra orange juice, if necessary. Heat the juice and sugar and stir until dissolved. Stir in the rum.

5 Mix the prepared fruit into the juice. Just before serving, heat gently to warm the fruit but not cook it.

6 Pile into orange shells and sprinkle with chopped pistachio nuts. Decorate with orange zest, if wished, and serve immediately.

Cook's Notes

TIME
Preparation takes about 15 minutes, cooking time is about 5 minutes.

VEGETARIAN SUITABILITY
This recipe is suitable for vegans.

VARIATION
Use any combination of your favourite fruit to fill the orange shells in this recipe.

PARFAIT AU CASSIS

S<small>ERVES</small> 4

A rich and creamy dessert with a delicious fruity tang.

*I*NGREDIENTS

340g/12oz blackcurrants
2 tbsps crème de cassis
3 free-range egg yolks
120g/4oz light muscovado sugar
280ml/½ pint single cream
280ml/½ pint double cream, whipped
Blackcurrants and mint leaves, to decorate

1 Purée the blackcurrants in a liquidiser or food processor and push through a sieve with a wooden spoon to remove the skin and pips.
2 Add the cassis to the fruit purée and freeze until it becomes slushy, stirring occasionally to prevent large ice crystals from forming.
3 Whisk the egg yolks and sugar together until they become very thick and mousse like.
4 Heat the single cream in a small pan until almost boiling.
5 Gradually add the scalded cream to the egg mixture, stirring constantly.
6 Place the bowl over a pan of gently simmering water and cook, stirring constantly, until the mixture thickens enough to coat the back of the spoon.

7 Cool quickly by standing the bowl in iced water.
8 Fold the whipped cream into the cooled egg mixture.
9 Freeze until the mixture is almost solid, then beat with an electric mixer or in a food processor until slushy.
10 Break up the blackcurrant mixture with a fork or electric whisk and fold into the cream mixture to give a marbled effect.
11 Divide the mixture between 6 freezer-proof glasses and freeze until required.
12 Move from the freezer to the refrigerator 30 minutes before serving. Decorate with blackcurrants and mint leaves.

T*IME*
Preparation takes about 30 minutes, plus freezing. Cooking time is about 30 minutes.

V*EGETARIAN* S*UITABILITY*
This recipe is suitable for lacto-vegetarians only.

RASPBERRY MERINGUES

SERVES 4

Light, pale pink meringues form the basis of this delightful summer dessert.

INGREDIENTS

2 free-range egg whites
120g/4oz unrefined caster sugar
Few drops raspberry flavouring
Few drops red food colouring (optional)
225g/8oz raspberries (optional)
60ml/4 tbsps raspberry liqueur or sherry
140ml/¼ pint double cream, whipped
Cocoa powder, for decoration

1 Line two baking sheets with non-stick baking parchment. Preheat the oven to 150°C/300°F/Gas Mark 2.
2 Whisk the egg whites until stiff, then gradually whisk in the two-thirds of the caster sugar.

3 Carefully fold in the remaining sugar, flavouring and a food colouring, if using.
4 Spoon into a piping bag fitted with a plain nozzle and pipe eight heart shapes or rounds.
5 Place in the oven for 1½ hours to dry out. Remove from the oven and allow to cool completely.
6 Meanwhile, place the raspberries and liqueur or sherry in a bowl and allow to marinate until required.
7 Whip the cream and use, together with a few of the soaked raspberries, to sandwich the meringues into pairs.
8 Sprinkle the tops with a little cocoa powder and serve any remaining raspberries separately.

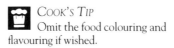

Cook's Notes

TIME
Preparation takes about 20 minutes, cooking time is about 1½ hours.

SERVING IDEA
Serve with extra fruit salad if a more substantial dessert is required.

VEGETARIAN SUITABILITY
This recipe is suitable for lacto-vegetarians only.

COOK'S TIP
Omit the food colouring and flavouring if wished.

PREPARATION
These meringues can be made several days in advance and kept in an air-tight container.

CRANBERRY CRISP

SERVES 2

Cranberries are often overlooked as being a fruity accompaniment to savoury dishes. However, their bittersweet flavour is complemented perfectly by the honey in this recipe to produce an interesting dessert you will want to try over and over again.

INGREDIENTS

140ml/¼ pint orange juice

120g/4oz fresh or frozen cranberries

2 tsps unrefined caster sugar

2 tsps cornflour

¼ tsp ground cinnamon

30g/1oz butter or vegetable margarine

225g/8oz crunchy oatmeal cereal

15g/½oz plain flour

2 tbsps clear honey

1 Preheat the oven to 180°C/350°F/Gas Mark 4.
2 Put the orange juice, cranberries and sugar in a small saucepan and cook gently for 10 minutes, stirring occasionally until the fruit softens.
3 Blend the cornflour with a little cold water and

Step 6 *Drizzle honey over the topping before baking.*

stir into the cranberries along with the cinnamon. Cook until thickened.
4 Pour into an ovenproof serving dish.
5 Melt the butter or margarine and stir in the cereal and flour, stir to mix well and pile on top of the cranberry mixture.
6 Drizzle the honey over the topping and bake for 15 minutes. Serve hot.

Cook's Notes

TIME
Preparation takes about 10 minutes, cooking time is about 25 minutes.

VEGETARIAN SUITABILITY
This recipe is suitable for vegans, if a suitable margarine is used.

VARIATION
Use this topping to cover any fruit filling.

SERVING IDEA
Serve with fresh cream (lacto-vegetarians only) or a fruit purée.

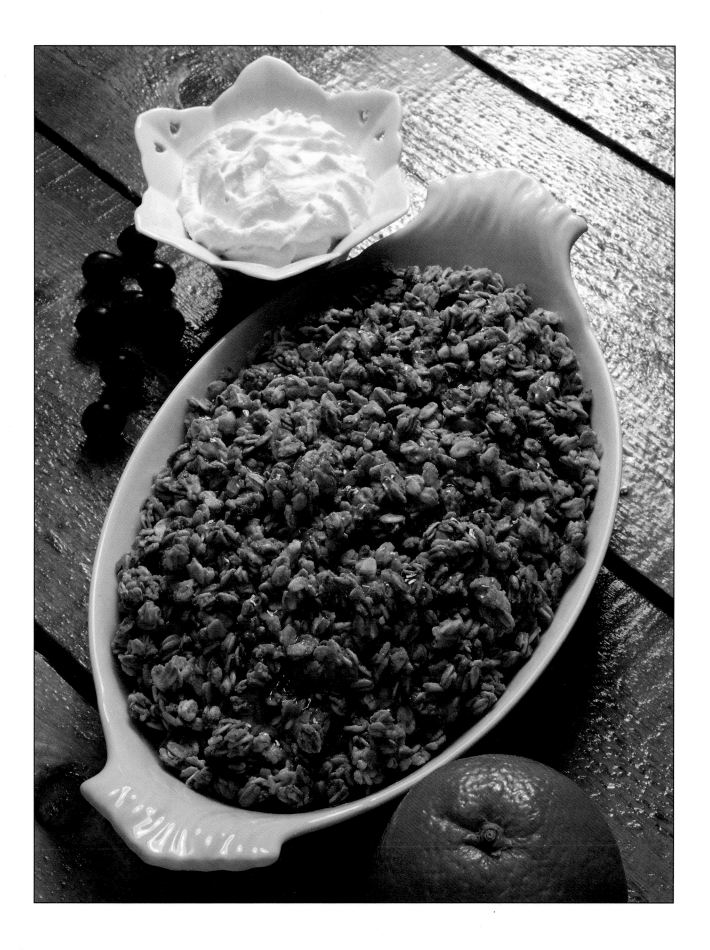

CRÈME CARAMEL

SERVES 6

This classic dessert with its light texture and flavour makes a perfect end to so many meals.

INGREDIENTS

120g/4oz unrefined granulated sugar
140ml/¼ pint water
4 free-range eggs
30g/1oz unrefined caster sugar
420ml/¾ pint milk
140ml/¼ pint single cream
Few drops vanilla essence
Strawberries or other fruit, to decorate

1 Place six individual ramekins or dariole moulds in a roasting tin. Preheat the oven to 160°C/325°F/ Gas Mark 3.
2 Put the granulated sugar and water in a small saucepan and heat gently, stirring until sugar dissolves.

3 Boil without stirring until the syrup begins to caramelise and turns golden.
4 Quickly pour a little caramel into each of the ramekins or dariole moulds.
5 Lightly whisk together the eggs and caster sugar. Heat the milk and cream in a saucepan until almost boiling then whisk into the eggs along with the vanilla essence.
6 Strain the custard and pour gently into the dishes. Fill the roasting tin with enough hot water to come halfway up the sides of the dishes and bake for 45 minutes or until a knife inserted into the custards comes out clean.
7 Remove from the water bath and chill. Serve turned out onto serving dishes, and decorate with strawberries or other fruit.

Cook's Notes

TIME
Preparation takes about 15 minutes, cooking time is about 55 minutes.

VEGETARIAN SUITABILITY
This recipe is suitable for lacto-vegetarians only.

SERVING IDEA
Serve with a little fresh pouring cream if wished.

RHUBARB, ORANGE AND STRAWBERRY COMFORT

SERVES 4

Delicious, easy to prepare and only 60 calories per serving, or a little more if honey is used. What more could anyone ask of a scrumptious dessert?

INGREDIENTS

450g/1lb canned rhubarb in natural juice

¼ tsp ground ginger

298g/10½oz can mandarin segments in natural juice

Liquid sweetener or honey to taste

2 tbsps low fat natural yogurt

175g/6oz strawberries, hulled and rinsed

2 tbsps crunchy oat cereal

Step 4 *Beat the rhubarb briskly until the fruit breaks up and the mixture thickens.*

1 Place the rhubarb and ginger in a saucepan.

2 Strain the juice from the mandarins and add to the pan, reserving the segments.

3 Cook the rhubarb mixture for about 10 minutes, stirring until mushy.

4 Beat the rhubarb briskly until the fruit breaks up and the mixture becomes thicker.

5 Sweeten with sweetener or honey to taste.

6 Stir in the yogurt along with the mandarin segments, taking care not to break them up too much.

7 Cover and allow to cool completely.

8 Slice the strawberries thinly and reserve a few slices for decoration.

9 Mix the strawberry slices into the cooled rhubarb mixture and spoon into serving dishes.

10 Just before serving sprinkle with the crunchy cereal and decorate with reserved strawberry slices.

Cook's Notes

TIME
Preparation takes about 20 minutes, plus chilling. Cooking time is about 10 minutes.

VEGETARIAN SUITABILITY
This recipe is suitable for lacto-vegetarians only. Vegans could substitute the yogurt with a vegetable cream substitute, but the calorie content will be higher.

VARIATION
Use canned apricots in place of the rhubarb and pitted cherries instead of the mandarin segments.

BOMBE AUX APRICOTS

SERVES 6-8

A few additions lift shop-bought ice-cream out of the ordinary, and turn it into a special dessert.

INGREDIENTS

120g/4oz no-soak dried apricots, chopped
2 tbsps brandy
850ml/1½ pints vanilla ice-cream
60g/2oz toasted hazelnuts, finely chopped

1 Put a 1150ml/2-pint bombe mould or decorative mould into the freezer to chill.
2 Place the apricots in a small saucepan with the brandy, heat until steaming then remove from the heat, cover, and allow to cool completely.
3 Put about two-thirds of the ice-cream in a large mixing bowl and allow to stand at room temperature until it becomes just soft enough to beat to a spreading consistency.
4 Quickly beat in the toasted hazelnuts, mixing well until evenly incorporated.
5 Carefully coat the base and sides of the chilled mould with the hazelnut ice-cream, leaving a well in the middle and keeping the ice-cream layer as even as possible.
6 Return the bombe mould to the freezer and

Step 5 Coat the base and sides of the mould with an even layer of the semi-frozen hazelnut ice-cream, leaving a well in the centre.

freeze until the ice-cream layer is solid.
7 Remove the remaining ice-cream from the freezer and allow to soften slightly. Beat the apricots and brandy into the ice-cream.
8 Spoon the apricot mixture into the centre of the mould, packing down well to remove any air pockets.
9 Freeze the bombe completely – overnight is best.
10 About 30 minutes before the dessert is to be eaten, remove the bombe from the freezer and stand in warm water for a few seconds. Upturn the mould onto a serving dish and shake the ice-cream out. Leave to stand in the refrigerator to soften slightly.

Cook's Notes

TIME
Preparation takes about 20 minutes, plus standing and freezing.

VEGETARIAN SUITABILITY
This recipe is suitable for lacto-vegetarians only.

BURGUNDY GRANITA

SERVES 4

The alcohol content in this water-ice stops the mixture from freezing solid, so you do not even have to beat it during the freezing process.

INGREDIENTS

90g/3oz unrefined caster sugar
140ml/¼ pint water
420ml/¾ pint Burgundy wine
2 tbsps brandy
Grated orange rind, to decorate

1 Place the sugar and water in a saucepan and heat gently until the sugar dissolves.
2 Bring to the boil and boil for 5 minutes. Allow the syrup to cool completely.
3 Combine the sugar syrup with the wine and brandy. Pour into a shallow freezer-proof container.

Step 4 *After freezing the Burgundy mixture, stir with a fork to break up the ice crystals.*

4 Freeze overnight until required. Remove from the freezer, stir to break up the ice crystals, pile into cocktail or wine glasses, and serve decorated with finely grated orange rind.

Cook's Notes

TIME
Preparation takes about 15 minutes, plus freezing.

VEGETARIAN SUITABILITY
This recipe is suitable for vegans.

SERVING IDEA
Serve as a refresher between dinner courses in small port or sherry glasses.

COOK'S TIP
Keeps for up to 2 weeks after which time the flavour will deteriorate.

Chapter 8
CAKES AND BAKING

RICH FRUIT CAKE

MAKES 1 X 20.5CM/8-INCH CAKE

This cake will improve both in flavour and texture if stored in an airtight container for 1 month before eating.

INGREDIENTS

650g/1lb 7oz mixed dried fruit

90g/3oz glacé cherries, quartered

60g/2oz flaked almonds

175g/6oz butter or vegetable margarine

175g/6oz light muscovado sugar

3 free-range eggs (size 2), beaten

215g/7½ oz plain flour, sieved

1 tsp mixed spice

1 tbsp black treacle

3 tbsps sherry or brandy

1 Lightly grease and line a 20.5cm/8-inch deep cake tin. Preheat the oven to 150°C/300°F/Gas Mark 2.

2 Mix together the dried fruit, cherries and almonds.

3 Beat together the fat and sugar until pale and creamy.

4 Gradually beat in the egg, adding a little of the

Step 5 *Fold the flour and spice into the cake mixture using a metal spoon.*

flour if the mixture begins to curdle.

5 Carefully fold in the flour and spice followed by the fruit.

6 Add treacle and stir until very well combined.

7 Carefully spoon into the prepared tin and level the top. Bake for about 2½ hours, or until a skewer inserted into the centre comes out clean.

8 Allow to cool completely in the tin.

9 When the cake is completely cold, prick the top with a skewer and sprinkle the sherry or brandy over the top and allow this to soak into the cake before covering with greaseproof paper and sealing in an airtight tin.

Cook's Notes

TIME
Preparation takes about 30 minutes, cooking time is about 2½ hours.

VEGETARIAN SUITABILITY
This recipe is suitable for lacto-vegetarians only.

SERVING IDEA
Cover with marzipan and royal or fondant icing for special celebrations.

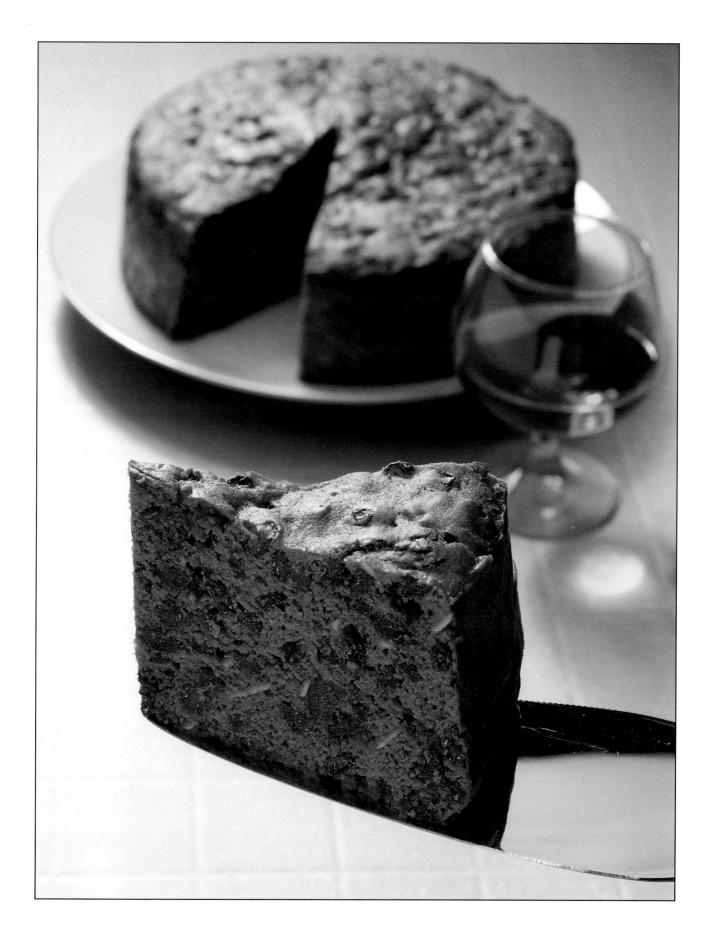

DATE AND WALNUT CAKE

MAKES 1 X 450G/1LB LOAF

*This traditional loaf is quick to prepare and a healthy alternative to
many other cakes.*

INGREDIENTS

140ml/¼ pint water
90g/3oz butter or vegetable margarine
120g/4oz fresh or dried dates, stoned and chopped
120g/4oz wholemeal flour
1 tsp baking powder
½ tsp bicarbonate of soda
1 tsp ground cinnamon
60g/2oz walnuts, chopped
60g/4 tbsps unrefined demerara sugar

1 Grease and base line a 450g/1lb loaf tin. Preheat the oven to 180°C/350°F/Gas Mark 4.
2 Place the water, buttter or margarine and dates into a saucepan and heat gently until simmering. Simmer for 3 minutes or until dates soften.

3 Using a fork, mash the dates coarsely into the cooking liquid.
4 Put the flour, baking powder, bicarbonate of soda, cinnamon and walnuts into a bowl and make a well in the centre.
5 Pour the date mixture into the well and beat gradually, incorporating the flour until well mixed.
6 Pour the cake mixture into the prepared tin and level the top.
7 Bake for 40 minutes or until a skewer inserted into the cake comes out clean.
8 Allow to cool slightly in the tin before transferring to a wire rack to cool completely.
9 Sprinkle with demerara sugar just before serving.

Cook's Notes

TIME
Preparation takes about 15 minutes, cooking time is about 40 minutes.

VEGETARIAN SUITABILITY
Use non-dairy margarine for vegans.

SERVING IDEA
Serve with morning coffee.

VARIATION
Use apricots instead of dates, and almonds instead of walnuts in this recipe.

APPLE SPICE RING

SERVES 8-10

*For those who are trying to cut down their sugar intake, this cake can
be made without sugar and is equally delicious.*

INGREDIENTS

450g/1lb dessert apples, cored
90g/3oz ground hazelnuts
120g/4oz wholemeal flour
30g/1oz bran
60g/2oz light muscovado sugar
1½ tsps baking powder
1 tsp ground cinnamon
Pinch of ground nutmeg
Pinch of ground cardamom
30g/1oz butter or vegetable margarine, melted
120ml/4 fl oz milk
Dessert apple slices and icing sugar, to decorate

1 Preheat the oven to 180°C/350°F/Gas Mark 4.
Lightly grease a 20.5cm/8-inch ring tin.
2 Grate the apples on the course side of a grater.
3 Place in a mixing bowl with the hazelnuts.

Step 6 *Stir the milk into
the apple cake mixture to
make a fairly stiff batter.*

4 Stir in the flour, bran, sugar (if using), baking
powder and spices. Mix well.
5 Add the butter or margarine and beat until it is
evenly blended.
6 Stir in the milk and mix to a stiff batter.
7 Carefully spoon into the prepared tin and level
the top. Bake for 45 minutes or until a skewer
inserted into the centre comes out clean.
8 Allow to cool in the tin slightly then turn out
on to a wire rack to cool completely.
9 Dust with icing sugar and decorate with apple
slices just before serving.

Cook's Notes

TIME
Preparation takes about 15
minutes, cooking time is about 45
minutes.

COOK'S TIP
If you do not have a ring tin,
place a empty jam jar in the centre of a
20.5cm/8-inch deep-sided cake tin.

VEGETARIAN SUITABILITY
Use soya milk and dairy-free
margarine for vegans.

VARIATION
Use almonds instead of
hazelnuts in this recipe.

SERVING IDEA
Serve hot as a dessert with
custard sauce (lacto-vegetarians only)
or apple purée if wished.

FRUIT AND ALMOND CAKE

MAKES 1 x 20.5CM/8-INCH RING CAKE

This delicious cake is sure to please every generation of the family.

INGREDIENTS

175g/6oz butter or vegetable margarine
175g/6oz light muscovado sugar
3 free-range eggs, beaten
175g/6oz self-raising flour, sieved
2-3 drops almond essence
2 tbsps milk
30g/1oz ground almonds
60g/2oz raisins
60g/2oz glacé cherries
Unrefined caster sugar

1 Lightly grease a 20.5cm/8-inch ring tin. Preheat the oven to 180°C/350°F/Gas Mark 4.
2 Beat together the butter or margarine and the muscovado sugar until pale and creamy.
3 Gradually beat in the eggs adding a little of the flour if the mixture begins to curdle.
4 Carefully fold in the flour, the almond essence, milk, ground almonds, raisins and cherries.
5 Spoon into the prepared tin and level the top. Bake for about 30 minutes or until a skewer inserted into the centre comes out clean.
6 Allow to cool in the tin slightly then transfer to a wire rack to cool.
7 Dust with caster sugar just before serving.

Cook's Notes

TIME
Preparation takes about 15 minutes, cooking time is about 45 minutes.

VEGETARIAN SUITABILITY
This recipe is suitable for lacto-vegetarians only.

COOK'S TIP
If you do not have a ring tin, place a empty jam jar in the centre of a 22.5cm/9-inch deep-sided cake tin.

SERVING IDEA
Drizzle a little almond flavoured icing over the top of the cake.

BANANA AND DATE LOAF

<u>MAKES 1 x 900G/2LB LOAF</u>

Banana cakes are an ideal way of using up over-ripe bananas. The riper they are, the more flavour they seem to add to the finished cake.

INGREDIENTS

60ml/4 tbsps milk

1 tbsp treacle

120g/4oz butter or vegetable margarine

90g/3oz light muscovado sugar

2 free-range eggs, beaten

175g/6oz self-raising flour, sieved

90g/3oz pitted dates, chopped

1 small ripe banana, peeled and sliced

60g/2oz walnuts, chopped

Glacé icing, walnut halves and banana slices, to decorate

1 Grease and base line a 900g/2lb loaf tin. Preheat the oven to 190°C/375°F/Gas Mark 5.

2 Put the milk, treacle, butter or margarine and sugar in a saucepan and heat, stirring, until the fat melts and the sugar dissolves.

3 Cool slightly then beat in the eggs.

4 Put the flour, dates, banana and nuts in a large bowl and make a well in the centre.

Step 4 *Put the flour, fruit and nuts into a large bowl and make a well in the centre.*

5 Pour the egg and treacle mixture into the centre and beat, gradually incorporating the flour, until a thick batter is formed.

6 Pour the batter into the loaf tin and bake in the centre of the oven for 50 minutes or until a skewer inserted into the loaf comes out clean.

7 Cool slightly in the tin, before transferring to a wire rack to cool completely.

8 Cover with glacé icing and arrange walnut halves on top.

9 Just before serving arrange banana slices, dipped in lemon juice to prevent discolouring, around the loaf.

Cook's Notes

TIME
Preparation takes about 15 minutes, cooking time is about 45 minutes.

VEGETARIAN SUITABILITY
This recipe is suitable for lacto-vegetarians only.

VARIATION
Use honey in place of the treacle in this recipe.

CHOCOLATE PEAR SPONGE

<u>MAKES 1 x 18CM/7-INCH CAKE</u>

Chocolate and pears make a delicious combination in this moist, dense cake.

INGREDIENTS

120g/4oz butter or vegetable margarine

120g/4oz unrefined caster sugar

2 free-range eggs

90g/3oz self-raising flour

15g/½oz cocoa powder

½ tsp baking powder

1 tsp mixed spice

1 tbsp milk

1 small ripe pear, peeled, cored and diced

1 Lightly grease an 18cm/7-inch deep cake tin. Preheat the oven to 180°C/350°F/Gas Mark 4.

2 Beat together the butter or margarine and the caster sugar until pale and creamy. Gradually add the eggs, beating well after each addition.

3 Sieve the flour, cocoa powder, baking powder

Step 4 Add the flour and cocoa mixture to the creamed margarine and sugar.

and mixed spice together.

4 Add the milk and flour mixture to the creamed mixture.

5 Add the diced pear and stir until all the ingredients are well combined.

6 Carefully spoon into the prepared tin and level the top. Bake for 40-45 minutes or until springy to the touch.

7 Allow to cool in the tin slightly then transfer to a wire rack to cool.

Cook's Notes

TIME
Preparation takes about 15 minutes, cooking time is about 30 minutes.

VEGETARIAN SUITABILITY
This recipe is suitable for lacto-vegetarians.

SERVING IDEA
Serve hot with chocolate sauce or pear purée as a delicious dessert.

WHOLEMEAL SODA BREAD

<u>MAKES 1 ROUND LOAF</u>

Soda bread is an excellent alternative to yeast baked bread and can be made in a fraction of the time.

INGREDIENTS

225g/8oz wholemeal flour
225g/8oz plain flour, sieved
Pinch of salt
2 tsps bicarbonate of soda
2 tsps cream of tartar
30g/1oz butter or vegetable margarine
2 tsps light muscovado sugar
280ml/½ pint milk
1 tbsp lemon juice or vinegar
15g/½oz rolled oats

1 Preheat the oven to 200°C/400°F/Gas Mark 6. Lightly grease a baking sheet. Place the flours in a mixing bowl, mix in the salt, bicarbonate of soda and cream of tartar.

2 Rub the butter or margarine into the flours and stir in the sugar.
3 Heat the milk in a small pan until lukewarm, then stir in the lemon juice or vinegar and mix until the milk sours and curdles.
4 Make a well in the centre of the flour mixture and pour in the milk. Mix to form a soft dough.
5 Turn out onto a lightly floured work surface and knead until smooth.
6 Shape the dough into a round and place on the baking sheet. Score a deep cross on the top of the bread to mark into four sections.
7 Sprinkle with the rolled oats.
8 Bake for 25-30 minutes or until risen and golden.

Cook's Notes

TIME
Preparation takes about 10 minutes, cooking time is about 40 minutes.

VEGETARIAN SUITABILITY
This recipe is suitable for vegans, if soya milk and non-dairy margarine are used.

PREPARATION
Use an electric mixer with a dough hook, to mix and knead the dough if you have one.

294

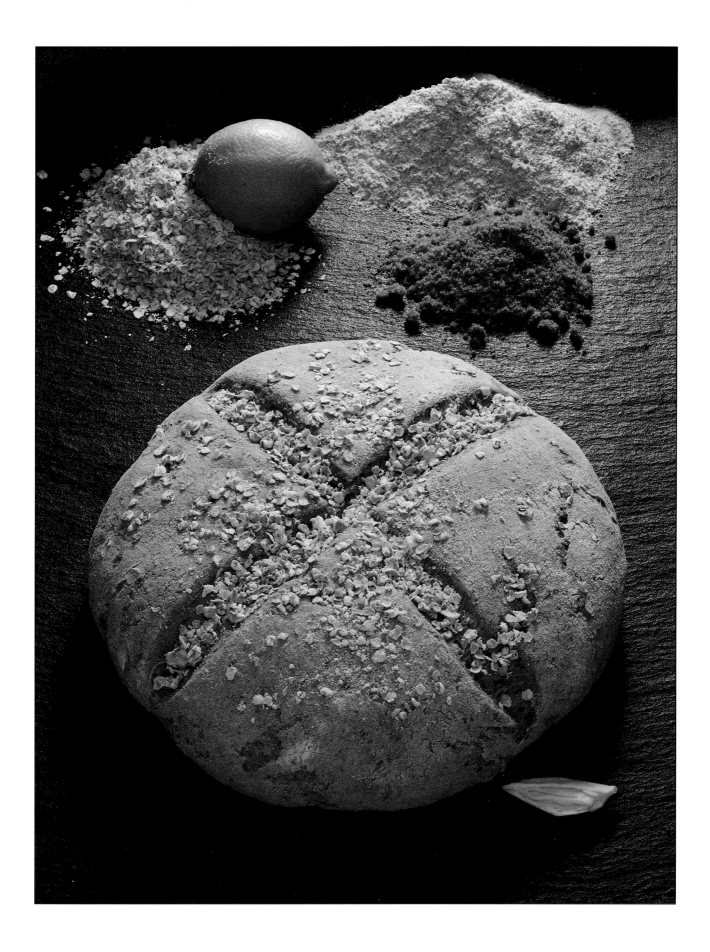

BOSTON BROWN BREAD

MAKES 1 x 900G/2LB LOAF

*This traditional American bread is served in Boston with baked beans.
However this variation of the traditional recipe is equally as good served
spread with butter for a sweet tea bread.*

INGREDIENTS

15g/½oz butter or vegetable margarine
90g/3oz treacle
280ml/½ pint natural yogurt
75g/2½oz wholemeal flour
75g/2½oz plain flour, sieved
90g/3oz cornmeal
1 tsp baking powder
1 tsp salt
60g/2oz raisins

1 Lightly grease a 900g/2lb loaf tin. Preheat the oven to 190°C/375°F/Gas Mark 5.
2 Melt the butter or margarine in a small pan, add the treacle and heat until softened. Remove from the heat and stir in the yogurt.

Step 4 *Beat the yogurt mixture into the dry ingredients until a soft batter is formed.*

3 Put the flours, cornmeal, baking powder and salt in a large mixing bowl. Stir in the raisins.
4 Beat the yogurt mixture into the dry ingredients until well combined.
5 Spoon into the prepared tin and level the top.
6 Bake for 30 minutes or until risen and springy to the touch.
7 Cool in the tin for 5 minutes, before turning out onto a wire rack to cool completely.

Cook's Notes

TIME
Preparation takes about 15 minutes, cooking time is about 30 minutes.

VEGETARIAN SUITABILITY
This recipe is suitable for lacto-vegetarians only. See variation for vegan alternative.

VARIATION
For vegans use 200ml/7 fl oz soya milk instead of yogurt and non-dairy margarine. Use more flour if needed.

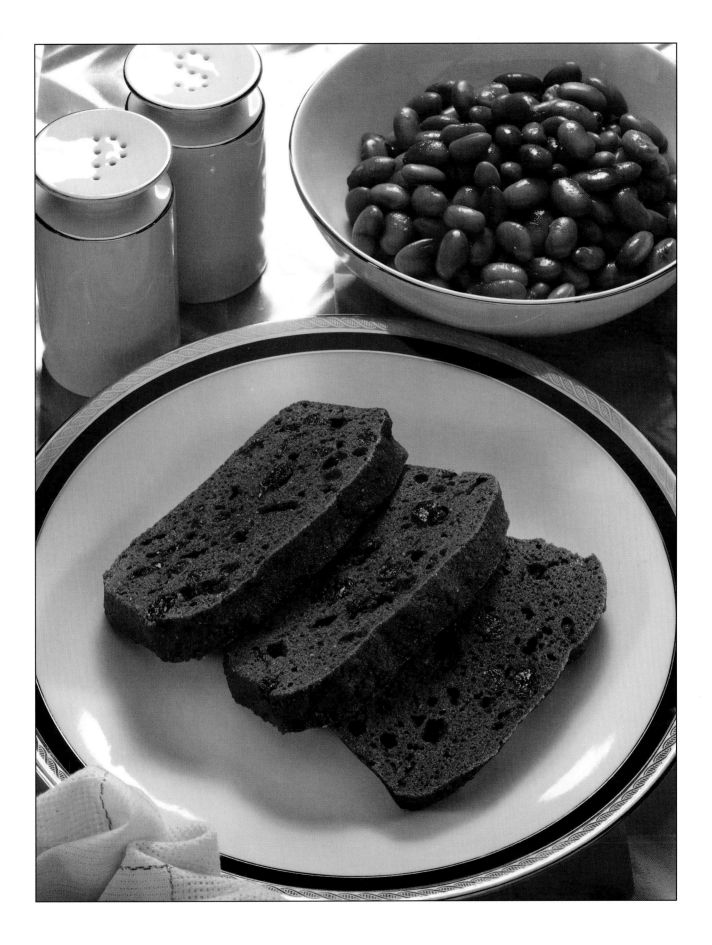

HAZELNUT BROWNIES

MAKES 16

These moist, cake-like brownies are an irresistible treat.

INGREDIENTS

120g/4oz butter or vegetable margarine
175g/6oz light muscovado sugar
2 free-range eggs
½ tsp vanilla essence
90g/3oz wholemeal flour
½ tsp baking powder
Pinch of salt
60g/2oz hazelnuts, chopped
Icing sugar, to dust

1 Grease and line a 20.5cm/8-inch square cake tin. Preheat the oven to 180°C/375°F/Gas Mark 5.
2 Melt the butter or margarine and beat in the sugar, stirring until smooth.
3 Add the eggs and essence, beating well to prevent the mixture from curdling.
4 Stir in all the remaining ingredients except the icing sugar, mixing well to blend evenly.
5 Pour into the prepared tin and bake for 25-30 minutes or until springy to the touch.
6 Allow to cool for 10 minutes in the tin, then turn out onto a wire rack to cool completely.
7 Cut into 16 squares and dust with icing sugar before serving.

Cook's Notes

TIME
Preparation takes about 15 minutes, cooking time is about 30 minutes.

VEGETARIAN SUITABILITY
This recipe is suitable for lacto-vegetarians only.

FREEZING
These brownies freeze well for up to 6 weeks.

SERVING IDEA
Serve with coffee or tea.

FRUIT SCONES

MAKES ABOUT 8

*These traditional teatime favourites are delicious served with butter
and jam.*

INGREDIENTS

225g/8oz plain flour, sieved

1 tbsp baking powder

60g/2oz butter or vegetable margarine

30g/1oz unrefined caster sugar

30g/1oz sultanas

1 free-range egg, beaten

About 60ml/4 tbsps milk

15g/½oz unrefined granulated sugar

1 tsp ground cinnamon

Step 5 *Cut out rounds
from the rolled out dough,
using a 5cm/2-inch plain
cutter.*

1 Preheat the oven to 200°C/400°F/Gas Mark 6.
Lightly grease a baking sheet.

2 Place the flour and baking powder in a mixing
bowl. Rub in the butter or margarine until the
mixture resembles fine breadcrumbs.

3 Stir in the sugar and sultanas.

4 Add the egg and enough milk to form a soft
dough.

5 Roll out the dough to about 1.25cm/½-inch
thick and cut into rounds with a 5cm/2-inch plain
cutter. Place on the baking sheet.

6 Mix together the granulated sugar and
cinnamon.

7 Brush the tops of the scones with a little milk
and sprinkle with the cinnamon mixture.

8 Bake for 10-15 minutes or until risen and
golden.

9 Transfer to a wire rack to cool.

Cook's Notes

TIME
Preparation takes about 20
minutes, cooking time is about 15
minutes.

VEGETARIAN SUITABILITY
This recipe is suitable for lacto-
vegetarians only.

FREEZING
These scones will freeze
successfully for up to 2 months.

VARIATION
Use 90ml/6 tbsps natural yogurt
instead of the egg in this recipe if
preferred.

CHEESE AND PAPRIKA SCONES

MAKES ABOUT 10

These moreish savoury scones are best eaten warm the same day they are made.

INGREDIENTS

225g/8oz self-raising flour, sieved

1 tsp paprika

Pinch of salt

60g/2oz butter or vegetable margarine

60g/2oz vegetarian Red Leicester cheese, grated

1 tsp English mustard

1 free-range egg

60ml/4 tbsps milk

1 tsp Marmite or other yeast extract

Little boiling water

Step 2 *Rub the butter or margarine into the flour with your fingertips until the mixture resembles fine breadcrumbs.*

1 Preheat the oven to 200°C/400°F/Gas Mark 6. Lightly grease a baking sheet.

2 Place the flour, paprika and salt in a mixing bowl and rub in the butter or margarine until the mixture resembles fine breadcrumbs.

3 Stir in the cheese.

4 Beat the mustard, egg and milk together in a small bowl and pour into the flour and cheese. Mix well to form a soft dough, adding a little extra milk if necessary.

5 Roll out the dough to about 1.25cm/½-inch thick and cut into 10 rounds with a 5cm/2-inch plain cutter.

6 Place on a baking sheet. Mix the Marmite or other yeast extract with a little boiling water and brush over the tops of the scones.

7 Bake for 10-15 minutes or until risen and golden.

8 Transfer to a wire rack to cool.

Cook's Notes

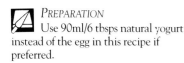

TIME
Preparation takes about 20 minutes, cooking time is about 15 minutes.

PREPARATION
Use 90ml/6 tbsps natural yogurt instead of the egg in this recipe if preferred.

VEGETARIAN SUITABILITY
This recipe is suitable for lacto-vegetarians only.

VARIATION
Omit the yeast extract and brush scones with a little milk, then sprinkle with sesame seeds and a little extra cheese.

CHOCOLATE FILLED MERINGUES

<u>MAKES 8-10</u>

Crisp meringues with a rich chocolate filling are perfect for special occasions, when they are hard to resist.

INGREDIENTS

2 free-range egg whites

120g/4oz unrefined caster sugar

175g/6oz chocolate butter cream or

140ml/¼ pint double cream and 60g/2oz plain chocolate, melted

Cocoa powder, for dusting

1 Preheat the oven to 150°C/300°F/Gas Mark 2.

2 Line two baking sheets with non-stick baking parchment.

3 Whisk the egg whites until stiff, then gradually whisk in two-thirds of the caster sugar until the meringue is smooth and glossy.

4 Carefully fold in the remaining sugar.

5 Spoon into a piping bag fitted with a plain nozzle and pipe 16 rounds.

6 Place in the oven for 1½ hours to dry out. Remove from the oven and allow to cool completely.

7 Soften the butter cream, or whip the double cream and fold the melted chocolate into the cream.

8 Sandwich the meringues together with the chocolate flavoured filling.

9 Dust with a little cocoa powder and serve.

Cook's Notes

TIME
Preparation takes about 20 minutes, cooking time is about 1½ hours.

VEGETARIAN SUITABILITY
This recipe is suitable for lacto-vegetarians only.

PREPARATION
These meringues can be made several days in advance and kept in an air-tight container.

PEANUT BUTTER BRAN COOKIES

<u>MAKES ABOUT 35</u>

*These rich, crumbly cookies are just the thing for hungry children,
when served mid-morning with a glass of milk.*

INGREDIENTS

120g/4oz butter or vegetable margarine
120g/4oz light muscovado sugar
1 free-range egg, beaten
225g/8oz crunchy peanut butter
60g/2oz bran
120g/4oz wholemeal flour
Pinch salt
½ tsp baking powder
½ tsp vanilla essence

1 Grease two baking sheets. Preheat the oven to 190°C/375°F/Gas Mark 5.
2 Beat together the fat and sugar until pale and creamy.
3 Gradually add the egg, beating well after each addition. Beat in the peanut butter.

Step 3 *Add the peanut butter to the well-beaten fat, sugar and egg mixture.*

4 Beat in the bran, flour, salt, baking powder and essence, mixing well to form a stiff dough.
5 Take small pieces of the dough and roll into balls. Place well apart on the baking sheets and flatten slightly with a fork or palette knife.
6 Bake one tray at a time for 5-10 minutes.
7 Cool slightly on the tray, then transfer to a wire rack to cool completely.

Cook's Notes

 TIME
Preparation takes about 15 minutes, cooking time is about 10 minutes.

PREPARATION
If the biscuit dough is too soft, add a little extra flour.

VEGETARIAN SUITABILITY
This recipe is suitable for lacto-vegetarians only.

 SERVING IDEA
Serve for tea or add to a packed lunch.

FREEZING
These biscuits freeze well, cooked, for up to 3 months, or the uncooked dough can be frozen and cooked when required.

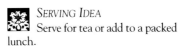

GINGER NUTS

MAKES 36

These spicy biscuits are given a delicious texture by including nuts in the recipe.

INGREDIENTS

175g/6oz butter or vegetable margarine

120g/4oz dark muscovado sugar

120ml/4 fl oz golden syrup

2 tsps vinegar

3 free-range eggs, beaten

2 tbsps milk

675g/1½lbs wholemeal flour

1½ tsp bicarbonate soda

2 tsp ground ginger

½ tsp ground cinnamon

Pinch of ground cloves

60g/2oz hazelnuts, chopped

1 Grease two baking sheets. Preheat the oven to 190°C/375°F/Gas Mark 5.

2 Put the butter or margarine, sugar, golden syrup and vinegar into a bowl and beat well together until they are smooth and well blended.

3 Beat in the eggs and milk.

4 Add the flour, bicarbonate of soda, spices and hazelnuts, mixing well to form a firm dough.

5 Take small amounts of the biscuit mixture and roll into balls. Place well apart on the baking sheets.

6 Press each biscuit down with a fork and bake for 5-10 minutes.

7 Cool slightly on the tray then transfer to a wire rack to cool completely.

Cook's Notes

TIME
Preparation takes about 20 minutes, cooking time is about 10 minutes.

VEGETARIAN SUITABILITY
This recipe is suitable for lacto-vegetarians only.

PREPARATION
If the biscuit dough is too soft, add a little flour to firm it.

CRANBERRY BARS

<u>MAKES 12-16 BARS</u>

Cranberries have a delicious flavour and are seldom used to their full potential. This recipe certainly rectifies this and these delicious bars are sure to become a firm family favourite.

INGREDIENTS

120g/4oz butter or vegetable margarine

150g/5oz light muscovado sugar

120g/4oz plain flour, sieved

Pinch of salt

90g/3oz rolled oats

120g/4oz cranberry sauce

60g/2oz walnuts, chopped

1 Preheat the oven to 180°C/350°F/Gas Mark 4.

2 Put the butter or margarine and the sugar in a bowl and beat together until thick and creamy.

3 Stir in the flour, salt and oats, and mix well.

4 Spread two-thirds of the mixture onto the base of a well greased 20.5cm/8-inch square baking tin, pressing down well.

Step 3 *Stir the flour, salt and oats into the creamed mixture.*

5 Mix together the cranberry sauce and nuts and spread over the oat mixture.

6 Crumble the remaining oat mixture over the top and spread out evenly over the top with a knife.

7 Bake for 20 minutes.

8 Allow to cool for about 10 minutes, then mark into bars.

9 Leave to cool completely in the tin before removing.

Cook's Notes

TIME
Preparation takes about 20 minutes, cooking time is about 20 minutes.

VEGETARIAN SUITABILITY
This recipe is suitable for vegans if non-dairy margarine is used.

SPICY TREACLE COOKIES

<u>MAKES ABOUT 24</u>

Treacle cookies are always a treat, with added spices they are even more delectable.

INGREDIENTS

225g/8oz wholemeal flour

2 tsps baking powder

1 tsp mixed spice

1 tsp ground ginger

Pinch of salt

120g/4oz butter or vegetable margarine

120g/4oz light muscovado sugar

1 free-range egg, beaten

2 tbsps treacle

Icing sugar, to dust

1 Grease two baking sheets. Preheat the oven to 190°C/375°F/Gas Mark 5.

2 Sieve together the flour, baking powder, spices and salt, mixing in any that is left in the sieve.

3 Beat together the fat and sugar until pale and creamy.

4 Gradually add the egg, beating well after each addition.

5 Beat in the treacle then, using a metal spoon, fold sieved dry ingredients.

6 Place spoonfuls of the mixture onto the baking sheets and bake one tray at a time for 5-10 minutes.

7 Cool slightly on the tray then transfer to a wire rack to cool completely.

8 Dust with icing sugar.

Cook's Notes

TIME
Preparation takes about 20 minutes, cooking time is about 20 minutes.

VEGETARIAN SUITABILITY
This recipe is suitable for lacto-vegetarians only.

VARIATION
Use golden syrup in place of the treacle and cinnamon in place of the mixed spice and ginger in this recipe.

SUNFLOWER CAROB COOKIES

MAKES ABOUT 28

These cookies come alive with the addition of sunflower seeds.

INGREDIENTS

120g/4oz butter or vegetable margarine

120g/4oz light muscovado sugar

1 free-range egg, beaten

1 tsp vanilla essence

½ tsp bicarbonate of soda

½ tsp salt

30g/1oz bran

90g/3oz rolled oats

120g/4oz wholemeal flour

60g/2oz sunflower seeds

120g/4oz carob drops

1 Grease two baking sheets. Preheat the oven to 190°C/375°F/Gas Mark 5.

2 Beat together the fat and sugar until pale and creamy.

3 Gradually add the egg, beating well after each addition.

4 Beat in the vanilla essence, then the bicarbonate of soda, salt, bran, oats and flour, mixing well until a stiff dough is produced.

5 Finally mix in the sunflower seeds and carob drops.

6 Place heaped spoonfuls of the mixture onto the baking sheets and bake for 5-10 minutes.

7 Cool slightly on the tray then transfer to a wire rack to cool completely.

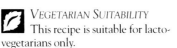

Cook's Notes

TIME
Preparation takes about 20 minutes, cooking time is about 10 minutes.

VARIATION
Use plain chocolate drops instead of carob drops in this recipe.

VEGETARIAN SUITABILITY
This recipe is suitable for lacto-vegetarians only.

SERVING IDEA
Serve sprinkled with a little icing sugar if wished.

FREEZING
Form the dough into a 5cm/2-inch diameter log and freeze uncooked. When required cut the required number of 6mm/¼-inch thick slices and bake as above.

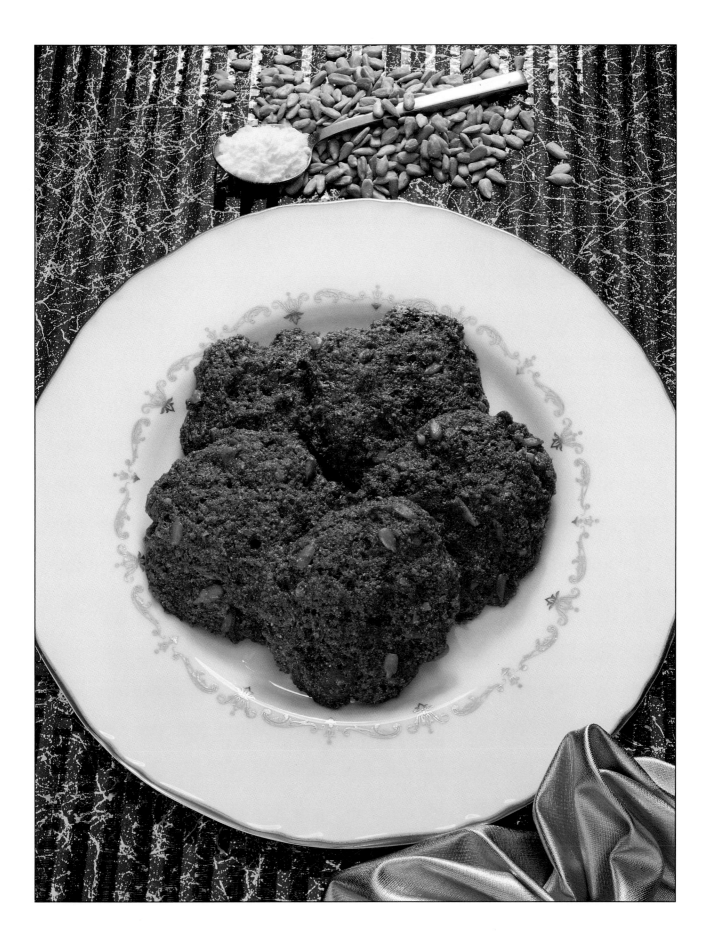

MUESLI COOKIES

MAKES ABOUT 36

These simple-to-make biscuits are full of wholesome ingredients.

INGREDIENTS

120g/4oz butter or vegetable margarine

120g/4oz light muscovado sugar

1 free-range egg, beaten

1 tsp vanilla essence

1 tsp baking powder

225g/8oz wholemeal flour

Pinch of salt

120g/4oz sugarless muesli

60g/2oz currants

1 Grease two baking sheets. Preheat the oven to 190°C/375°F/Gas Mark 5.

2 Beat together the fat and sugar until pale and creamy.

Step 4 *Mix the dry ingredients into the egg mixture to form a stiff dough.*

3 Gradually add the egg, beating well after each addition.

4 Beat in the vanilla essence, then beat in the baking powder, flour, salt, muesli and currants to make a stiff dough.

5 Place heaped spoonfuls of the mixture on to the baking sheets and bake for 5-10 minutes.

6 Cool slightly on the tray then transfer to a wire rack to cool completely.

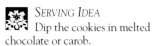
Cook's Notes

TIME
Preparation takes about 15 minutes, cooking time is about 20 minutes.

SERVING IDEA
Dip the cookies in melted chocolate or carob.

VEGETARIAN SUITABILITY
This recipe is suitable for lacto-vegetarians only.

FREEZING
This recipe can be frozen uncooked. Make a double batch, then cook as many biscuits as you need, and freeze the remaining mixture in batches until required.

PREPARATION
If the dough is not stiff enough then add a little extra flour to make it firm enough to heap into piles.

LEMON ICED TREACLE COOKIES

MAKES ABOUT 30

Children in particular will love these colourful little biscuits.

INGREDIENTS

2 tsps baking powder
1 tsp ground allspice
½ tsp ground ginger
225g/8oz wholemeal flour
Pinch of salt
120g/4oz butter or vegetable margarine
120g/4oz light muscovado sugar
1 free-range egg, beaten
2 tbsps treacle
450g/1lb icing sugar
Grated rind and juice of 1 lemon
Yellow food colouring (optional)
140ml/¼ pint water
Candied lemon slices (optional)

1 Grease two baking sheets. Preheat the oven to 190°C/375°F/Gas Mark 5.

2 Sieve together the baking powder, spices, flour and salt, adding any bran to the mixture that is left in the sieve.

3 Beat together the fat and sugar until pale and creamy.

4 Gradually add the egg, beating well after each addition.

5 Beat in the treacle, then using a metal spoon fold in the sieved dry ingredients.

6 Place spoonfuls of the mixture onto the baking sheets and bake one tray at a time for 5-10 minutes.

7 Cool slightly on the tray then transfer to a wire rack to cool completely.

8 When all the biscuits are cooked, sieve the icing sugar into a bowl and add the lemon rind and juice. Add colouring if using.

9 Gradually stir in enough water to form a thin coating icing and spread equal amounts onto each biscuit.

10 Decorate, if wished, with candied lemon slices and allow icing to set before serving.

Cook's Notes

TIME
Preparation takes about 20 minutes, cooking time is about 20 minutes.

VEGETARIAN SUITABILITY
This recipe is suitable for lacto-vegetarians only.

COLLETTES

MAKES 12

These attractive home-made sweets are ideal for serving at the end of a dinner party or formal meal.

INGREDIENTS

175g/6oz plain chocolate
60g/2oz white chocolate
2 tsps brandy or coffee essence
60ml/4 tbsps double cream
Chopped pistachio nuts, to decorate

1 Arrange 12 paper sweet cases on a tray or plate.
2 Break the plain chocolate into pieces and melt in the top of a double boiler or in a bowl placed over a pan of gently simmering water.
3 Using a small paint brush or teaspoon, coat the inside of each paper case with an even layer of chocolate.

Step 3 *Using a teaspoon or small paint brush, coat the base and sides of each paper sweet case with an even layer of the melted chocolate.*

4 Thicken this layer gradually as the chocolate sets inside the case by brushing extra thin layers over the top of the previous one.
5 Continue layering up the chocolate cases until all the melted chocolate has been used. Chill in the refrigerator until the chocolate has set completely.
6 Melt the white chocolate in the same way as the plain chocolate. Stir in the brandy or coffee essence.
7 Whip the cream until just holding its shape.
8 Carefully fold the whipped cream into the chocolate mixture using a metal spoon. Mix well to blend evenly.
9 Chill the mixture until just firm enough to pipe.
10 Carefully peel away the paper cases from the chocolate shells and put these into fresh paper cases to serve.
11 Place the cream mixture into a piping bag fitted with a 1.25cm/½-inch star nozzle. Pipe swirls of the mixture into the chocolate shells.
12 Sprinkle with chopped pistachio nuts and chill until required.

Cook's Notes

⏱ TIME
Preparation takes about 40 minutes, plus chilling.

🍃 VEGETARIAN SUITABILITY
This recipe is suitable for lacto-vegetarians only.

CHERRY NUT BALLS

MAKES 16

These crunchy textured sweets are a delicious treat and a favourite with children.

INGREDIENTS

120g/4oz butter or vegetable margarine

175g/6oz unrefined caster sugar

225g/8oz glacé cherries

1 free-range egg, beaten

2 tbsps evaporated milk

60g/2oz crisp rice cereal

60g/2oz walnuts, chopped

About 3 tbsps desiccated coconut

Step 2 *Chop the rinsed cherries into small pieces using a sharp knife.*

Step 7 *Roll each cherry ball in the desiccated coconut, pressing it on with your fingers to coat evenly.*

1 Melt the butter or margarine and the sugar over a low heat, stirring constantly, until the sugar dissolves.

2 Rinse the cherries in hot water and pat dry on kitchen paper, then chop and stir into butter mixture.

3 Beat the egg into the milk, then gradually add to the hot cherry mixture, stirring well after each addition.

4 Cook gently, stirring, until the mixture comes together in a ball.

5 Remove from the heat and beat in the cereal and nuts.

6 Divide into 16 pieces and roll into balls.

7 Roll each cherry ball in the desiccated coconut and cover evenly, pressing the coconut onto the balls if necessary.

8 Chill well before serving in individual sweet cases.

Cook's Notes

TIME
Preparation takes about 20 minutes, cooking time is about 10 minutes.

VEGETARIAN SUITABILITY
This recipe is suitable for lacto-vegetarians only.

VARIATION
Use any combination of glacé fruit and nuts in place of those suggested in this recipe.

CHOCOLATE TRUFFLES

MAKES ABOUT 30

*These delicious truffles are ideal for serving after dinner or for giving as
a special home-made present.*

INGREDIENTS

175g/6oz plain chocolate

15g/½oz butter or vegetable margarine

2 free-range egg yolks

2 tsps brandy or black coffee

2 tsps single cream

3 tbsps each cocoa powder and ground almonds

1 Break the plain chocolate into pieces and melt
in the top of a double boiler or in a bowl placed
over a pan of gently simmering water.

2 Stir in the butter or margarine.

3 Lightly beat the egg yolks and add to the
chocolate, beating well until evenly incorporated.

4 Beat in the brandy or coffee, and cream and
chill in the refrigerator for at least 1 hour or until it
is firm.

5 Divide the mixture into about 30 even-sized
pieces and roll these into small balls using your
hands.

Step 5 *Roll the mixture
into small balls using your
hands.*

Step 6 *Roll the truffles
either in the cocoa or
almonds before placing
them in sweet cases and
refrigerating.*

6 Put the cocoa powder and almonds onto
separate plates and gently roll half the chocolates
in each one to coat.

7 Put the coated truffles into paper sweet cases
and chill until required.

Cook's Notes

 TIME
Preparation takes about 20
minutes, plus chilling.

PREPARATION
If the chocolate balls become
too soft while you are rolling them,
return them to the refrigerator for a
few minutes, and then continue.

VEGETARIAN SUITABILITY
This recipe is suitable for lacto-
vegetarians only.

SERVING IDEA
Serve with coffee or liqueurs.

VARIATION
Use white or milk chocolate in
place of plain chocolate and a fruit
liqueur instead of the brandy or coffee.

ROCKY ROAD FUDGE

MAKES 450G/1LB

Home-made fudge is always welcome as a special treat or gift.

INGREDIENTS

450g/1lb unrefined caster sugar
60g/2oz plain chocolate, grated
60g/2oz butter or vegetable margarine
175ml/6 fl oz milk
2 tsps vanilla essence
60g/2oz walnuts, chopped
30g/1oz crisp rice cereal

1 Line a 20.5cm/8-inch square tin with non-stick baking parchment.
2 Place the sugar, chocolate, butter or margarine and milk in a saucepan and heat gently, stirring, until sugar dissolves.
3 Increase the heat and bring to the boil.

Continue to boil, stirring frequently, until the temperature of the mixture reaches 115°C/239°F or 'soft ball' stage on a sugar thermometer. This should take about 10 minutes.
4 Remove from the heat and allow the fudge to cool for about 10 minutes, then beat in the vanilla essence.
5 Continue to beat the fudge until it begins to lose its shiny appearance and starts to become thick and grainy.
6 Quickly beat in the nuts and cereal, mixing them well.
7 Spread the fudge mixture evenly into the prepared tin and mark the fudge into squares.
8 Refrigerate until it is completely cold before removing from the dish and breaking into squares.

Cook's Notes

TIME
Preparation takes about 20 minutes, cooking time is about 20 minutes.

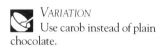

VARIATION
Use carob instead of plain chocolate.

VEGETARIAN SUITABILITY
This recipe is suitable for lacto-vegetarians only.

PREPARATION
If you do not have a sugar thermometer you can test for 'soft ball' stage by dropping a small amount of the mixture into cold water. If it forms a soft ball the mixture is ready to be cooled.

COOK'S TIP
Stir the fudge very frequently during cooking to prevent the mixture from burning and tainting the flavour.

HONEYCOMB

MAKES 450G/1LB

As well as being a great family favourite, this traditional sweet is also fascinating to watch being prepared.

INGREDIENTS

225g/8oz unrefined granulated sugar
225ml/8 fl oz golden syrup
1 tbsp white wine vinegar
1 tbsp bicarbonate of soda

1 Line a 20.5cm/8-inch square cake tin with well-oiled aluminium foil, pressing well into the corners of the tin, and pressing it as smoothly as possible against the sides and base.
2 Place the sugar, syrup and vinegar in a large saucepan and heat gently, stirring until the sugar dissolves.

Step 1 *Line a square cake tin with well-oiled aluminium foil, pressing well into the corners to remove as many creases as possible.*

Step 6 *Break the honeycomb into irregular-shaped pieces after peeling off the aluminium foil.*

3 Increase the heat and bring to the boil. Continue to boil, stirring frequently, until the temperature of the mixture reaches 146°C/295°F or 'hard crack' stage on a sugar thermometer.
4 Remove from the heat. Quickly add the bicarbonate of soda to the hot sugar syrup and stir well. The mixture will foam very quickly once the soda has been added.
5 Pour the foaming sugar syrup into the prepared tin and leave in a cool place until set.
6 Remove the honeycomb from the dish and break it up into irregular shaped pieces.

Cook's Notes

 TIME
Preparation takes about 5 minutes, cooking time is about 10 minutes.

VEGETARIAN SUITABILITY
This recipe is suitable for vegans.

 SERVING IDEA
Serve dipped in or drizzled with chocolate.

PREPARATION
Take great care when handling the hot syrup as it can give a very nasty burn if spilt onto the skin.

Chapter 9

DRINKS

BLUEBERRY CORDIAL

MAKES: APPROXIMATELY 570ML/1 PINT

Until recently blueberries were not that readily available, but now larger supermarkets and green grocers often have them in stock and they are well worth hunting out, if only just to make this fabulous cordial.

INGREDIENTS

675g/1½lbs blueberries, fresh or frozen
140ml/¼ pint water
1 tbsp lemon juice
340g/12oz unrefined granulated sugar

1 Cook the blueberries in the water and lemon juice for 45 minutes, crushing them against the side of the pan occasionally.
2 Strain through a scalded jelly bag, and reserve the juice.
3 Return the juice to the pan and add the sugar. Heat gently, stirring, until the sugar dissolves.

4 Boil for 5 minutes.
5 Pour into warm screw top bottle or jars. Seal, then release the lids a quarter turn.
6 Stand the bottles apart in a pan with enough water to come nearly up to the base of the caps. (First line the bottom of the pan with a few sheets of newspaper to prevent the bottles from breaking.)
7 Bring very slowly to simmering point, this should take about 30 minutes, and maintain the simmering for 30 minutes.
8 Remove bottles, tighten the lids and allow to cool. Label and store in a cool dark place.

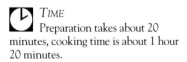

Cook's Notes

⏱ TIME
Preparation takes about 20 minutes, cooking time is about 1 hour 20 minutes.

🌿 VEGETARIAN SUITABILITY
This recipe is suitable for vegans.

❄ SERVING IDEA
Serve diluted with soda water or dry white wine, or undiluted over ice creams or desserts.

🍃 VARIATION
Use cranberries or damsons in place of the blueberries in this recipe.

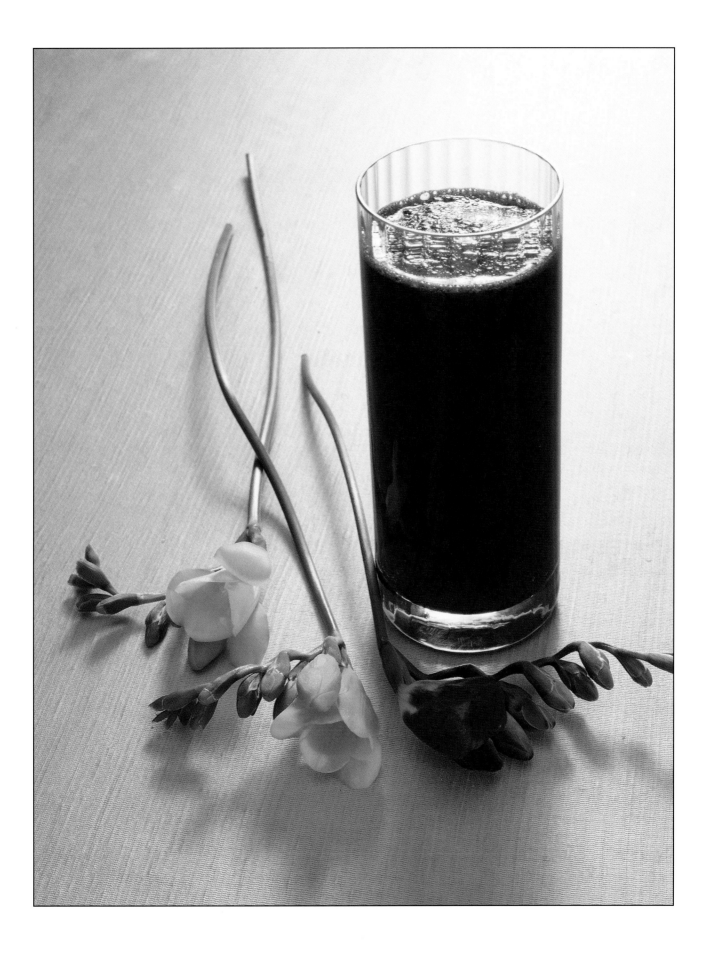

RASPBERRY CORDIAL

MAKES: APPROXIMATELY 570ML/1 PINT

This delicious cordial makes a refreshing change from conventional squashes or soft drinks.

INGREDIENTS

900g/2lbs raspberries, fresh or frozen
340g/12oz unrefined granulated sugar
200ml/7 fl oz water
½ a cinnamon stick
1 tbsp lemon juice
60ml/4 tbsps raspberry liqueur (optional)

1 Crush the raspberries and place in a saucepan. Heat gently to simmering and cook for 5-10 minutes or until they break up, then push through a sieve.

2 Place the raspberry juice, sugar, water, cinnamon and lemon juice in a pan, bring to the boil and simmer gently for 30 minutes.

3 Remove the cinnamon stick and strain through muslin or a jelly bag.

4 Stir in the liqueur if using and pour into warm screw top bottles or jars. Seal tightly, then release the lids a quarter turn.

5 Stand the bottles apart in a pan with enough cold water to come nearly up to the base of the caps. (First line the bottom of the pan with a few sheets of newspaper to prevent the bottle from breaking.)

6 Bring very slowly to simmering point, this should take about 30 minutes, and maintain the simmering for 30 minutes.

7 Remove bottles, tighten the lids and allow to cool. Label and store in a cool dark place.

Cook's Notes

TIME
Preparation takes about 30 minutes, cooking time is about 1 hour 35 minutes.

VEGETARIAN SUITABILITY
This recipe is suitable for vegans.

VARIATION
Use strawberries in place of the raspberries used in this recipe.

EAU DE FRAMBOISE

<u>MAKES 570ML/1 PINT</u>

*Raspberry liqueurs are delicious and just that little bit different to serve
to friends after dinner.*

INGREDIENTS

450g/1lb fresh or frozen raspberries
340g/12oz unrefined caster sugar
420ml/¾ pint vodka

1 Put the raspberries in a saucepan and cook
gently until the juices run. Crush the raspberries
slightly with the back of a wooden spoon as they
cook.

2 Strain the juice into another pan and reserve
the fruit pulp.

3 Add the sugar to the juice and heat gently,
stirring, until the sugar dissolves.

4 Cool the syrup completely then stir in the
reserved fruity pulp.

5 Add the vodka and mix well.

6 Put the liqueur into a wide-necked jar and seal
well.

7 Stand the jar in a cool dark place for 1 month,
shaking occasionally to blend the flavours
completely.

8 After this time, strain the liqueur through a
nylon sieve into a jug. Discard the fruit pulp and
pour the liqueur into a coloured bottle. Seal this
with a cork or screw top and serve as required.

Cook's Notes

TIME
Preparation takes about 5
minutes, plus standing. Cooking time
is about 5 minutes.

VEGETARIAN SUITABILITY
This recipe is suitable for
vegans.

COOK'S TIP
Do not crush the raspberries too
much as this will result in making the
liqueur cloudy. Storing in a coloured
bottle prevents the liqueur loosing its
colour.

VARIATION
Use strawberries or redcurrants
in place of the raspberries in this
recipe.

MULLED WINE

MAKES 4 GLASSES

This warming beverage is traditionally served at Christmas, but is so easy to prepare, why not serve it on any cold winter's evening.

INGREDIENTS

½ lemon

570ml/1 pint red wine

2 tbsps light muscovado sugar

2 cinnamon sticks

6 cloves

90ml/6 tbsps brandy

1 Using a potato peeler, carefully pare away the rind from the lemon without including too much of the white pith.

2 Place the lemon rind, wine, sugar, cinnamon sticks and cloves in a heavy-based saucepan, and heat gently over a low heat.

3 Bring the wine to simmering point, stirring occasionally. Do not let it boil.

4 Simmer very gently for 5-10 minutes, then strain into a jug or punch bowl.

5 Stir in the brandy and serve.

Step 1 *Carefully pare away the rind from the lemon, using a potato peeler or very sharp knife.*

Step 4 *Strain the spiced wine into a jug or punch bowl.*

Cook's Notes

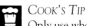 TIME
Preparation takes about 5 minutes, cooking time is about 10 minutes.

 VARIATION
Use cider instead of wine for this recipe.

VEGETARIAN SUITABILITY
This recipe is suitable for vegans.

 SERVING IDEA
Serve each glass of wine with a cinnamon stick placed in it.

COOK'S TIP
Only use whole spices in this recipe, as ground spices will impart too strong a flavour and will make the wine cloudy and grainy when drinking.

CREME DE MENTHE

MAKES 570ML/1 PINT

This favourite liqueur is simple to make and deliciously different when made with fresh ingredients.

INGREDIENTS

340g/12oz unrefined caster sugar
280ml/½ pint water
8 large sprigs of fresh mint or 1 tsp natural mint essence
Few drops of green food colouring (optional)
420ml/¾ pint vodka

1 Place the sugar and water in a saucepan and heat gently, stirring until the sugar dissolves.
2 Bring to the boil, remove from the heat and add the mint sprigs. Cover and allow to stand for 10 minutes to allow the flavour to infuse. Remove the mint sprigs.
3 If you are using the mint essence, there is no need to allow the syrup to infuse, simply cool slightly before proceeding.
4 Stir in the food colouring if using. Add the vodka to the syrup and stir well to combine.
5 Pour the liqueur into a clean, coloured bottle and allow to stand for at least a month before using.

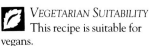

Cook's Notes

TIME
Preparation takes about 5 minutes, plus standing. Cooking time is about 2 minutes.

VEGETARIAN SUITABILITY
This recipe is suitable for vegans.

PREPARATION
Do not use a raw cane sugar, such as golden caster sugar, to make liqueurs as this will spoil the colour of the liqueur.

COOK'S TIP
Never allow a mixture to boil once the mint has been added as boiling destroys the delicate flavour.

LIQUEUR À L'ORANGE

MAKES 850ML/1½ PINTS

This delicious liqueur should be made no less than one month before it is required. Although it may seem expensive, you only drink a small quantity at a time and a cheaper variety of brandy can be used.

INGREDIENTS

3 oranges
225g/8oz unrefined caster sugar
570ml/1 pint brandy

1 Using a potato peeler, thinly pare off the rind from one of the oranges, taking care not to include the bitter white pith.

2 Cut all the oranges in half and squeeze the juice.

3 Place the orange rind, juice and sugar in a saucepan and heat gently, stirring, until the sugar has dissolved.

4 Allow the syrup to cool completely then strain through a nylon sieve to remove the peel and any orange flesh that may be in the syrup.

5 Mix the orange syrup with the brandy, and pour into a clean, coloured bottle.

6 Seal the bottle with a cork or screw top and leave in a cool, dark place for at least 1 month,

Step 1 *Thinly pare off the rind from one of the oranges, using a potato peeler.*

Step 4 *Strain the orange syrup through a nylon sieve to remove the orange rind and any membranes remaining in the juice.*

shaking the bottle vigorously, from time to time, to ensure the flavours combine well. Serve as required.

Cook's Notes

TIME
Preparation takes about 15 minutes, plus standing. Cooking time is about 5 minutes.

VARIATION:
Use 175g/6oz fresh raspberries or strawberries in place of the oranges in this recipe.

VEGETARIAN SUITABILITY
This recipe is suitable for vegans.

COOK'S TIP
Using a coloured bottle greatly improves the colour of this liqueur. Always store liqueurs of any type in a cool, dark place to help preserve the colour and flavour.

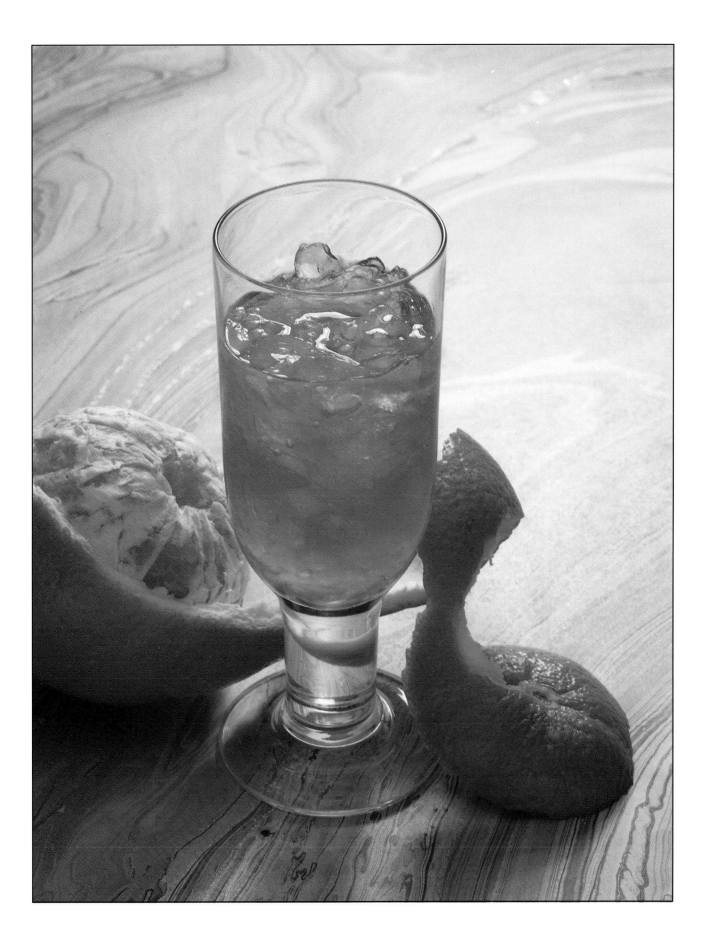

SPICED ORANGE TEA

MAKES 4 CUPS

This refreshing tea-based drink makes a delicious change from the traditional cuppa!

INGREDIENTS

½ orange

3 whole cloves

1 stick cinnamon

700ml/1¼ pints water

2 tea bags, Assam or Darjeeling variety

1 Using the fine side of a grater, carefully grate the rind from the orange, taking care not to get any of the white pith into the peel.
2 Put the grated rind and spices in a saucepan and add the water.
3 Bring slowly to the boil, allowing time for the spices to infuse.

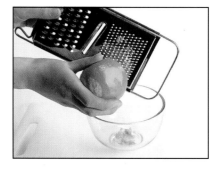

Step 1 *Using the fine side of a grater, carefully grate the orange rind.*

4 Place the tea bags into a pot or heat-resistant jug and strain the boiling water onto the tea bags.
5 Stir and allow the tea to brew for a few minutes. Remove and discard the tea bags.
6 Serve the tea hot, or chill it completely and serve very cold.

Cook's Notes

 TIME
Preparation takes about 5 minutes.

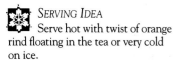 SERVING IDEA
Serve hot with twist of orange rind floating in the tea or very cold on ice.

VEGETARIAN SUITABILITY
This recipe is suitable for vegans.

COOK'S TIP
Only use whole spices in this recipe, as ground spices will impart too strong a flavour and will make the tea cloudy and grainy when drinking.

VARIATION
Use lemon rind in place of the orange rind and allspice berries instead of the cloves.

Chapter 10

JAMS AND PRESERVES

WHOLE STRAWBERRY CONSERVE WITH GRAND MARNIER

MAKES: APPROXIMATELY 2.8KG/6LBS

This luxury preserve will make an attractive gift for a 'foodie' friend or relative. Make sure that you use only firm, unblemished berries.

INGREDIENTS

1.8kg/4lbs strawberries
1.8kg/4lbs preserving sugar with added pectin
60ml/4 tbsps lemon juice
60ml/4 tbsps Grand Marnier

1 Hull the strawberries, wash them and leave to dry.
2 Layer the strawberries into a preserving pan, sprinkling sugar between each layer.
3 Set aside until the juice begins to run.

4 Heat gently, stirring until the sugar has dissolved. Add the lemon juice and boil rapidly for 5 minutes.
5 Remove from the heat and test for the setting point, if necessary boil for a few more minutes. (When the setting point is reached, a little of the jam spooned onto a cold saucer will wrinkle when pushed with a finger after 1 minute.)
6 Stir in the Grand Marnier. Allow the jam to cool considerably, then stir to distribute the strawberries and pot into warm, sterilized jars. Seal and label.

Cook's Notes

TIME
Preparation takes about 10 minutes, plus standing. Cooking time is about 10 minutes.

VEGETARIAN SUITABILITY
This recipe is suitable for vegans.

PREPARATION
Take great care not to over stir this conserve, otherwise the berries will break and the attractive appearance will be spoilt.

VARIATION
Use whole pitted cherries instead of strawberries and Kirsch instead of the Grand Marnier.

GINGER PEAR JAM

MAKES: APPROXIMATELY 2.3KG/5LBS

Often a glut of pears leaves you wondering how you can use them up.
This recipe is an ideal way, allowing you to savour that fresh taste of
pears right through the winter.

INGREDIENTS

1.8kg/4lbs firm pears
850ml/1½ pints water
60g/2oz grated fresh ginger root
Juice of 1 lemon
1.4kg/3lbs unrefined granulated sugar

1 Peel and core the pears, and cut them into thick slices. Place in a preserving pan with the water, ginger and lemon juice.
2 Tie the peel and core in a square of muslin and add to the pan. Cook the pears for about 30 minutes until soft and pulpy.
3 Remove the muslin bag. Mash the fruit or push through a sieve.

Step 1 *Peel and core the pears, and cut into thick slices.*

4 Stir in the sugar, and heat gently, stirring, until sugar is dissolved.
5 Boil rapidly until setting point is reached. This should take about 20 minutes. Test with a wooden spoon, if the spoon leaves a channel, setting point has been reached.
6 Pour into hot, sterilized jars, seal and label.

Cook's Notes

TIME
Preparation takes about 20 minutes, cooking time is about 50 minutes.

VEGETARIAN SUITABILITY
This recipe is suitable for vegans.

RHUBARB AND RASPBERRY JAM

MAKES: APPROXIMATELY 2KG/4¼LBS

Raspberries can be expensive but when mixed with rhubarb, which is both cheap and plentiful when in season, just a few will produce a delicious, fruity jam.

INGREDIENTS

675g/1½lbs rhubarb, cut into small pieces
140ml/¼ pint water
675g/1½lbs raspberries
3 tbsps lemon juice
1.4kg/3lbs unrefined granulated sugar

1 Place the rhubarb with the water in a preserving pan and simmer gently for 10 minutes or until the rhubarb is just soft.

2 Add the raspberries and lemon juice and continue to cook for 10 minutes or until all the fruit is very soft.
3 Stir in the sugar and cook gently stirring until all the sugar has dissolved.
4 Boil rapidly until setting point is reached; a little spooned onto a cold plate should wrinkle after a minute, when pushed with a finger. Allow to stand for 20 minutes, then stir.
5 Pour into hot, sterilized jars, seal and label.

Cook's Notes

TIME
Preparation takes about 30 minutes, plus standing. Cooking time is about 40 minutes.

VEGETARIAN SUITABILITY
This recipe is suitable for vegans.

SERVING IDEA
Serve warm with a sponge pudding as a delicious sauce.

THREE FRUIT MARMALADE

MAKES: APPROXIMATELY 1.6KG/3½LBS

This marmalade can be made at any time of the year, unlike those which include Seville oranges in the ingredients.

INGREDIENTS

4 limes
2 oranges
2 grapefruits
1.1litres/2 pints water
900g/2lbs unrefined granulated sugar
30g/1oz butter (if necessary)

Step 2 *Cut the citrus fruit peel into shreds using a small, sharp knife.*

1 Wash the fruit and pare off the peel with a sharp knife, taking care not to include too much of the white pith.
2 Cut the peel into shreds and squeeze the juice from the fruit. Tie the remaining pith and seeds in a square of muslin.
3 Put the juice, peel and muslin bag into a preserving pan with the water and simmer gently for about 1 hour, or until the peel is soft and the mixture has been reduced by about half.

4 Remove the muslin bag, squeeze out well. Stir in the sugar and heat gently, stirring until all the sugar is dissolved.
5 Boil rapidly, without stirring, until setting point is reached. (A little spooned onto a cold plate should wrinkle after a minute, when pushed with a finger.)
6 If the marmalade looks bubbly and cloudy, stir the butter through the mixture to help clear it.
7 Allow to stand for 20 minutes before pouring into hot, sterilized jars. Seal and label.

Cook's Notes

TIME
Preparation takes about 45 minutes, plus standing. Cooking time is about 1½ hours.

VEGETARIAN SUITABILITY
This recipe is suitable for vegans.

SERVING IDEA
Serve with hot buttered toast for breakfast

VARIATION
Use any combination of citrus fruit so long as you have about 3½lbs of fruit.

MARMALADE WITH WHISKY

MAKES: APPROXIMATELY 1.4KG/3LBS

This delicious breakfast marmalade could be used as a very welcome home-made present for Christmas or the New Year.

INGREDIENTS

3 oranges
3 grapefruit
1.1litre/2 pints water
675g/1½lbs light muscovado sugar
30g/1oz butter (if necessary)
60ml/4 tbsps whisky

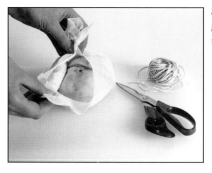

Step 2 *Tie the pith and pips into a square of muslin.*

1 Wash the fruit and pare off the coloured part of the skin with a sharp knife, taking care not to include too much of the white pith.
2 Cut the peel into shreds and squeeze the juice from the fruit. Tie the remaining pith and seeds in a square of muslin.
3 Put the juice, peel and muslin bag into a preserving pan with the water and simmer gently for about 1-1½ hours, or until the peel is soft and the mixture has been reduced by about half.
4 Remove the muslin bag and squeeze out well.

Stir in the sugar and heat gently, stirring, until all the sugar is dissolved.
5 Boil rapidly without stirring until setting point is reached. (A little spooned onto a cold plate should wrinkle when pushed with a finger.)
6 If the marmalade looks bubbly and cloudy, stir the butter in to help it to clear.
7 Stir in the whisky, then allow to stand for 20 minutes before pouring into hot, sterilized jars. Seal and label.

Cook's Notes

TIME
Preparation takes about 50 minutes, plus standing. Cooking time is about 1½ hours.

VEGETARIAN SUITABILITY
This recipe is suitable for vegans as long as the butter isn't used.

PINEAPPLE GRAPEFRUIT MARMALADE

MAKES: APPROXIMATELY 2.3KG/5LBS

The flavours of pineapple and grapefruit complement each other wonderfully, as highlighted in this delicious and unusual recipe.

INGREDIENTS

2 large pineapples
3 grapefruit
570ml/1 pint water
675g/1½lbs unrefined granulated sugar
15g/½oz butter (if necessary)

1 Peel and cut the pineapples into small pieces.
2 Wash the grapefruit and pare off the coloured part of the skin with a sharp knife, taking care not to include too much of the white pith.
3 Cut the peel into shreds, and squeeze the juice from the fruit.
4 Tie the remaining pith and seeds in a square of muslin.
5 Put the juice, peel, muslin bag and pineapple into a preserving pan with the water and simmer gently for about 1 hour, or until the peel is soft.
6 Remove the muslin bag, squeeze out well. Stir in the sugar and heat gently, stirring until all the sugar is dissolved.

Step 1 *Peel the pineapples and remove any brown 'eyes' using the end of a potato peeler or a very sharp knife.*

Step 4 *Tie the grapefruit pith and seeds into a square of muslin.*

7 Boil rapidly, without stirring, until setting point is reached.
8 If the marmalade looks bubbly and cloudy, stir the butter through the mixture to help clear it.
9 Allow to stand for 20 minutes before pouring into warm, sterilized jars. Seal and label.

Cook's Notes

TIME
Preparation takes about 1 hour, plus standing. Cooking time is about 1½ hours.

VEGETARIAN SUITABILITY
This recipe is suitable for vegans as long as the butter isn't used.

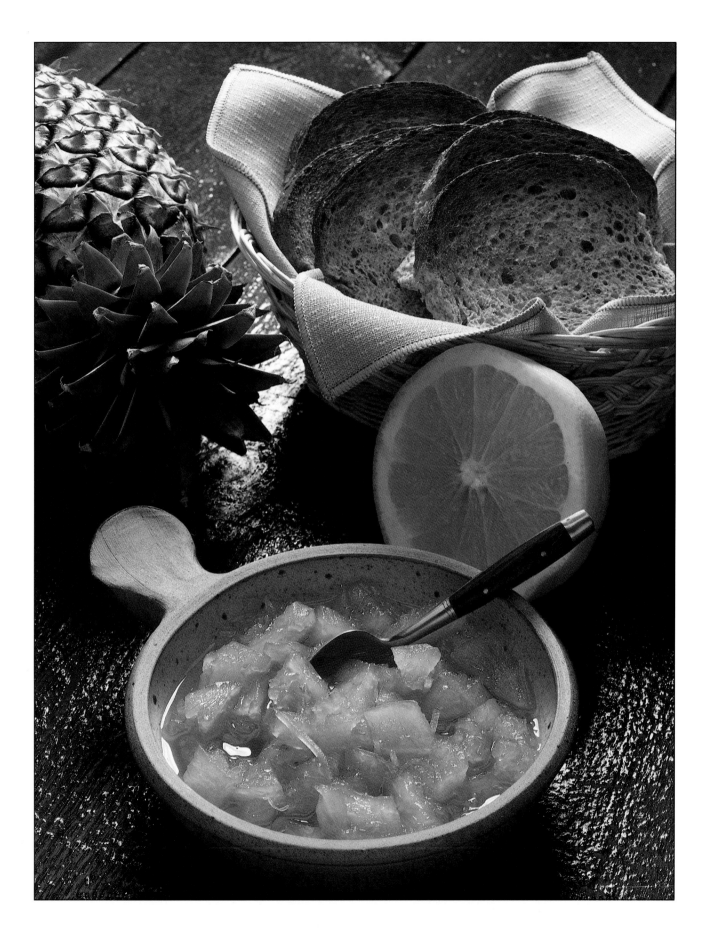

APPLE CIDER JELLY

MAKES: APPROXIMATELY 675G/1½LBS

This delicious fruit jelly can be made at any time of the year.

INGREDIENTS

420ml/¾ pint dry cider
140ml/¼ pint clear unsweetened apple juice
450g/1lb preserving sugar with added pectin
1 tsp lemon juice
1 cinnamon stick

1 Pour the cider and apple juice into a preserving pan and stir in the sugar and lemon juice. Add the cinnamon stick.
2 Heat gently until the sugar dissolves. Boil rapidly for 5 minutes, then test to see if the setting point has been reached. A small amount will set on a cold plate within 2 minutes. Boil for a few minutes longer if necessary, before testing again.
3 Remove the cinnamon stick and pour into hot, sterilized jars. Seal and label.

Cook's Notes

TIME
Preparation takes about 5 minutes, cooking time is about 8 minutes.

VEGETARIAN SUITABILITY
This recipe is suitable for vegans.

SERVING IDEA
Serve on warm buttered bread or scones.

VARIATION
Add a good handful of chopped fresh mint leaves for a delicious savoury variation.

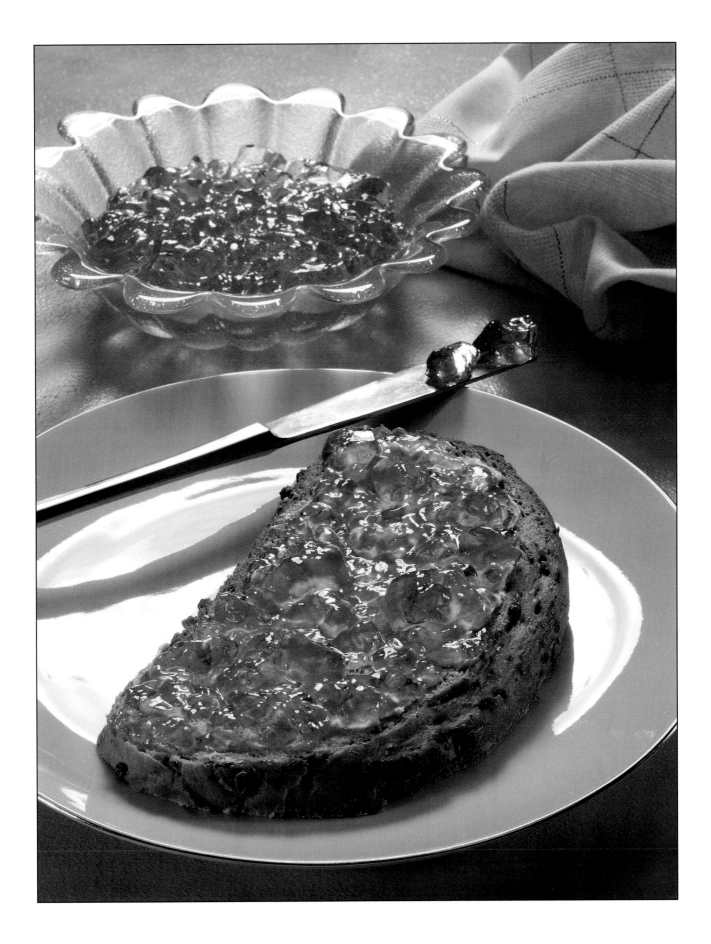

CHRYSANTHEMUM AND GREEN PEPPERCORN JELLY

MAKES: APPROXIMATELY 450G/1LB

This exotic flavoured jelly is best made with the old fashioned type of chrysanthemum, often found in gardens.

INGREDIENTS

570ml/1 pint unsweetened clear apple juice
340g/12oz preserving sugar with added pectin
1 tbsp lemon juice
1 tbsp green peppercorns, packed in brine, well drained
Handful chrysanthemum petals, rinsed and dried

1 Pour the apple juice into a preserving pan and stir in the sugar and lemon juice. Heat gently until the sugar dissolves.

2 Add the peppercorns and boil rapidly for 5 minutes, then test to see if the setting point has been reached. A small amount will set on a cold plate within 2 minutes. Boil for a few minutes longer if necessary, before testing again.
3 Remove from the heat and skim away any scum.
4 Allow to cool slightly, stirring until beginning to set. Stir in the petals.
5 Pour into warm sterilized jars. Seal and label.

Cook's Notes

TIME
Preparation takes about 10 minutes, cooking time is about 8 minutes.

VEGETARIAN SUITABILITY
This recipe is suitable for vegans.

SERVING IDEA
Serve with salads.

VARIATION
Use nasturtium or carnation petals in this recipe instead of the chrysanthemum petals.

HOT PEPPER JELLY

MAKES: APPROXIMATELY 900G/2LBS

This savoury jelly will add a touch of spice to a barbecue or picnic.

INGREDIENTS

3 red peppers, seeded
1 green pepper, seeded
2 red or green chillies, seeded
280ml/½ pint white wine vinegar
675g/1½lbs preserving sugar with added pectin

1 Chop the peppers and chillies finely in a food processor or by hand. Place in a large saucepan or preserving pan with the vinegar.
2 Stir in the sugar and heat gently until the sugar dissolves.

Step 1 *Using a sharp knife or food processor, carefully chop the peppers and chillies very finely.*

3 Boil rapidly for 5 minutes, then test to see if the setting point has been reached. Boil for a few minutes longer if necessary, before testing again.
4 Pour into hot, sterilized jars. Seal and label.

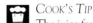

Cook's Notes

TIME
Preparation takes about 20 minutes, cooking time is about 10 minutes.

VEGETARIAN SUITABILITY
This recipe is suitable for vegans.

COOK'S TIP
The juice from chillies will stay on unprotected fingers for several hours, even after washing. It is therefore a good idea to wear rubber gloves to avoid this happening.

PREPARATION
Remember, great care must be taken when preparing chillies. Avoid getting the juice into your eyes or mouth. If this should happen, rinse with lots of cold water.

FENNEL PRESERVE WITH AQUAVIT

MAKES: APPROXIMATELY 900G/2LBS

This highly flavoured, aniseed preserve would make an unusual accompaniment to cold nut roasts or vegetable pies.

INGREDIENTS

3 heads fennel
225g/8oz unrefined granulated sugar
280ml/½ pint distilled malt vinegar
280ml/½ pint water
Pinch of salt
1 tbsp caraway seeds
140ml/¼ pint aquavit

1 Cut the root ends off the fennel and cut fennel into 1.25cm/½-inch slices. Include the green tops.
2 Place the sugar, vinegar, water, salt and caraway seeds into a large saucepan and heat gently. Stir until the sugar dissolves and boil for 5 minutes.
3 Add the sliced fennel and cook for 10 minutes or until the fennel looks translucent.
4 Stir in the aquavit.
5 Pour into hot, sterilized jars. Seal and label.

Step 1 *Slice the trimmed fennel into 1.25cm/ ½-inch slices, including the green tops.*

Step 5 *Seal the jars either with coated screw tops or with cellophane circles held in place with elastic bands.*

Cook's Notes

TIME
Preparation takes about 10 minutes, cooking time is about 15-20 minutes.

VEGETARIAN SUITABILITY
This recipe is suitable for vegans.

SERVING IDEA
Serve with nut roasts or vegetable pies.

PREPARATION
If you prefer a less chunky preserve, grate the fennel rather than slicing it.

LEMON LIME CURD

MAKES: APPROXIMATELY 675G/1½LBS

Delicious spread on bread or as a filling for cakes.

INGREDIENTS

Grated rind and juice of 2 lemons
Grated rind and juice of 1 lime
45g/1½oz unsalted butter
225g/8oz unrefined caster sugar
3 eggs, beaten

1 Place the rind and juice into the top of a double boiler or in a bowl placed over a pan of gently simmering water.
2 Add the butter and heat until melted. Stir in the sugar and continue cooking until the sugar has dissolved, stirring occasionally.
3 Strain the beaten eggs into the juice mixture and cook gently until the curd thickens, stirring constantly. Take care not to over heat the mixture or it will curdle. If the mixture does start to curdle remove from the heat immediately, set the base of the pan or bowl into cold water and whisk rapidly.
4 The curd is cooked when the mixture coats the back of a spoon.
5 Pour into dry jars, seal and label. Store in the refrigerator until required.

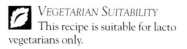

Cook's Notes

TIME
Preparation takes about 10 minutes, cooking time is about 50 minutes.

VEGETARIAN SUITABILITY
This recipe is suitable for lacto vegetarians only.

PICKLED ORANGE SLICES

MAKES: APPROXIMATELY 450G/1LB

*These orange slices make a luxurious accompaniment for a nut roast or
an elegant garnish for many other main courses.*

INGREDIENTS

3-4 thin-skinned oranges
280ml/½ pint white wine vinegar
340g/12oz unrefined granulated sugar
1 cinnamon stick
2 whole allspice berries
4 whole cloves

1 Slice the oranges into 5mm/¼-inch rounds,
discard the ends and remove any pips.
2 Place in a saucepan with enough water to cover.
Simmer gently for about 40 minutes or until the
peel is tender. Drain the fruit and discard the
water.
3 Heat the vinegar, sugar and spices in a shallow
pan, add a layer of oranges to the pan and simmer
gently until the peel becomes transparent.

Step 1 *Slice the oranges
into 5mm/¼-inch thick
rounds.*

4 Remove the oranges with a draining spoon and
pack into sterilized jars.
5 Repeat the process until you have cooked all the
orange slices.
6 Increase the heat and boil the liquid for about 5
minutes or until it starts to thicken. Pour over the
fruit in the jar.
7 Seal the jars and label.

Cook's Notes

TIME
Preparation takes about 15
minutes, cooking time is about 1 hour
10 minutes.

VEGETARIAN SUITABILITY
This recipe is suitable for vegans

PREPARATION
If preferred, the vinegar mixture
can be strained to remove the spices
before pouring over the oranges.

SERVING IDEA
 Serve with nut roasts or as a
garnish to other dishes.

KUMQUATS IN COINTREAU

MAKES: APPROXIMATELY 675G/1½LBS

Preserved whole fruits look and taste deliciously exotic. This recipe is an ideal way of using kumquats which are now available from most greengrocers and supermarkets.

INGREDIENTS

450g/1lb whole kumquats
225g/8oz unrefined granulated sugar
420ml/¾ pint water
3 tbsps Cointreau

1 Cut a cross in the top of each kumquat and pack into screw-top preserving jars.
2 Heat the sugar and water gently until the sugar dissolves, then boil for 1 minute. Stir in the Cointreau.
3 Pour the syrup over the kumquats to within 1cm/½-inch of the top of the jar. Screw the lids onto the jars, then release a quarter turn.
4 Place several layers of folded newspaper in the bottom of a pan which is deep enough to fill with water to the top of the jars. Place the jars in the pan.
5 Fill the pan with cold water, up to the necks of the jars, and heat slowly to simmering point, this should take about 30 minutes.
6 Maintain the water at simmering point for 10 minutes or until the kumquats look clear.
7 Remove the jars from the water and place on a wooden surface. Immediately fully tighten the lids and allow to cool completely.
8 Label and store in a cool, dark place.

Step 1 *Cut a small cross in the rounded end of each kumquat with a sharp pointed knife.*

Cook's Notes

TIME
Preparation takes about 15-20 minutes, cooking time is about 45-60 minutes.

VEGETARIAN SUITABILITY
This recipe is suitable for vegans.

PREPARATION
Put 1 or 2 lime leaves into the jar with the kumquats for an attractive decoration.

PINEAPPLE, MANGO AND MINT CHUTNEY

MAKES: APPROXIMATELY 1.4KG/3LBS

This fresh tasting chutney makes an ideal accompaniment for salads, or is equally delicious served simply with cheese and homemade bread.

INGREDIENTS

1 large pineapple

Salt

2 large mangoes, peeled, stoned and chopped

225g/8oz sultanas

850ml/1½ pints distilled white vinegar

3 tbsps chopped fresh mint

1 tbsp chopped fresh root ginger

½ tsp ground nutmeg

450g/1lb unrefined granulated sugar

1 Peel the pineapple and chop. Layer in a shallow dish, sprinkle liberally with salt and leave for several hours, or overnight.

2 Rinse pineapple and drain well.

3 Place the pineapple, mangoes, sultanas, vinegar, mint, ginger and nutmeg in a preserving pan and simmer gently for 10 minutes or until the fruits are tender.

4 Stir in the sugar and heat gently until the sugar dissolves, then boil rapidly until thickened, stirring frequently to prevent it from burning on the bottom of the pan.

5 Test by stirring with a wooden spoon, if the spoon leaves a channel then the mixture is ready.

6 Pour into hot, sterilized jars, seal and label.

Cook's Notes

TIME
Preparation takes about 20 minutes, plus standing. Cooking time is about 35 minutes.

VEGETARIAN SUITABILITY
This recipe is suitable for vegans.

COOK'S TIP
If fresh pineapples are not available, use the equivalent amount of drained canned pineapple, but make sure that the fruit has been canned in natural juice and not in sugar syrup.

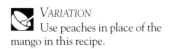
VARIATION
Use peaches in place of the mango in this recipe.

SERVING IDEA
Serve with vegetarian curries, ploughman's lunches or cold pies.

SWEET PICKLED ONIONS

MAKES: APPROXIMATELY 1.8KG/4LBS

Nothing can compare with the flavour of home-made pickled onions –
perfect for picnics or salads.

INGREDIENTS

1.4kg/3lbs button or pickling onions
850ml/1½ pints cider, malt or distilled vinegar
340g/12oz light muscovado sugar
2 tbsps mustard seeds
1 cinnamon stick
1 tsp salt

1 Pour boiling water over the onions to loosen the skins, and then peel.

Step 1 *Pour boiling water over the pickling onions, drain, and then peel away the skins using a sharp knife.*

2 Bring a large pan of water to the boil and add a couple of tablespoons of the vinegar and blanch the onions for 5 minutes.

3 Drain and pat dry. Pack into preserving jars.

4 Heat the remaining ingredients together until boiling and pour over the onions to within 1cm/½-inch of the top of the jar. Screw the lids onto the jars then release a quarter turn.

5 Place several layers of folded newspaper in the bottom of a pan which is deep enough to fill with water to the top of the jars. Place the jars in the pan.

6 Fill the pan with water up to the neck of the jars and heat slowly to simmering point – this should take about 30 minutes.

7 Maintain the water at simmering point for 10 minutes.

8 Turn off the heat, tighten the lids, and allow the jars to cool completely in the water.

9 Label and store in a cool dark place.

Cook's Notes

TIME
Preparation takes about 20 minutes, cooking time is about 1 hour.

VEGETARIAN SUITABILITY
This recipe is suitable for vegans.

SERVING IDEA
Serve these onions with fresh bread and cheese for a delicious lunch.

CURRIED FRUIT

MAKES: APPROXIMATELY 1.2KG/2½LBS

This rich, spicy chutney pickle is very quick to make and goes particularly well with Indian food.

INGREDIENTS

225g/8oz light muscovado sugar

140ml/¼ pint distilled malt vinegar

140ml/¼ pint water

4 whole cloves

2 tbsps mild curry powder

1 tsp coriander seeds

3 apples, peeled, cored and thickly sliced

175g/6oz pineapple chunks

90g/3oz raisins

6 apricots, pitted and halved

1 Place the sugar, vinegar, water, cloves, curry powder and coriander seeds in a large saucepan or preserving pan and heat gently, stirring until the sugar dissolves.

2 Boil for 2 minutes.

3 Add the apples, pineapple and raisins and cook for 5 minutes. Add the apricots and cook for another 3 minutes. The apple should look translucent.

4 Pour into hot, sterilized jars, seal and label. After opening, store in the refrigerator.

--- *Cook's Notes* ---

TIME
Preparation takes about 15 minutes, cooking time is about 15 minutes.

VEGETARIAN SUITABILITY
This recipe is suitable for vegans.

SERVING IDEA
Stir a tablespoon of this chutney into some mayonnaise and serve over hard-boiled eggs for a delicious starter.

VARIATION
Use a hot curry powder in this recipe in place of the mild one suggested.

Index